W9-BIT-607

A GIFT FOR YOU!

OUR iNNER
NATURE
iS BEING
RENEWED
DAY BY
DAY

What a
blessing
... to be
thought
of and
loved!

© Copyright 1997 by Creative Com—

This gift comes to you with best wishes and this gift card signed:

11042X04

FROM, MILLY

USA, BC-E

A TREASURY OF

LIVING FAITH®

VOLUME THREE

*Catholic Devotions For
Every Day Of The Year*

✠

Daily Devotions
from
LIVING FAITH

James E. Adams
Editor

Living Faith Publications

Imprimatur
Most Rev. Michael J. Sheridan
St. Louis Archdiocese

An imprimatur is an official declaration that published material is free of doctrinal and moral error. It does not imply agreement with all the opinions and statements in the book.

Copyright © 1998
Creative Communications for the Parish, Inc.
All Rights Reserved

A Treasury of *LIVING FAITH*
Volume Three
Catholic Devotions For
Every Day Of The Year

International Standard Book Number
1-889387-13-4

Cover Art and Design by
Sally Beck

Printed in the United States

Contents

This is the third volume in the **Treasury of Living Faith** series that makes available the best devotions from past issues of our quarterly magazine *LIVING FAITH*. The following 366 devotions, one for each date of the year, were selected from *LIVING FAITH* issues published from 1992 through 1997.

What stands out in this new Treasury is the increasingly strong contributions from such *LIVING FAITH* writers as Sr. Ruth Marlene Fox, Sr. Macrina Wiederkehr, Nancy Summers, Elizabeth-Anne Vanek (Stewart) and Sr. Joyce Rupp. A special word of thanks to them and to all our writers who know the difficulty—and the satisfaction—of writing short devotionals that are helpful to many readers.

The discipline behind these devotions is simple: It consists of reading a brief reflection on a Scripture passage and using a short reflection to inspire one's daily prayer. The practice has a long and rich tradition in the Church, one that is being renewed in our time.

The noted spiritual writer Henri J.M. Nouwen wrote that daily Scriptural reflection and prayer—particularly when centered on the Gospels—was an invaluable spiritual discipline. "It wasn't that the Gospel proved useful for my many worries but that the Gospel proved the uselessness of my worries."

The duty for such daily personal reflection on Scripture is perhaps most simply stated by Dietrich Bonhoeffer: "I must seek each day in prayer the word that my Lord wants to say to me that day."

It is our hope that the devotions herein will help you find that word the Lord wants you to hear each day.

James E. Adams

A New Year Of Hope

■ **The Lord bless you and keep you! The Lord let his face shine upon you, and be gracious to you! The Lord look upon you kindly and give you peace!**

Numbers 6:24-26

Though we may try to drown out our regret, no amount of merry-making can silence the fact that there are some realities about the old year we wish we could leave behind—realities that produce feelings of sadness, nostalgia, disappointment, shame and hurt. We hope that the new year will treat us more kindly, and that those Christmas holiday cards wishing us blessings of "Peace, Health and Prosperity" will indeed come our way.

"How will fate treat us?" we may ask ourselves. "Will this be a good year?" From the perspective of faith, however, we know that all time is good because God, the Timeless One, *is* goodness. Like Mary, whose motherhood we celebrate today, we need to believe that even in times of confusion—even when angels bear terrifying messages, even when there are hazardous journeys, closed doors and murderous plots—still there is the possibility of amazing grace and the certainty of God's abundant love.

Regardless of what we carry with us into this new year, we can be certain God looks upon us in kindness, ready to give us the gift of peace.

Fill us with your peace; let your light shine on us.

Elizabeth-Anne Vanek

Begin Prayer With Praise

■ **Let young men too, and maidens, old men and boys, praise the name of the Lord, for his name alone is exalted.**
Psalm 148:12-13

Always begin your prayer by praising God. Praise puts you in a right relationship with God. By praising him, you are submitted to him; he is the master and you are his servant. He is the glorious, almighty eternal, everlasting one and you are a struggling, sinful creature dependent upon him for redemption and grace, faith and hope, salvation and truth. This is the perspective we should have. It isn't, "God, old buddy, come into my corner here and snuggle up by the fireplace." God is God and we are mere mortals, and we should relate to him accordingly.

In the Book of Revelation, we see the vision of a heavenly host praising the Lamb: "Amen! Praise and glory, wisdom and thanksgiving and honor, power and might, to our God forever and ever. Amen!" That is what we are called to do forever. That's the right relationship to God, that's the response we should have. That kind of awesome respect, filled at the same time with the love and mercy of God, is what we are called to do.

By beginning your prayer with praise, you establish the right relationship with God. You become aware of who you are and who God is.

Fr. Michael Scanlan, T.O.R.
Appointment With God

What Am *I* Looking For?

■ **Jesus turned and saw them following him and said to them, "What are you looking for?" They said to him, "Rabbi" (which translated means Teacher), "where are you staying?" John 1:38**

Prayerful questions sometimes rise up out of the Gospels. I call them eternal questions. Jesus' question to the first disciples is one of those eternal questions that continues to confront me. I offer you this simple gospel question for your prayer today— What are you looking for?

I have often used this question as a prayer-line to guide me through my day. Stressful and anxiety-ridden, I am impatient at the red light. Jesus' voice finds me in the midst of my distress, asking, What are you looking for? Pouring my fifth cup of morning coffee, the voice of wisdom breaks through, asking, What are you looking for?

In my restless roaming and wandering the question startles me back to the reality of the present moment. What are you really looking for? Attempting to heal the gaping hole of my loneliness, that eternal question follows me through the day—What are you looking for? It's such a good question.

Help me, Jesus, to put an end to all my guardedness, my reluctance and evasion, and with the first disciples, answer your question with my own—Where are you staying, where do you live?

Sr. Macrina Wiederkehr, O.S.B.

The Extravagant Love Of God

■ **You must see what great love the Father has lavished on us by letting us be called God's children—which is what we are.** 1 John 3:1

"Lavished"—what a bountiful word!

God's love has been generously shared with us, poured out abundantly into our hearts. We have only to be open and receptive in order for this extravagant outpouring of goodness to be ours. Have you ever thought about the profuse nature of God's great love? What a marvelous gift it is.

Somedays it may be difficult to believe in this generous gift. It may not seem like we are lavished with God's love when we are experiencing our weaknesses or when life seems full of troubles and unwanted difficulties. Yet, this abundant gift of God's love never stops being offered to us.

John tells us that if we accept this lavish gift of God into our lives, it will begin to transform us. Like God, we will become generous with our kindness and acceptance of others. The goodness of God's love will shine through our lives.

Today close your eyes and picture God's love surrounding you and filling you with deep abiding peace and acceptance.

Sr. Joyce Rupp, O.S.M.

Supply And Demand

■ **Jesus asked them, "How many loaves have you? Go and see." And when they had found out they said, "Five loaves and two fish."** Mark 6:38

This question haunts me every time I pray this scripture passage. When I try to dodge the responsibility my ministry demands of me, I often hear Jesus asking me to check my supply. The one who walked along the shores of Galilee pursues me with questions. Are you sure the cupboard of your heart is bare? Is your supply really exhausted?

"You see," he continues, "it doesn't take all that much to prepare a banquet."

To one who is hungry a few crumbs is a feast.

To one who is lonely a few words is a healing presence.

To one who is afraid a few minutes of attention can be a great comfort.

To one who is in sorrow sitting quietly nearby without trying to take away that sorrow can be a blessing.

Look carefully into your larder before you proclaim that nothing is there. How many loaves do you have?

Sr. Macrina Wiederkehr, O.S.B.

Listening To God

■ **Then Eli understood that the Lord was calling the youth. So he said to Samuel, "Go to sleep, and if you are called, reply, 'Speak, Lord, for your servant is listening.'"** 1 Samuel 3:8-9

God usually chooses to deal with people through other people. Of course, he can reveal himself directly to anyone he wishes, as with Samuel in the temple. It is helpful to note, however, that Eli, the priest, had to make clear to Samuel that the voice he was hearing was the voice of God. Incidentally, Eli was not the most saintly of men; God was displeased with him because he had not reproved his sons who were guilty of blasphemy. The point is that God often works through people, and sometimes they are not necessarily very holy.

God wants to act through us now. Perhaps we do not think that we are especially holy or that we are suitable instruments for God. Such is a thought we must put from our minds. We must be as eager as Samuel was to know what God's will is for us and then to be as zealous as he was in following God's will. Actually, we find God's will all around us in people who are in need. The sick, the lonely, the discouraged—all these are signs to us that God wants us to act.

Lord, open my heart so I can hear when you speak.
Fr. Charles E. Miller, C.M.
Opening The Treasures

The Miracle Of Change

■ **Jesus did this as the beginning of his signs in Cana in Galilee and so revealed his glory, and his disciples began to believe in him.** John 2:11

Who needed this miracle, Lord?

The bride and groom, to be saved from embarrassment?

The waiters, to escape accountability?

The guests, to continue their feasting?

Your mother, to salvage the celebration?

The disciples, to recognize your power?

You, to mark the beginning of your public ministry?

Do I need this miracle? Yes, two thousand years after the event, I know that I need this miracle as much as any of the participants or bystanders did then. The image of water being turned into wine reminds me of the possibility of transformation in my own life. As I imagine the revelry spilling over the brims of the water jars, filling the house with laughter and amazed delight, I know that I, too, can become heady with desire for new wine.

Come, Lord, pour your life into me. Let this dull water ferment and sparkle with your effervescence.

Elizabeth-Anne Vanek

The God Of Silence

■ **He said to them, "Come by yourselves to an out-of-the-way place and rest a little." People were coming and going in great numbers ... So they went off in the boat by themselves to a deserted place.** Mark 6:31-32

Silence of the heart, not only of the mouth, is necessary. Then you can hear God everywhere; in the closing of the door, in the person who needs you, in the birds that sing, in the flowers, the animals—that silence which is wonder and praise. Why? Because God is everywhere, and you can see and hear him. That crow is praising God. That stupid crow! I can hear it. We can see and hear God in that crow.

We need to find God, and he cannot be found in noise and restlessness. See how nature, the trees, the flowers and the grass grow in perfect silence. See the stars, the moon and the sun, how they move in silence ... "God is the friend of silence. His language is silence." *Be still and know that I am God.* He requires us to be silent to discover him. In the silence of the heart, God speaks to us ... We need silence to be alone with God, to speak to him, to listen to him, to ponder his words deep in our hearts. We need to be alone with God in silence to be renewed and to be transformed. Silence gives us a new outlook on life. In it we are filled with the grace of God, which makes us do all things with joy.

Mother Teresa
Total Surrender

Living Up To My Calling

■ **Humbly welcome the word that has taken root in you, with its power to save you. Act on this word. If all you do is listen to it, you are deceiving yourselves.**

James 1:21-22

Not enough of us live Christ fully enough. Too many of us are in some measure faithless, hopeless, loveless. I believe that God's only Son died for me. Do I, in return, live for him?

I profess to love God above every creature, to love my sisters and brothers as deeply as I love myself. Is it clear to the pagan that I really rank God above power and pride, above sex and self, above wealth and status and comfort? Is it clear to the pagan that, literally for Christ's sake, my heart goes out not only to the beauty but to the beast, to pauper as well as prince, to anyone who needs me?

We keep saying it is a form of pride to want to be different, better than others. But is it too much to expect that I who have been gifted with God's revelation of Himself in Christ, I who have the Spirit of Christ indwelling in me, I who share Christ's presence in the gathered assembly and the proclaimed word, I who feed on the very body and blood of Christ—is it too much to expect that Christ will transpire in me, come to light in me?

Help me, Lord, to begin today to live up to my awesome calling to become your disciple.

Fr. Walter J. Burghardt, S.J.
Still Proclaiming Your Wonders

A Prayer To Accept Crosses

■ **Jesus summoned the crowd with his disciples and said to them, "Whoever wishes to come after me must deny his very self, take up his cross and follow me."**

Mark 8:34

Lord, let me receive the cross gladly. Let me recognize your cross in mine. Let me always remember that those sufferings known only to myself, which seem to be without purpose and without meaning, are part of your plan to redeem the world. Make me patient to bear the burdens of those nearest at hand. To welcome inconvenience for their sake, frustration because of them. Let me accept their temperament, nurse them in sickness, share with them in poverty, enter into sorrows with them.

Teach me to accept myself—my own temperament, my temptations, my limitations, my failures, the humiliation of being myself as I am.

Allow me, Lord, all my life long, to accept both small suffering and great suffering, certain that through your love both are redeeming the world.

And in communion with all and with you, let me accept death joyfully, and the fear of death—my death and the deaths of my loved ones. Not with my will but with yours, knowing that you have changed sorrow to joy, and death to life.

Caryll Houselander
The Stations Of The Cross

Impertinent Prayer

■ **O Lord, to you I call; hasten to me; hearken to my voice when I call upon you.** Psalm 141:1

There is something audacious, almost impudent, in the way the psalmist addresses his prayers to God for help. It's "Come," "Be quick," "Hear me," "Make haste"—not a single "please" in the whole lot.

Yet what an acknowledgement of God's power, God's greatness in these bold and forthright prayers! "Yahweh," they say, "You are God. You are great. You are powerful. You are able to do all things. If I am to be helped, the help must come from You." All the focus is on God. The trust is absolute. "Unless you help me, Yahweh, the help of man is vain."

Could it be that our "Please, God . . ." prayers have more of our own self in them than consideration of God? Do we say "please" as if we had to condition God to be generous, as if we needed to wheedle from God what we need? Are we thinking more of what we want than of the great wonder of the God to whom we speak?

May it not be so. "For I am needy and poor, O God. Help me!"

Sr. Mary Terese Donze, A.S.C.

Prayer Of The Word

■ **For just as from the heavens the rain and snow come down and do not return there till they have watered the earth, making it fertile and fruitful . . . so shall my word be that goes forth from my mouth; it shall not return to me void, but shall do my will, achieving the end for which I sent it.** Isaiah 55:10-11

O God, may I always and everywhere listen to your word, reverence it, cherish it, nurture it—and never hinder it from doing its work of striving to make me more genuinely holy.

Words these days are common as dirt. Billions of human words crowd the airwaves each day, ready to fly into my ears at the flick of a switch. Billions more are printed each day, all of them trying to sell, to entertain, to inform—and at times to confuse or even to deceive. I could easily drown in this daily flood, sucked into this bottomless whirlpool of words.

Your word, O God, is not like a screaming verbal vortex. Your word is like the soft rain and melting snow that quietly penetrates and slowly nourishes. Your word comes, not in noisy fanfare, irritating shouts and information overload, but rather in silence and in restful peace.

May your word, O God, be ever more fruitful in me. Help me to do my part so that the goal you want to achieve in me with your word is realized.

James E. Adams

God Gives Second Chances

■ **The word of the Lord came to Jonah a second time: "Set out for the great city of Nineveh, and announce to it the message that I will tell you." So Jonah made ready and went to Nineveh, according to the Lord's bidding.**

Jonah 3:1-3

Jonah had heard the word of the Lord before. He ran away from it, had a hair-raising adventure and, eventually, a change of heart.

Are there not times when we, too, live out this pattern? We fear the intrusion of God's word into our lives, so we choose other alternatives and suffer the consequences. We come to regret our decisions, perhaps wishing we could go back in time and do it all over again.

Luckily, this is not the end of our story, any more than it was for Jonah. God's word came to him a second time. One of the significant lessons in the story of Jonah is that our God offers second chances!

We have made many choices in our lives for which we know there is no going back. But have we forgotten the option of going forward? Never mind being too late, too old, too busy. Those are flimsy excuses when weighed against the extraordinary opportunity of a second chance from God.

Dear God, you give me many opportunities to know, love and serve you. May I never ignore those chances, but always try to make the most of them.

Nancy F. Summers

God Delights In Mercy

■ **While he was still a long way off, his father caught sight of him, and was filled with compassion. He ran to his son, embraced him and kissed him.** Luke 15:20

In the story of the Prodigal Son, the father was not caught off guard by the son's return. It seems he kept a vigil, probably scanning the horizon day and night, anxiously yearning for a glimpse of the beloved child. The long watch ends dramatically with the son's appearance—no cool and cautious welcome here! Rather, we are treated to the remarkable scene of the father racing down the road, full of kisses and hugs, joy and forgiveness. All this before the son could even present his well-practiced apology!

The image of God Jesus sketches in this parable is so much more than a stern but just judge. This is a seeking, eager, can't wait, one-step-ahead-of-you God. Neither hesitant nor grudging in forgiveness, our God actually delights in mercy (*Who is there like you, the God who removes guilt and pardons sin for the remnant of his inheritance; who does not persist in anger forever, but delights rather in clemency, and will again have compassion on us, treading underfoot our guilt?* Micah 7:18-19).

In spite of the familiarity of the often-told story, can we not still be astounded by a God so touchingly thrilled to see us coming home?

Nancy F. Summers

What Is Our Hope?

■ **God is our refuge and our strength, an ever-present help in distress. Therefore we fear not, though the earth be shaken and mountains plunge into the depths of the sea.** Psalm 46:2-3

What is this marvelous Christian gift we call hope? It is not a wimpy "maybe things will turn out okay."

Rather it is a confident expectation that wherever you turn, whatever your problem, God will be there. Not always with an answer, but always with a presence, a strength, a courage out of this world. A confident expectation that your life will not end in six feet of dirt, will in fact never end, that you will always be alive to God, that the spiritual part of you will survive the corroding of your flesh, that one day, the whole person that is "you" will come together again, but without the pain, without the tears.

Unless such is your hope, there is no point in your being at Mass (or practicing your religion in other ways, for that matter). And if I may quote one of my few memorable sentences: "If heaven is not for real, I shall be madder than hell."

O God, grant me a firm and confident hope that keeps me grounded in you and your promises.

Fr. Walter J. Burghardt, S.J.
Dare To Be Christ

Love Is A Gift

■ **Whoever is without love does not know God, for God is love.** 1 John 4:8

God is much like the sun. The sun only shines. We can stand under the sun, share its gifts of warmth and light, or we can leave it. We can even lock ourselves in the dungeons of darkness. But the sun does not go out because we have left it. In the same way we can leave God, but he does not change. He only loves. We are free to reject the warmth and light of his love. If we do, we grow dark and cold and can even fall into spiritual death. But we are always free, and even when we are languishing in the dark, we know we can always go back into the warm light of God's love.

Would God love me more if I tried harder and became a better Christian? I feel sure that God would reply, "I couldn't love you more. I have given you all my love. Like all real love, my love is a gift. You are free to accept or reject it. Even if a mother were to forget the child of her womb, I would never forget you."

God could not love us more because he has already offered us all his love for us to accept or reject. I truly believe this is the way it was in the beginning, is now, and ever shall be. God is love.

Fr. John Powell, S.J.
Through The Eyes Of Faith

God Creates Us Out Of Love

■ **God is love, and whoever remains in love remains in God and God in him.** 1 John 4:16

We must not begin with mysticism, with the creature's love for God, or with the wonderful foretastes of union with God given to some in their earthly life.

We begin at the real beginning, with love as the Divine Energy. This primal love is Gift-love. In God there is no hunger that needs to be filled, only plenteousness that desires to give. The doctrine that God was under no necessity to create is not a piece of dry scholastic speculation. It is essential. Without it we can hardly avoid the concept of what I can only call a "managerial" God, a Being whose function or nature is to "run" the universe, who stands to it as a headmaster to a school or a hotelier to a hotel . . .

God, who needs nothing, loves into existence wholly superfluous creatures in order that he may love and perfect them . . .

If I may use a biological image, God is a "host" who deliberately creates his own parasites, causes us to be so that we may exploit and "take advantage of" him. Herein is love. This is the diagram of Love Himself, the inventor of all loves.

C.S. Lewis
The Four Loves

Love—A Power That Unites

■ **The commandment we have from him is this: those who love God must love their brothers and sisters also.**

1 John 4:21

Love is the only basis for human relationships that respects in one another the dignity of the children of God created in his image and saved by the death and resurrection of Jesus; love is the only driving force that impels us to share with our brothers and sisters all that we are and have. Love is the power that gives rise to dialogue, in which we listen to each other and learn from each other. Love gives rise, above all, to the dialogue of prayer in which we listen to God's word, which is alive in the Holy Bible and alive in the life of the Church. Let love, then, build the bridge across our differences and contrasting positions. Let love for each other and love for truth be the answer to polarization, when factions are formed because of differing views in matters that relate to faith or to priorities of action. No one should ever feel alienated or unloved, even when tensions arise in the course of our common efforts to bring the fruits of the Gospel to society. Our unity as Christians, as Catholics, must always be a unity of love in Jesus Christ Our Lord.

Lord, forgive me for the times I have made others in the Church feel alienated or unloved.

Pope John Paul II
from *The Pope Speaks To The American Church*

Humility—A Dose Of Reality

■ **He must increase; I must decrease.** John 3:30

Self-love is destructive of self. If we allow an unwarranted, unlimited kind of self-concern to consume us, our very mental health is in question.

In 1980, so corrosive had the effects of exaggerated self-importance become that the American Psychiatric Association began to identify narcissism as a personality disorder. Clearly, the cultural effects of rampant individualism have come home to haunt us. The symptoms . . . include a grandiose and exaggerated sense of self-importance; preoccupation with fantasies of success; exhibitionism and insatiable attention-getting maneuvers; disdain and disproportionate rage in the face of criticism; a sense of entitlement that undermines any hope of success in personal relationships; talk that is more self-promotion than communication . . . In humility, life is put before us raw . . .

Life is not about "me." Life is about God. What the psychiatrists have begun to hint at, (the saints) already knew. Self-preference, self-will, self-love and radical egotism are attempts to make ourselves our God. I become the ultimate arbiter of good and evil in my life. Growth becomes impossible.

Sr. Joan Chittister, O.S.B.
Wisdom Distilled From The Daily

Resting In The Lord

■ **Whoever enters into God's rest, rests from his own works as God did from his. Therefore, let us strive to enter into that rest.** Hebrews 4:10-11

People seek to secure divine favor with works; they try to redeem themselves or keep in God's good books by what they do. This commercial way of thinking is very widespread, and extends right into our modern spiritual communities.

Certain of good will and with the utmost generosity, with growing zeal people offer God more and more hours of work and promise to spend them in pious service for him . . .

The time comes when God speaks to the overzealous, because when they do too much of his work, it destroys their inner peace: "That's enough! Stop! Break off! Relax and find rest with me. Smile, let yourself go for a while and feel that I love you. I love you. Can't you feel it? I love you. Can't you accept it?" The true Christian attitude does not consist primarily in loving so much as in knowing and accepting the love of God. It is much simpler to give than to receive. We don't understand that. In zeal of our faith we grit our teeth and go on working, but letting go and surrendering to God is also an attitude of faith and is evidence of our trust.

Fr. Henri Boulad, S.J.
All Is Grace

No Love Is Lost Or Wasted

■ **God is not unjust so as to overlook your work and the love you have demonstrated for his name by having served and continuing to serve the holy ones.** Hebrews 6:10

W e need have no hesitation about the power of God's mercy. Infinite mercy is so far beyond our comprehension it would be folly to describe it. . .

It seems that no moment of love is ever wasted. This is a very consoling thought for parents who are disappointed by their children. It is a great mystery how, in time, God's life emerges. Even at the very end, there is time. God's eternal mercy envelopes our temporal order. Time as we know it has no meaning in God's eternity. Today's prayers keep alive those tiny flames of light in ourselves and in those we love. They reach out to loved ones, through God's mercy, across the limitations of time and space. They become part of the all-consuming fire of Divine love and eventually achieve their objective. This is why Christianity is a religion of hope. This is why we are Easter people and *Alleluia* is our song. We are not overcome by guilt. We rise above it and become a new creation.

Thank you, O Lord, for creating me, for redeeming me and for calling me to Christian holiness.

Fr. John Catoir
Enjoy The Lord

Come Into The Light

■ **You are the light of the world.** Matthew 5:14

Depression could be considered one of the major epidemics of the 20th century. Brought on by fear and hopelessness, intensified by disappointment and loss, it can entangle all of us, young and old, without warning. The outer darkness which we see imaged in senseless violence, economic chaos and the exploited environment often becomes internalized. We grow weak and lethargic, susceptible to physical ailments, unresponsive to others' needs. The world is no longer home to us, but a hostile prison.

When we are caught up in outer darkness and weighed down by inner darkness, we can often see no way out. Time and time again, however, small rays of light surprise us into joy. Chance meetings, unexpected phone calls and small acts of kindness can rouse us from inertia, re-awakening in us the memory of what it is to be alive. Grateful for this deliverance, we need to let our light shine so that we may do our part to help others again find meaning.

Come, Lord! Let your light rise for us in the darkness.

Elizabeth-Anne Vanek

Led By The Lord

■ **I have waited, waited for the Lord, and he stooped toward me and heard my cry. He drew me out of the pit of destruction, out of the mud of the swamp; he set my feet upon a crag; he made firm my steps.** Psalm 40:2-3

Many times I have felt that I was sinking into a swamp of confusion and indecision, sinking fast into a pit of personal disaster. It seemed that God had deserted me. My own efforts to rise up out of the morass only seemed to make matters worse, so like the psalmist, I waited.

And then the answer came, the required course of action became obvious and the energy to pursue it returned. From a vantage point of trust and faith, I could see my way again. My steps became quicker and more sure, and I seemed to be on steadier ground. Like the psalmist, I praised the Lord.

When I look back on my life, I can see the swamps and high places more clearly. I can recognize how carefully and surely the Lord was leading me: the trails to the high places were generous gifts, but even the swamps were places of learning and growth.

Lord, each time I see the trail grow dark and feel the earth less firm beneath my feet, help me to wait in humility and trust.

Denise Barker

Mary, A Christian Realist

■ Behold, this child is destined . . . to be a sign that will be contradicted (and you yourself a sword will pierce). . .
Luke 2:34-35

Mary hoped for the best, like we all do, but she was prepared to face dark times. To be prepared for dark times is not to be a pessimist, but to be well-informed about life. Everyone has been around long enough to know that any life is marked with sorrow—and that any good and virtuous Christian's life is necessarily going to be marked by a number of special sorrows. We are going to have sorrows and difficulties as a result of our belief in Christ . . . Recall the prediction of Simeon in the Gospel of St. Luke.

Mary is a figure of realism, of the cross, of self-emptying suffering . . . There is no other Christianity than that of the cross. If you get deluded into thinking that if you follow Christ, it will be all peaches and sunshine, you will be plunged into darkness. When the sorrows and dark days arrive and you have believed this nonsense, you will be utterly unprepared. It is a psychologically devastating thing to teach someone that everything is going to be wonderful. It's the worst thing you could ever tell anybody.

Fr. Benedict J. Groeschel, C.F.R.
Five Figures From The Passion

Called To Conversion

■ **"I fell to the ground and heard a voice saying to me, 'Saul, Saul, why are you persecuting me?' I replied, 'Who are you, sir?' And he said to me, 'I am Jesus the Nazorean whom you are persecuting.'"** Acts 22:7-8

What a conversion! As Saul, he was famous for his persecution of Christians; as Paul, he himself experienced persecution. The first dramatic moment of being knocked off his horse and blinded was just the beginning of Paul's conversion.

Whether we were "born" Christian or are a "convert," we all have to go through some kind of conversion, and it is a lifelong process. Jesus touches us daily and invites us to turn from the values and ways of our society that contradict his Gospel. Sometimes, Jesus' touch is dramatic, as it was with Paul. Most often, it is far less dramatic and may even go unnoticed. Jesus comes to us in our encounters on the telephone, in our offices and classrooms, on the street and in our homes. Each encounter is a moment for conversion: will I follow Jesus' sacrificial love or pull back from that call?

Jesus, if need be, please knock me from my high horse of selfishness. Help me hear your ordinary invitations today. Help me see you and hear you in each person I encounter.

James McGinnis

The Value Of Suffering

■ **He began to teach them that the Son of Man must suffer greatly and be rejected by the elders, the chief priests, and the scribes, and be killed, and rise after three days.**

Mark 8:31

When Jesus tried to explain to his disciples that he must "suffer greatly," Peter would not hear of it. He couldn't bear the thought that his dear friend would have to go through such great pain. One can imagine Peter saying to Jesus, "Now just stop that kind of talk. Nothing terrible is going to happen to you." He denied the suffering that Jesus knew would happen.

Peter refused to accept the fact that suffering was a part of Jesus' journey. He did not understand that this suffering was to be a source of transformation. His response was very normal, very human. None of us wants the suffering that comes our way. But if we have faith to see it as a part of our own journey of transformation, it can be a grace-filled experience. Peter apparently did not hear what Jesus said about rising from the dead. Perhaps if Peter had really heard this hopeful statement, he would not have been so quick to fight Jesus' journey of suffering.

Jesus, help me to learn from the suffering that is a part of my life and not to deny the possibility of my growing from it.

Sr. Joyce Rupp, O.S.M.

I Need Self-Examination

■ **I have set before you life and death, the blessing and the curse. Choose life.** Deuteronomy 30:19

Who among us would knowingly choose doom, to be cursed rather than blessed? No one! And yet, do we not find that certain segments of our lives are neither life-enhancing nor holy? Perhaps a part of us has ended up on the side of death without our having chosen it to be so. We may have an addiction that has so subtly ensnared us that we are almost unaware of the idol it has become. Perhaps a genuine desire to serve has led us into a situation where personal power has become a weapon of control or coercion.

Such life-denying behaviors are difficult to detect, for we never intended to choose death. Through courageous self-examination, we can seek greater awareness: what do those who know us well say about our choices? Are there parts of our lives we label "not open for discussion"? In what or in whom have we placed all our faith, our hope, our love?

Today, as every day, we have this great challenge and opportunity: we can choose again, we can choose life.

Nancy F. Summers

Standing By Jesus

■ **Whoever is not with me is against me, and whoever does not gather with me scatters.** Luke 11:23

Speaking very forcefully, Jesus challenged his listeners to make good decisions. But what does it mean to be "with" Jesus? When we are with someone, we are supportive and understanding. We are willing to stand up for them and to stand by them when times are tough.

What does it mean to "gather" with Jesus? Think of the image Jesus used to describe his love of the people: a hen longing to gather up her chicks under her wing to protect them. There is strength in gathering with Jesus. When we bond with Jesus, we are not alone. We can be more resilient and more loving.

Being "with" Jesus or "gathering" with him is not always easy. Our emotions and our will may pull us in other directions and urge us to go our own way rather than the Gospel's way. Jesus urges us to go with him and to gather strength from this experience of bonding.

Jesus, thank you for your challenge to go with you. I want to live your values and to accept your call to follow you even when it is difficult for me to do so.

Sr. Joyce Rupp, O.S.M.

A Prayer From The Heart

■ **Not as you see does God see, because you see the appearance but the Lord looks into the heart.**

1 Samuel 16:7

I take comfort in your seeing me, Lord. Your vision penetrates beneath the surface, beneath the masks I wear, beneath the roles I play. You search my heart and find there what the world cannot see—my hurts and disappointments, my feelings of foolishness and inadequacy, dreams that have faded to nothing, wounds that still fester.

You also see how much I have struggled to do what I perceived to be your will. Often, I have fallen short of your expectations, Lord, but your keen gaze takes note of the hardships I have encountered along the way. You know I've tried.

Others may think I "have it all together." Only you can see the storms which sometimes batter my heart, the fears which almost immobilize me. Only you can see that it is your grace alone which gives me strength, that it is your presence which is my life.

Please, Lord, continue to look into my heart—and may what you find there move you to compassion.

Elizabeth-Anne Vanek

Mary Says "Yes" To God

■ **Mary said, "Behold, I am the handmaid of the Lord. May it be done to me according to your word."** Luke 1:38

With those words Mary sums up the faith of Abraham following Yahweh's call across the desert, the faith of Moses kneeling before the burning bush, the faith of the prophets listening to the word which came to them, the faith of Job standing in the midst of the whirlwind.

Mary responds to God in an attitude of listening to the really real. She attunes herself to the word which is coming to her, and she trusts that it is speaking truth to her. By participating in that dialogue with reality, she allows the truth which is spoken to become real. She does not hide from truth; she faces it. She does not run from truth; she embraces it. She sees the truth of what is, and in doing so, she lets it be.

Mary is therefore the model of prayer for all Christians. Prayer is getting in touch with reality, letting it speak to us, and incarnating the word which comes to us. We let it happen; we don't make it happen. For saying "yes" to God in prayer does not just mean acknowledging that we heard it. It means changing our lives in accordance with that word.

Fr. Richard Rohr, O.F.M. and Joseph Martos
The Great Themes Of Scripture: New Testament

Breaking The Spiral Of Fear

■ **There is no fear in love, but perfect love drives out fear because fear has to do with punishment . . .** 1 John 4:18

The opposite of love may not be hate, but fear. We all hunger for the experience of loving and of being loved, but something blocks us from reaching out to satisfy the hunger. The more we separate ourselves from healing love, the more we experience isolation and fear. The fear may show itself as apprehensions, as worries and anxieties, as a discomfort with life that blooms into hostility toward others.

Instead of loving others, we wind up feeling threatened by them. The spiral of fear grows and we can be unable to love.

Most of our fears stem from illusions about ourselves. We think we are not lovable, and so do not love. That often results in feelings of hostility toward others. The hostilities flow from illusion too, because they stem from fears of unworthiness. We are worthy because God loves us unconditionally. One who accepts this is gradually freed from the illusion of unworthiness and the fear it generates. Becoming free from fear through our trust in God's love, we can overcome our hostilities and reach out to others.

Lord, help me to know and to break down whatever mental traps are keeping me in fear and hostility.

Fr. Kenneth E. Grabner, C.S.C.
Focus Your Day

Love Of Others Must Be First

■ **I give you a new commandment: love one another. As I have loved you, so you also should love one another. This is how all will know that you are my disciples, if you have love for one another.** John 13:34-35

We must learn to move beyond ourselves, to say no to instant gratification, to set limits on our own needs and somehow to start meeting somebody else's needs. That's why Jesus *commanded* us to love. He didn't suggest it. He didn't say, "When you get healed, love." Or "when you grow up, love." Or "when you get it together and have dealt with all your mother/father/husband/children wounds, then start loving." No, the commandment for all of us is, LOVE.

Until we love, we really do not even know who we are. In fact, we can buy into all the self-discovery the world has to offer and *still* not know ourselves.

Contemporary wisdom says we're supposed to keep telling people they're good and beautiful; they're great and fantastic; Jesus loves them—and eventually they'll believe it. But I haven't seen that work. I think we know the love of God is within us when we ourselves can "do love" much more than when people tell us we are lovable. We can always disbelieve the second, but the first has an unexplainable power.

Fr. Richard Rohr, O.F.M.
Radical Grace

The Home Of Jesus

■ **So they went and saw where he was staying, and they stayed with him that day.** John 1:39

John's disciples are curious and cautious. One imagines them following at a safe distance rather than trying to catch up with Jesus or engage him in conversation. They want to see for themselves whether or not this is indeed the "Lamb of God" before making any commitment.

Jesus, however, surprises them by turning around. Somewhat sheepishly, they ask him where he lives. Jesus' casual, "Come and see" lets them hear and observe without having to express their hearts' desires. Seeing where Jesus lives becomes a metaphor for understanding *who* Jesus is.

We learn a great deal from a single visit to a person's home. Artwork, the presence or absence of pets or plants, furniture, color schemes and spatial arrangement all reflect aspects of that resident's personality, heritage, values and self-image. What do John's disciples find on entering Jesus' home? What would Jesus find were he to visit our dwelling places? Would there be any signs of our discipleship? Would there be anything to indicate the ways in which we have responded to his call?

Satisfy our curiosity, Lord, that we may follow you with eager hearts.

Elizabeth-Anne Vanek

The Human Touch

■ **My daughter is at the point of death. Please, come lay your hands on her that she may get well and live.**

Mark 5:23

Studies have shown that infants die when deprived of human touch. And it would not be surprising to find a similar effect on adults. Physical contact with others is not merely life-enhancing, it is life-sustaining. This was no less true in the time of Jesus, when followers continually sought to touch or be touched by him. In today's Gospel, the hemorrhaging woman was cured by believing in the power of Jesus' touch, and Jesus raised Jairus' daughter by taking her hand.

We are to be the hands of Christ, extending outward to everyone we encounter. We must strive to make our touch pure, as his was, free of any perversion or cloying demand. With our hands, we wordlessly communicate sympathy, acceptance, concern, joy, relief and understanding. While we may not be able to cure specific diseases, Christ's healing touch lives on in our hands. May we always be reaching out to heal one another.

Lord Jesus, let me be your healing hands today.

Nancy F. Summers

Taking Time To Grow

■ **The child grew and became strong, filled with wisdom; and the favor of God was upon him.** Luke 2:40

Although we say we believe that Jesus emptied himself to take on human existence, it is not uncommon to lapse into an idealized, superhuman portrait of him. Our best inclinations toward respect and awe may mislead us to re-create the Jesus of the Gospels into an image of an otherworldly God-man.

As an antidote to this falsely elevated concept of Christ, Luke shows us Jesus growing, developing and learning. The lifelong process of maturing physically, emotionally and intellectually was the way of Jesus and of all humanity, and God finds favor in this. Finding the pace of human growth too slow and too imperfect for our standards, we may disdain our own humanity and therefore even tend to deny the humanity of Christ.

Jesus' own growing and learning sanctifies the process of human growth and gives evidence of the holiness of gradual human development. Jesus seen in his humanity, rather than above it, begins to take on truly heroic proportions.

Lord Jesus, may I embrace my humanity lovingly as you did.

Nancy F. Summers

Heeding The Call To Repent

■ **"Whatever place does not welcome you or listen to you, leave there and shake the dust off your feet in testimony against them." So they went off and preached repentance.**
Mark 6:11-12

To answer the call to repentance one must feel a kind of dissatisfaction, and want something better. The seed of repentance and conversion is the realization, however vague, that we are not what we could and should be.

Repentance demands openness, honesty, humility, and, above all, courage—the courage to put an end to self-deception and confront a painful reality. People can become so set in their ways that it becomes close to impossible to move them. It's almost as if they were set in concrete. Still, it's not that they *can't* be moved, but rather that they *won't* be moved. People can get so used to being dressed in rags, and feel so comfortable in them, that even if you gave them a new suit for nothing they wouldn't wear it.

The hardest people of all to convert are the good, because they don't see any need of conversion. It's hard enough to get people who are sick, and who know it, to go to a doctor. But try getting those who are sick, but who are convinced they are well, to go!

Fr. Flor McCarthy
Windows On The Gospel

No Substitute For Prayer

■ **Rising very early before dawn, he left and went off to a deserted place, where he prayed.** Mark 1:35

Interspersed among all the accounts of Jesus' healing ministry are scattered reminders that he took time to pray.

While we could say that everything he did was prayer, what Jesus models for us is the need to spend quiet, uninterrupted time with God. Doing "God's work" is no substitute for sustaining a relationship with God; in fact, we can only "do" it effectively if we are grounded in prayer.

Prayer is not to be confused with obligation or penance. It is a matter of friendship, of mutuality. It is a sacred moment in which God's heart can meet our heart. If we are to open our hearts toward God in the way that Jesus taught us, we need to come to prayer as we really are—without fear and without shame. God longs for the day when we will learn to pray with passion and authenticity, when we will express all that is deepest and dearest to us. God waits for each of us to remember that we are indeed made in the divine image and that we are priests in the sanctuary of our hearts.

Jesus, teach us to pray as you prayed.

Elizabeth-Anne Vanek

Blunt Words From Jesus

■ **Well did Isaiah prophesy about you hypocrites, as it is written: "This people honors me with their lips, but their hearts are far from me."** Mark 7:6

The harshest words of Jesus are aimed at hypocrites, and the second harshest at the people who are primarily concerned with possessions. He says that power, prestige and possessions are the three things that prevent us from recognizing and receiving the Reign of God.

When he says that to the good, upright people, their reaction is indignation and scandal. They call him an unbeliever, an enemy of the law, and finally a devil—because they *own* too many things that they have to defend. The only ones who can accept the proclamation of the Reign are those who have nothing to protect, neither their own self-image nor their reputation, their possessions, their theology, their principles, nor their certitudes. And these are called "the poor."

I'm convinced that many of the guilt feelings the middle class is haunted by, much of its widespread negative self-image and much of its self-hatred and self-centeredness are due to the fact that we live in, and have settled down in, a world that Jesus says we should never be at home in.

Fr. Richard Rohr, O.F.M.
Simplicity

Our Little Becomes A Lot

■ **Still he asked them, "How many loaves have you?" "Seven," they replied.** Mark 8:5

There is something bordering on the absurd in the apostles mentioning their having seven loaves of bread when Christ speaks of wanting to give food to 4,000 people. Yet Christ took the bread. It was as if, by making their bread the basic element of his miracle, Christ wanted to demonstrate for the apostles that their input was necessary in order for him to allow them to share in the glory of what was to follow.

The same is true with us, and it will probably be one of the greatest surprises of heaven to learn that Christ has taken our "seven loaves," our less than heroic attempts to be kind, our awkward efforts at forgiveness, our haphazard striving to be patient, our distracted prayers, our fragile compassion, our tarnished purity, our overall humanness . . . that he has taken all these and made them into a glorious crown of glory that he seems proud to bestow upon us as we stand before him when life's journey is done.

Christ may not "need" anything we can offer him, but he chooses to accept our less-than-perfect acts as the necessary condition toward releasing the power of his love in our regard.

Sr. Mary Terese Donze, A.S.C.

When Attitudes Are Crucial

■ **A leper came to him and kneeling down begged him and said, "If you wish, you can make me clean."**
Mark 1:40

A major aspect in any kind of healing is the desire to be made whole.

Whether one is afflicted physically, spiritually or emotionally, wanting to be healed is always the first step. Neither miracle drugs, nor expensive therapy, nor the most discerning spiritual guidance is likely to have any impact unless the "patient" participates in the healing process. One's very attitude, then, can be the deciding factor between health and sickness.

Jesus, the Divine Physician, does indeed desire that we should be whole. We may not always be restored to full health, but if we ask for the grace of healing, we may be surprised at how fully we *can* live, in spite of limitations. Through his help, we can move beyond whatever afflicts us by learning acceptance, by developing new gifts, by finding new ways to cope. What we do with our lives, then, does not depend upon the whims of fate so much as on our own wills and God's abundant grace.

In our weakness, make us strong, O Lord, that we may continue to serve you.

Elizabeth-Anne Vanek

Divine Exasperation

■ **Jesus sighed from the depth of his spirit and said, "Why does this generation seek a sign?"** Mark 8:12

Jesus was exasperated because the Pharisees were testing him. He found it irritating when they asked for a sign. How Jesus must have longed for them to believe his message without asking him to prove it.

I rarely think of Jesus as the Exasperated One. Most often I see him as the Loving or Compassionate One. Yet to deny Jesus' exasperation is to deny Jesus a part of his humanity. There were times when Jesus was frustrated, irritated and upset. These emotional responses did not make him any less good or holy. Rather, his responses confirmed that he was fully human. Jesus continued to love and care for others even when he sighed deeply at their sin and failures.

That we are all fully human is something we should always keep in mind. We may be loved dearly by someone but also experience their irritability and exasperation at times, just as we can get upset with others whom we love. While it is essential to have some control over our emotions, it is also necessary to accept our natural human responses.

Jesus, help us to accept our humanity even while we try our best to be kind and loving people

Sr. Joyce Rupp, O.S.M.

Right Place—Right Time

■ **All good giving and every perfect gift is from above, coming down from the Father of lights . . .** James 1:17

I can recognize God's gifts, however small, by their quality and depth.

They may be unexpected and even offbeat, spectacular or almost imperceptible. They may be found in the most unlikely people or places. Yet all God's gifts are exquisite and deeply satisfying. God's gifts answer my secret longings, my unknown needs and deepest desires.

God offers each one of us countless opportunities to receive genuine benefits. I have often found that these benefits can come disguised in some slightly unpleasant tasks or experiences. I have often wondered aloud how God could find any real value in what God gave me at a particular time. Much later I have discovered why I was the one who needed to be there or to perform that action. The people involved needed my particular gift as I needed theirs.

God's gifts are tailored to fit exactly. God knows where I am best needed and what I need. God sees to it that I am often at the right place at the right time to be both giver and recipient.

O God, thank you for all your good gifts. May I learn to recognize and appreciate them.

Jean Royer

Our Crosses Are 'Optional'

■ **If any want to become my followers, let them deny themselves and take up their cross and follow me.**

Mark 8:34

The phrase "Take up your cross" has been softened by usage. We've all heard it since we've been kids. We don't get the punch of it anymore. The cross is not simply enduring your hangnail for the day for the love of Jesus, or putting up with the inconvenience that your air conditioner doesn't work. That's what it's become in affluent societies.

The "cross" in the New Testament is precisely the suffering that comes into our lives by the choices we make for the Kingdom.

In that sense it is always optional and voluntary.

Lord, give me grace to see what I am called to do for the Kingdom—and the courage to do it.

Fr. Richard Rohr, O.F.M.
Radical Grace

Healing Isn't Neat And Tidy

■ **Putting spittle on his eyes, he laid his hands on him.**
                                                    Mark 8:23

Why didn't Jesus just say, "You're healed" or simply place his hands on the blind man's eyes? One reason may be that some cultures considered spittle to have healing powers and used it to ward off evil. I think there may be another symbolic reason. Spittle is messy, intrusive, and repulsive. Healing does not always happen in neat and tidy ways. Sometimes our inner healing comes from a painful, difficult life experience which eventually brings about greater clarity in our lives. We begin to see in a new way.

I remember a time when I was reprimanded for my independence and my arrogance. That comment deeply hurt me, but eventually I began to see the truth of what was said to me. That led me to reflect on my feelings of insecurity and to see my over-compensation of trying to care for everything myself. I wasn't allowing others to help me. I didn't like the "spittle" of that comment but it was a gift in that it led me to change some blind attitudes and actions. I believe God works through experiences like this and helps us to grow when "spittle" is put upon us.

Healing God, help me to count on your grace when the spittle of life comes my way.
                                    Sr. Joyce Rupp, O.S.M.

Our Time Is Not Our Own

■ **And people were bringing children to him . . . he embraced them and blessed them, placing his hands on them.** Mark 10:13, 16

Christ's days were full of activity, and he often spent the night in prayer. A certain urgency pervaded all he said and did. Yet he also took time out from his busy routine to "waste" it on a troop of youngsters.

If there is one thing over which most of us keep a jealous control, it is our time. Even when it comes to supporting a good cause, we often would rather part with a bit of money than give of our time. And we find it difficult not to resent others for breaking in on our schedules.

Yet time is really not ours at all. We have no rightful claim to even the next minute. If, then, Christ should come to us today in one of his "little ones"—a lonely neighbor, a frustrated teenager, a boring acquaintance—may we have the grace to forget the false notion of "our time" so that we may welcome Jesus in one of these "children" of his.

Lord, let me have time for others as I count on your having time for me.

Sr. Mary Terese Donze, A.S.C.

Stop Talking And Listen

■ **Behold, I stand at the door and knock. If anyone hears my voice and opens the door, I will enter his house and dine with him, and he with me.** Revelation 3:20

The three rules for becoming a good listener are, Stop Talking, Stop Talking and Stop Talking!

These same rules might be aptly applied to the life of prayer as well. Of course, there are many things that we need to say to God, and we should let these prayers flow when they come to us. Nonetheless, there comes a point at which we shall be unable to hear God's voice unless we "stop talking." Listening for God takes great determination and courage. We must die to our desires for quick fixes, dramatic results and unambiguous directives. We simply sit in stillness, calming our voices, our hearts and our minds. We may fall asleep, become distracted, despair of success or begin to feel fearful. If we persevere, gently accepting the obstacles as well as the gifts, we will find ourselves gradually more at home in the silence, making the silent waiting itself into a prayer of surrender and communion. On this ground we are led by God beyond words into the life and into the very heartbeat of God.

Lord God, help me to wait in silence for your voice.
Nancy F. Summers

Old Habits Die Hard

■ **Jesus knew that he had been ill for a long time . . . said to him, "Do you want to be well?"** John 5:6

This question of Jesus to the paralytic seems very insensitive. The man has been infirm for 38 years. Of course he wants to be liberated so he can walk! Of course he doesn't want to be the object of others' pity! Why does Jesus ask this poor man such a question?

Jesus knows the human heart well. Many of us do not want to be healed. We've grown comfortable with our infirmities. Our illness becomes our excuse from growing up. We come to enjoy being taken care of and having others do things for us. Above all, if we are sick we do not have to "pick up our mat and walk." We can continue to simply lay still and watch the world go by. We don't have to change.

Jesus reminds us of the pain that comes with all true healing. We must relearn to walk on our own and take responsibility for our actions. We must be willing to accept our healing and give up our sins. We must live out our healing in our daily lives. This is frightening. We find it much easier to lay on our mats and simply let others do things for us.

Jesus, give me courage to accept healing.

Fr. William F. Maestri
My Lenten Journal

Trust The Lord Completely

■ **The Lord is my shepherd; I shall not want. In verdant pastures he gives me repose. Beside restful waters he leads me; he refreshes my soul. He guides me in right paths for his name's sake. Even though I walk in the dark valley I fear no evil; for you are at my side.** Psalm 23:1-4

Why must we give ourselves fully to God? Because God has given himself to us. If God, who owes nothing to us, is ready to impart to us no less than that, shall we answer with just a fraction of ourselves?

One thing Jesus asks of me: that I lean on him; that in him and only in him I put complete trust; that I surrender myself to him unreservedly. Even when all goes wrong and I feel as if I am a ship without a compass, I must give myself completely to him. I must not attempt to control God's action; I must not count the stages in the journey he would have me make. I must not desire a clear perception of my advance upon the road, must not know precisely where I am upon the way of holiness.

I ask God to make a saint of me; yet I must leave to him the choice of the saintliness itself and still more the means which leads to it.

Jesus, daily I will lean on you. Help me to trust you and to love you completely.

Mother Teresa
Total Surrender

Selling Out Cheaply

■ **They paid him thirty pieces of silver, and from that time on he looked for an opportunity to hand him over.**
Matthew 26:15-16

After many years of reading and hearing the story of how Judas betrayed Jesus, I still find it incredible and repulsive. I wonder how Judas could ever have given away his loving friend for such a paltry reason. Yet, when I look into my own life I see that there are times when the betrayer in myself rears its wretched head and I meet my own Judas.

I can sense the betrayer in myself when I do not live up to the values and ideas I proclaim. It also happens when I sell the best part of myself by trying to keep up with what the culture tells me I ought to be, to own, to wear, to admire. I can sell my belief and my dreams for very little sometimes when I am anxious and tired and fearful and hurt.

At a long exhausting meeting not so long ago, I knew that there was an older woman there who did not have a ride home and would be asking for one. When the meeting ended, I walked out quickly so that I wouldn't hear her request and have to be inconvenienced by the extra miles. In that moment, I sold my compassion and care for my own convenience and comfort.

Forgive me, Jesus, for the times I have betrayed you.

Sr. Joyce Rupp, O.S.M.

Humble Prayerfulness

■ **Guide me in your truth and teach me, for you are God my savior.** Psalm 25:5

God certainly has preferences regarding every choice we face, whether the matter at hand seems big or small, important or insignificant. He wants to reveal his preferences to us and will do so if we seek his help and remain receptive to his inspirations.

Try to fathom the unique privilege we have. The transcendent God of heaven and earth, the sustainer and energizer of the whole universe, wants to communicate with each one of us personally and individually. Yet God will not force his preferences on us and even permits us to choose otherwise.

So how can we know God's preferences? And how could we possibly choose any more of action which we know he doesn't want for us? Because God's is not the only voice we hear. We must learn to recognize the presence of conflicting spirits at work within us at all times: the Holy Spirit, the evil spirit, and our own perverse spirit . . . To learn the Lord's preferences, we need to develop a vibrant faith and a spirit of humble prayerfulness . . . which helps us recognize our own inability and the utter helplessness either to know or fulfill God's will in our lives without his special help.

Fr. David E. Rosage
Beginning Spiritual Direction

A Clear Choice To Hear God

■   **Oh, that today you would hear his voice: Do not harden your hearts as at Meribah, as on the day of Massah in the desert.** Psalm 95:7-8

I began to understand this verse after a few years of marriage, when during some argument or misunderstanding, I could feel myself resisting any resolution of the matter. For some perverse reason that I can no longer recall, I just wanted the dispute to go on, most likely because I didn't want to admit I was wrong or to apologize.

I can be exactly the same way with God, particularly during a time of spiritual confusion and turmoil. My heart hardens, perhaps because I am trying to protect myself against being hurt, but very soon cynicism and bitterness have the upper hand.

Now I realize I have a choice: to go on hardening my heart or simply stop doing it. I have the option to cultivate gratitude for even the simplest of blessings, to look for signs of hope, to recognize and accept my own feelings whatever they may be. If I am able to receive the grace to relax my heart in such ways, then I will have already heard God's voice in my life.

Mark Neilsen

A Little Help From Friends

■ **They came bringing to him a paralytic carried by four men.** Mark 2:3

When I read this story, I think of all those people in my life who have helped me grow. I may not have been flat down on a stretcher but I was definitely in need of some help so that I could get myself together and be more whole. I think of people who never gave up on me, even when I was complaining and out of sorts constantly. I think of parents, teachers and mentors who saw a potential for wisdom and leadership in me that I had no inkling was there. I think of my religious community members who offered me spiritual nourishment and the blessing of kinship.

Each of us has been that person on the stretcher at some time. How blessed we are if there has been someone who cared enough about us not to give up on us! How thankful we can be if they somehow brought us to Jesus for greater healing and wholeness. Take a few extra minutes today to think about the people in your life who carried you when you were on "the stretcher" of mental, emotional, spiritual or physical pain. Take time to thank God for these gifts, and if possible, to write a note to one of these people to thank them for helping you to be more whole.

Sr. Joyce Rupp, O.S.M.

Wanting What God Wants

■ **Here are my mother and my brothers. [For] whoever does the will of God is my brother and sister and mother.**
Mark 3:34-35

We must intend our own salvation in the way God intends it.

God desires that we should be saved. We too need constantly to desire what God desires. God not only means us to be saved, but actually gives us all we need to achieve salvation. So we are not to stop at merely desiring salvation, but go a step further and accept all the graces God has prepared for us, the graces constantly offered to us.

It is all very well to say, "I want to be saved." It is not much use merely saying, "I want to take the necessary steps." We must actually take the steps. We need to make a definite resolution to take and use the graces God holds out to us. Our wills must be in tune with God's. Because God wants us to be saved, we should want to be saved. We should also welcome the means to salvation that God intends us to take . . . that is why general acts of devotion and prayer should always be followed by particular resolutions.

Lord, I resolve to pray daily for the courage to do your will.

St. Francis de Sales
Francis de Sales: Finding God Wherever You Are

Self-Control Vs. Self-Surrender

■ **Jesus said to them, "Amen, I say to you, tax collectors and prostitutes are entering the kingdom of God before you. When John came to you in the way of righteousness, you did not believe him; but tax collectors and prostitutes did."** Matthew 21:31-32

Jesus often says that the tax collectors and the drunkards are more open to the Reign of God than theologians who have only theories in our heads.

This statement of Jesus is an eternally valid judgment and a warning to those who deal with the Christian faith professionally: It's very dangerous to be a "professional Christian," to be possessed by theories of conversion and salvation. I believe that religion is the safest place to avoid God, because God wants to lead us to self-surrender, and all too often religion teaches us only self-control. And these are two completely different movements: Self-control is a different movement from self-surrender. Genuine self-control is a fruit of the Spirit, but it's not the *cause* of the Spirit.

Jesus, may I not use my religion and my piety just for self-control, but to learn self-surrender.

Fr. Richard Rohr, O.F.M.
Simplicity

Jesus Shows Us God Cares

■ **Teacher, do you not care that we are perishing?**

Mark 4:38

The first followers of Jesus seemed to need regular reassurances that he cared about them. For instance, in the calming of the sea, the disciples didn't doubt Jesus' ability to rescue them, they doubted whether he cared! Jesus, with unending patience, never fails to prove his compassion. In all the situations and various needs that Jesus encountered, he never suggested to petitioners that the purpose of their illness was personal growth, or that a certain catastrophe was their destiny, or that helping them would violate their free will. Jesus always cared enough to alleviate whatever suffering he came across. In doing so, he revealed to us the great heart of God—always loving, always caring, always on our side.

The existence of suffering is a mystery that continues to haunt us today. While theories abound, we still have more questions than answers. One question, though, was put to rest by every action in the life of Jesus. Does God care? Yes. Yes, God cares.

Lord, wherever I am mystified by the presence of suffering, help me to recall your perfect love and compassion.

Nancy F. Summers

Strive For Perfect Contrition

■ **Let us rid ourselves of every burden and sin that clings to us and persevere in running the race.** Hebrews 12:1

We must reject the phony image of holiness. A saint is just a sinner who is more repentant than most of us. If there is any place for perfection in our lives, it is perfect contrition for our sins. Perfect contrition is grief of the soul because we have offended God who is infinitely good, coupled with a firm resolve to cease offending him. Imperfect contrition is sorrow for our sins because we know we have been caught and fear the punishment due to them. A little boy caught with his hand in the cookie jar is a good example. Most of us are a mixture of holiness and selfishness, and hopefully we grow in grace and love of God as we mature in our spiritual lives. Some of us unfortunately never grow enough to take responsibility for our failings.

The journey to holiness begins anew each day when we begin to see some fault of our own, some egotism, some narcissism, some self-pity, something we haven't yet given up. It can look like a seven-storey mountain to us. We will despair of ever getting past such a huge barrier . . . until slowly the grace of God shows us the only clear path over it.

Fr. Benedict Groeschel, C.F.R.
Healing The Original Wound

What Am I Full Of?

■ **Woe to you who are full; you shall go hungry.** Luke 6:25

The fullness Jesus names as a curse is not merely restricted to food. Any kind of fullness "not of God" can only lead to emptiness.

The root of the word "sad" is the Anglo-Saxon word "saed" meaning "sated" or "full." Just as over-indulging on holidays can produce feelings of discomfort and "the blues," so cramming oneself in other ways leads to "woe." Whether we become full through acquiring possessions, indulging our addictions, in workaholism or dependent relationships, the comfort we experience is temporary and is invariably followed by a sense of "letdown."

Fullness is a major stumbling block in the spiritual life. It creates the illusion that we can find happiness, that we can "pursue happiness" as if it were a commodity. It makes us imagine we can achieve it through our own striving, struggling and exertion. It distracts us from our search for God. If we allow ourselves to experience the terror of our core emptiness, if we allow ourselves to be still enough and silent enough to recognize our basic loneliness, then, perhaps, we will finally realize that we need God. God alone is the answer to emptiness.

Elizabeth-Anne Vanek

A Whole-hearted Return

■ **Yet even now, says the Lord, return to me with your whole heart . . .** Joel 2:12

Each year when I hear the phrase "return with your *whole* heart" at the start of Lent—I gulp. Surrendering one's whole being to God is some challenge! I look again into my heart to discover those places that have not yet returned to the One who calls me. This is the wisdom behind having a Lenten journey each year. Knowing that I will be re-invited to return to God keeps me from being discouraged as I struggle to give my whole self to this loving Creator.

What does it mean to "return"? Re-turning indicates that I have been there, that I am making a shift, turning around and heading there again. I cannot re-turn to a place where I have not already been. I find this thought very comforting because I know that if I go to the very depths of my being, I belong totally to God. Some places of my heart have strayed and lost their way, but I know they belong to God. Lent is a time to go looking for these places. Lent is also a time to remember that God's invitation stands forever. Always God waits for us to return with our whole heart. What a loving God we have!

Thank you, loving God, for the challenging invitation to return to you with my whole heart.

Sr. Joyce Rupp, O.S.M.

Learn To Be A Healthy Sinner

■ **You will cast into the depths of the sea all our sins.**
                                                    Micah 7:19

During Lent we are encouraged to hold close to our hearts the memory of the mercy of God. Keeping this in mind, Lent can be a comforting time to reflect on our sins.

Regarding sin in our lives, we seem to be standing between two heresies. The old heresy put too much stress on our limitations. There was a tendency to call everything a sin. The new heresy reflects an almost casual attitude about sin, suggesting that nothing is a sin. Neither of these positions offers us a healthy attitude about sin.

The old tendency to live in constant guilt is not healthy. The new reluctance to call ourselves sinners is not healthy either. Perhaps we need to pray for the grace to be healthy sinners. If we are healthy, we are not afraid to name the sin in our lives. Yet even while facing our sinfulness, we must be aware that we are more than our sins.

Jesus, we hold the memory of your mercy in our hearts. You have cast our sins into the depths of the sea. Teach us to be healthy sinners.
                                    Sr. Macrina Wiederkehr, O.S.B.

The Time For Pruning

■ **Figs are not taken from thornbushes nor grapes picked from brambles.** Luke 6:44

Certain foods evoke strong memories in me. For the first time since coming to the United States many years ago I recently found fresh figs in a grocery. Eagerly, I bought a pint of small black figs, fully expecting they would carry me back to the fig tree of my childhood—one of massive girth reputed to be as old as my parents' 500-year-old home in Malta. This tree yielded two abundant crops each year. The figs were often pear-sized, succulent and rich in flavor. To my disappointment, however, most of the figs I bought had grown moldy under the plastic wrap. Their limp forms made me wonder whether they had already begun to spoil when they were harvested.

Jesus presents the image of a "good tree," one whose fruit is the measure of its worth. In Lent, it is time, once again, to evaluate our own yield. Do we allow God to be the source of all that we are and of all that we do, or is the divine image obscured by thorns and brambles? Do we produce a harvest that moves others to faith or is our fruit like the rotting figs I bought? Do we allow God to prune away the dead wood, or do we resist change and transformation?

Elizabeth-Anne Vanek

Accepting Our Crosses

■ **If any want to become my followers, let them deny themselves and take up their cross daily and follow me.**
Luke 9:23

A significant aspect of the human condition is our tendency to refuse to accept limits. There is within us, to use the image of Albert Camus, a rebel. The opening pages of Scripture attest to our refusal to accept limits. Paradise is lost because Adam and Eve cannot accept the limitation of their situation. They will not abide by the will of God. By contrast, Jesus, the new Adam, humbly accepts the cross. He counters pride with humility, rebellion with acceptance, the love of power with the power of love.

The cross comes to each of us in a personal way. The temptation is always to rebel. Our basic instinct is to follow the advice of Peter: turn from Jerusalem and seek security elsewhere. Yet we know this is the way of Satan. It is only by accepting our cross, and uniting it with Jesus, that we have the hope of eternal life. There is great wisdom and deep peace in accepting the cross. This is not an acceptance of despair or resignation. We accept the cross because it is the way to life in abundance.

Lord, help me to accept my cross with courage and without complaint.

Fr. William F. Maestri
My Way Of The Cross Journal

When The Dew Is Enough

■ **I will be like the dew for Israel.** Hosea 14:6

One of my fond memories of childhood on an Iowa farm is the dew of summer mornings. The coolness of a new dawn and the grass would be deliciously wet for my small bare feet. I remember my father speaking one time of how his corn crop could be saved in a dry season if there was enough heavy dew each day. If there was enough moisture on the leaves, it could be absorbed by the plant and would help it to survive.

In this message spoken through Hosea, God promises to be like dew for Israel. It is this dew which will help Israel to "blossom like a lily." This is a very significant promise because Israel then was in a tough place, a dry summer—struggling with the sin of the people and with the terrors of enemies of the land. Undoubtedly, Israel wanted more than "dew." A nice, full rainfall of help would have been greatly welcomed, but the dew was enough to get Israel through to better times. Isn't that like our lives? Sometimes we are in a tough spot and all we have is a little dew. Yet, this bit of spiritual moisture or help from God is enough to see us through until better times.

God, help me to appreciate the dew which comes instead of bemoaning the lack of a great rainfall.

Sr. Joyce Rupp, O.S.M.

Coping With Life's Suffering

■ **O Lord, my God, I cried out to you and you healed me. Lord, you brought me up from Sheol; you kept me from going down to the pit.** Psalm 30:3-4

Today's welfare and consumer state has accommodated itself to a permanent lie. That lie is the universally given impression that serene happiness is everywhere the rule, or if that is not strictly true in every case, it soon will be the case given goodwill and the irresistible progress of humankind.

No one would wish to quarrel with the ideals of more health, wealth, freedom, and so on by which modern persons set such store. The fact is that many things remain: pain, old age, sickness, disappointment in marriage, in one's children, in one's job, and at the end of it all death, which no one escapes and which is already a controlling factor of life because of the fear it generates. So the question can only be *how* one is to cope with this reality of suffering and death.

Cynicism and stoicism do not go very far. In faith, hope and love a Christian understands this aspect of her life as a sharing in the Lord's passion . . . The free, loving participation in the passion of Christ— that is what we try to do in our Lenten practices.

Fr. Karl Rahner, S.J.
The Great Church Year

Embracing Our Brokenness

■ **The Lord is close to the brokenhearted, saves those whose spirit is crushed.** Psalm 34:19

The first response to our brokenness is to face it squarely and befriend it. This may seem quite unnatural. Our first, most spontaneous response to pain and suffering is to avoid it, to keep it at arm's length; to ignore, circumvent or deny it. Suffering— be it physical, mental or emotional—is almost always experienced as an unwelcome intrusion into our lives, something that should not be there. It is difficult, if not impossible, to see anything positive in suffering; it must be avoided at all costs.

The first step to healing is not a step away from the pain, but a step toward it. We have to find the courage to embrace our brokenness, to make our most feared enemy into a friend and to claim it as an intimate companion. Healing is often so difficult because we don't want to know the pain . . . and that is so true of the pain that comes from a broken heart.

The deep truth is that our human suffering need not be an obstacle to the joy and peace we so desire, but can become, instead, the means to it.

Fr. Henri J. M. Nouwen
Life Of The Beloved

Why I Believe In Eternal Life

■ **And this is the promise he made us: eternal life.**

1 John 2:25

The hope we have for eternal life, for our loved ones . . . and for ourselves is not founded on stories of people coming back from the dead. It is not based on provocative ideas about reincarnation, nor on some expectation that somehow, some day, science may be able to preserve life indefinitely with substitute body parts. Our hope for eternal life is founded on our trust in Jesus who proclaimed his power over life and death. His promise justifies our belief in immortality.

But there is another justification for that belief. Our hope for eternal life is not based on our inability to accept our own death, nor on the fact that we will live on vicariously in our descendants or in someone's memory. The basis of our expectation of eternal life is founded on something very simple, yet powerful— the unconditional love that God has for us . . .

God loves each of us so as to give us life in the first place. But God's love does not change; it is unchanging and eternal. As a true lover, God wishes us to live forever, and God's love, which has power over life, guarantees that we will never perish.

O God, thank you for the gift of eternal life.

Michael R. Kent
Bringing The Word To Life

Our Plea For Healing

■ **Behold, the Lamb of God.** John 1:36

The priest says, "This is the Lamb of God who takes away the sins of the world. Happy are those who are called to his supper." And we respond: "Lord, I am not worthy to receive you, but only say the word and I shall be healed."

We pray this short, simple prayer at Mass immediately before we stand and walk forward to receive Holy Communion. For me, it contains the entire richness of the liturgy of the Eucharist. If for some reason I was kept from going to Mass, I believe it would be this prayer that would sustain me. For this is what our liturgy and the mystery of the Eucharist is all about. We are never truly worthy to receive such a divine gift as the body and blood of our Savior. Nonetheless, we can hear the Word of God burning within us and know that we do not need to be worthy. We present ourselves as we are before our God and plead for forgiveness and love. With our acceptance of that grace, we become healed. Healed of our sins. Healed of our inordinate drive for perfection. Healed of all our human frailties. Healed by the hand of God.

Lord, only say the word and I shall be healed.

Steve Givens

How Long Is Eternity?

■ **I write these things to you so that you may know that you have eternal life . . .** 1 John 5:13

Imagine (as someone has) a brass ball as large as the earth. Picture a bird flying past that ball once every million years and brushing lightly against it with its wing-feather. After the millionth million year the slightest scuff might begin to show on the brassy surface. Following the logic of the supposition, should the ever-so-slight friction of the wing go on endlessly, a moment would come when the brass would disappear. The mind boggles at the thought of the countless eons needed for such an event.

Yet the ever-present **now** of eternity lasts longer. And the awesome mystery of it all is that, whether we will it or not, you and I are destined to be part of that enduring reality. Whether that existence will be everlasting life and joy for us or everlasting frustration lies in our power to choose right now, today, this moment. God hovers over us in love, urging us to make the choices we will wish we had made those million years hence, but we are free to choose.

God, help me to use my freedom wisely.

Sr. Mary Terese Donze, A.S.C.

God's Mighty Works

■ **To what shall we compare the kingdom of God, or what parable can we use for it? It is like a mustard seed.**
Mark 4:30-31

Grace is like a mustard seed sown in us, the smallest of all seeds. It is growing, but it is not going to turn us into a cedar of Lebanon. We will be doing well if we become a modest shrub. . . .

Where are the mightiest works of the kingdom accomplished? In our attitudes and hence in secret. Where there is charity, there is God. Opportunities to work for the homeless, the starving, the aging, are all readily available. No one may notice our good deeds, including ourselves. The kingdom of God manifests itself in the modest changes in our attitudes and in the little improvements in our behavior that no one may notice, including ourselves. These are the mighty works of God, not great external accomplishments.

"To what shall I liken the kingdom of God?" Jesus asked. The kingdom is manifested in ordinary daily life and how we live it. Can we accept the God of everyday life? If we can, then we can enjoy the kingdom here and now, without having to wait for an apocalypse or someone to deliver us from our difficulties.

Fr. Thomas Keating, O.C.S.O.
The Kingdom Of God Is Like . . .

'Those Who Count For Nothing'

■ **I will leave as a remnant in your midst a people humble and lowly.** Zephaniah 3:12

As I was admiring a simple Japanese building recently in a botanical garden, the tour guide pointed out that its replacement value would exceed a million dollars. Instead of being impressed, I felt my enthusiasm drain. The beauty of the structure had been reduced to dollars. Size, cost and numbers seem to be indicators of worth, particularly in America. The success of our work is measured by these factors, as is the value of one's possessions. "How much is he or she worth?" is one common expression. And an event is deemed significant only if it draws crowds.

The idea of a "faithful remnant" is in radical opposition to this notion that numbers are everything or that status and wealth are requirements if we are to make a difference in the world. But St. Paul assures us that God has chosen "those who count for nothing" to keep alive the promise of the covenant. The simple of heart will earn the blessings Jesus announces in the Beatitudes; from their example, the rest of the world will learn the way to holiness.

Keep us faithful to your word, O Lord, that we may become a blessing to others.

Elizabeth-Anne Vanek

Facing Up To The Reality Of Sin

■ **Then I declared my sin to you; my guilt I did not hide. I said, "I confess my faults to the Lord," and you took away the guilt of my sin.** Psalm 32:5

The world that the Son of Man entered deserved condemnation because of the sin that had dominated all of history, beginning with the fall of our first parents. This is absolutely unacceptable to post-Enlightenment thought. *It refuses to accept the reality of sin, and, in particular, it refuses to accept original sin.* When, during my last visit to Poland, I chose the Decalogue and the commandment of love as a theme for homilies, Polish followers of the "enlightened agenda" were upset. The Pope becomes *persona non grata* when he tries to convince the world of human sin . . . But convincing the world of the existence of sin is not the same as condemning it for sinning. "God did not send his Son into the world to condemn the world, but that the world might be saved through him." (John 3:17) *Convincing the world of sin means creating the conditions for its salvation.* Awareness of our own sinfulness, including that which is inherited, is the first condition for salvation; the next is the confession of this sin before God, who desires only to receive this confession so that He can save.

Pope John Paul II
Crossing The Threshold Of Hope

The Majesty Of The Night Stars

■ **Yours, O Lord, are grandeur and power, majesty, splendor, and glory.** 1 Chronicles 29:11

Living in a rural area offers me the privilege of viewing the majesty of the stars at night. The night sky is a display case of God's jewels. Astronomers estimate that with the naked eye a person can see about 3,000 stars, but there are 400 billion stars in the Milky Way galaxy alone. There are probably billions of galaxies! The distance and magnitude of these stars which appear in our skies call me to awesome wonder. Each night I am irresistibly drawn to my window to marvel at them. And each night I come up with only questions. *What is beyond these stars? Why were they created? What is the importance of our minuscule earth in the midst of this untold splendor that God has created? What mysteries do these celestial bodies hold for us in the future?*

If I cannot grasp the dimensions of nighttime space which seems to reach toward eternity, why do I even try to understand God? How incomprehensible that the stars are there and I am here! At night all I can do is gaze in awe at the sacredness of the infinite twinkling darkness, knowing that I am somehow getting a glimpse of God through my window.

Sr. Ruth Marlene Fox, O.S.B.

A Prayer For Self-Esteem

■ **If you fulfill the royal law according to the scripture, "You shall love your neighbor as yourself," you are doing well.** James 2:8

The royal law of loving others as ourselves is quite a challenge. First of all, it requires us to love ourselves well. I meet many, many adults who struggle with their self-worth. If they make mistakes, they call themselves "stupid." If they don't match up to what people think is the right physical size, shape or color, they consider themselves "ugly." If they say the wrong thing or lack some social skill, they abuse themselves verbally and feel guilty or ashamed.

St. Teresa of Avila developed a prayer that I find very helpful in gaining self-esteem. Sit in a chair and imagine Jesus looking upon you with great love. That's it. Just sit there and be loved. This is not easy at first but gradually day after day, it becomes easier and more acceptable. As we learn to love ourselves fully, we will find that it is much easier to love others in a non-judgmental way as well.

Jesus, on those days when my mistakes and personality flaws glare at me, help me to continue to extend generous and non-judgmental love to both myself and to others.

Sr. Joyce Rupp, O.S.M.

What God Does Matters Most

■ **For whoever wishes to save his life will lose it, but whoever loses his life for my sake and that of the gospel will save it.** Mark 8:35

We can take ourselves, our striving, our efforts to be better, too seriously. Our striving itself, our hot pursuit of excellence, above all in our relation to God, can be another form of the self-centeredness and self-concern we all recognize as part of the problem.

To forget ourselves is obviously part of the solution according to Jesus. If all our effort is centered on making me better, more virtuous, more spiritual, more perfect, isn't this a matter of just more *self*ishness, even if it isn't concerned with getting me more power over others, more wealth, more material security? It may, as someone has said, feed the very vice it intends to destroy, self-centeredness, self-concern.

We need an occasional reminder—really more than occasional—that our perfection is more a matter of allowing God to act in us than our own striving . . .

Do not try to hold on to God, to perfection. Just hope, trust, that God will hold on to you.

Help me to remember, Holy Spirit, that what God does for me, not what I do for God, is most important.
Fr. Don Talafous, O.S.B.
A Word For The Day

Love From The Heart

■ **The tongue . . . is a restless evil, full of deadly poison. With it we bless the Lord and Father, and with it we curse human beings who are made in the likeness of God. From the same mouth come blessing and cursing.** James 3:8-10

Jesus taught us how to forgive out of love, how to forget out of humility. So let us examine our hearts and see if there is any unforgiven hurt—any unforgotten bitterness!

The quickest and surest way is the tongue—use it for the good of others. If you think well of others, you will also speak well of others and to others. From the abundance of the heart the mouth speaketh. If your heart is full of love, you will speak of love. If you forgive others the wrong they have done, your heavenly Father will also forgive you; but if you do not forgive others, then the wrongs you have done will not be forgiven by your Father.

It is easy to love those who are far away. It isn't always easy to love those who are right next to us. It is easier to offer a dish of rice to satisfy the hunger of a poor person than to fill up the loneliness and suffering of someone lacking love in our own family.

Lord, help me to speak lovingly, to bless rather than to curse.

Mother Teresa
Daily Readings

True Love

■ **Do you not know that to be a lover of the world means enmity with God?** James 4:4

"**L**ove" is such an overused word today that we can easily forget the power behind it. The experience of real lovers teaches us that love is passionate, all-consuming. Who or what we love becomes the desire of our lives, the object of our every waking moment, the source of our happiness. Meet someone in love and you will soon find that there's room for little else in his or her life.

It is in this ultimate sense that James uses the word. The simple fact is that if we choose to love the world in this way, to make the pursuit of its blessings the great goal of our existence, our *raison d'etre*, we haven't time or energy for God. By this we make ourselves enemies of God and of the abundant life which only God can bestow.

Jesus calls us to love properly—to love God with our whole heart, being, strength, and mind. Then we can appreciate and accept the good things of this life for what they truly are.

God, help me freely and wholeheartedly to embrace you as the love of my life, and my only lasting joy.

Fr. Anthony Schueller, S.S.S.

Beware Of Being Too Critical

■ . . . **the leading Pharisees, and the people there were observing Jesus carefully.** Luke 14:1

Whenever I read of Jesus being constantly scrutinized, criticized, and pressured by harsh judgments, I think of how I would never have done that had I known him. Then something happens to remind me that I am not all that different from the Pharisees.

Recently, I was in a grocery and I saw a woman who looked like someone I had known who had treated me harshly. I began thinking about this woman and soon all kinds of negative thoughts flooded my mind. This continued until I drove home, got out of the car—and realized that I was so busy thinking unpleasant thoughts about that woman that I had completely forgotten to fetch my bags of groceries!

I laughed right out loud when I saw what I had done, and I said, "Okay, God, you got me." I instantly recognized how self-absorbed I had been in something similar to the Pharisees, judging unlovingly and looking at another's life with an unkind viewpoint. It taught me a good lesson to be more careful about the negative energy that can easily creep into my thoughts and feelings.

Jesus, when I focus on others' failings, return me to positive thinking with your love and kindness.

Sr. Joyce Rupp, O.S.M.

Seeing Evil For What It Is

■ **The woman saw that the tree was good for food, pleasing to the eyes, and desirable for gaining wisdom.**

Genesis 3:6

Would we sin if sin were not pleasurable? Our first parents were lured into disobedience by the attractiveness of the tree—not that the tree itself could be blamed for their perversity, but its very attractiveness became an excuse for them to indulge in the fruit. They could rationalize eating the forbidden fruit because to do so held definite benefits—or so they thought. So it is with most sins. We calculate the risks, weigh the "advantages"—and then sin merrily.

Evil is seductive. It masquerades so well that we see desirability rather than insidiousness. Often, we are blind to our motives and ruthless in our pursuit of what we want. In Matthew's account of the tempting of Jesus in the desert, the tempter packages the lust for power in three different ways, each of which has ego appeal. Jesus, however, sees beneath the packaging and recognizes what is at stake: his very relationship with God, a relationship in which God has absolute primacy. Unlike our first parents—and unlike us at times—he recognizes that to say "yes" to the tempter means nothing less than to betray God.

Give us clarity, O God of Truth, that we may always see evil for what it is.

Elizabeth-Anne Vanek

The Lessons Of Repented Sin

■ **My sacrifice, God, is a broken spirit; God, do not spurn a broken, humbled heart.** Psalm 51:19

Sin is not the end of the world—and, in fact, may actually be the beginning of a number of things that can be gained hardly any other way in life. A bout with greed may be precisely what teaches us the freedom of poverty. A struggle with lust may well be what teaches us about the real nature of love. A strong dose of anger may be what it takes to teach us the beauty of gentleness.

There are things to be learned from sin. One is compassion. Another is understanding. A third is humility. A fourth is perception. Without the ability to own our own sins, these qualities are all hard to come by indeed . . .

Unless we can accept our incompleteness, we can never grow from it. Whatever the heights of our present virtue, the bottomless pit of life stretches always before us, always to be respected, always in the throes of challenging us to look at ourselves again. Humility reminds us that we are all in process always, and that to be in process is perfectly all right.

As the proverb says, "It is not where we are that counts. It is where we are going that matters."

Sr. Joan Chittister, O.S.B.
There Is A Season

A Loving Companion

■ **When Joseph awoke he did as the angel of the Lord had commanded him . . .** Matthew 1:24

What must it have been like for Joseph to have walked the journey of life with Mary? He was part of Mary's questions, anxieties, sorrows and struggles. He listened as Mary tried to explain the mystery of the Annunciation. He stood by her when she delivered the baby Jesus. He hurried with her to Egypt to save their child's life. He worried with her when their son was lost in the temple.

Joseph had great inner strength. He knew that God was his refuge and that he could count on God to be an ever-present help.

We, too, have our "Joseph moments" when we are called to walk with someone who is anxious, or depressed, or seriously ill, or caught up in a life situation that seems overwhelming or intolerable. It is not easy to be like Joseph. We may greatly desire to free the other person from their struggles but be unable to do so. However, we can be patient, understanding, considerate and kind. We cannot do this by ourselves. We, too, need the inner strength that comes from drawing near to God.

Jesus, when I live with or accompany someone in great distress, help me to be a loving companion like Joseph, relying always on your strength.

Sr. Joyce Rupp. O.S.M.

Our Potential To Become Divine

■ **After six days Jesus took Peter, James, and John his brother, and led them up a high mountain by themselves. And he was transfigured before them; his face shone like the sun and his clothes became white as light.**

Matthew 17:2

The statement, "God became human so that human beings might become divine" startles us even though it was made 1,700 years ago by Athanasius, who led the Council of Nicaea to proclaim the divinity of Christ. Athanasius believed that salvation meant such a full restoration of love between God and humanity that people could achieve "deification." *In* Jesus, the fullness of God's life is present. *Through* Jesus, that fullness is offered to us.

What Peter, James, and John saw on Mt. Tabor was human nature transformed beyond anything they could have imagined—as if the humanity of Jesus had no limits. Yet the transfiguration is not just an indication of Christ's divinity; it also reveals *our* potential to become divine. If the goal of the spiritual life is to grow in likeness to God, then the more we progress, the more we participate in God's own life. When the journey reaches its end and we have been stripped of all obstacles to holiness, God's life will become our life and we will be one with God.

Keep us faithful to the journey, loving God, that we may grow in holiness.

Elizabeth-Anne Vanek

When Under Stress, Stretch

■ **Blessed is the man who trusts in the Lord, whose hope is in the Lord. He is like a tree planted beside the waters that stretches out its roots to the stream: it fears not the heat when it comes, its leaves stay green . . .**

Jeremiah 17:7-8

Years ago, when I first began trying to trust in the Lord, I thought I was about to reach a goal: when things got hot, I would stay cool. But like all other would-be disciples, I found out that being Christian did not mean avoiding distress. I began to have second thoughts about the value of "carrying one's cross."

Now I read this verse from Jeremiah and appreciate a little more what it means for the tree to "stretch out its roots": it stretches *because* it is in distress. And it stretches in the depths of darkness, not quite sure when or how relief will come.

That's the way it seems to work for me: in the "heat" of my life's difficulties, I look for help. Sometimes I find only "drought" around me and I am pushed to depend on God. More and more I find that trust in God is a response to stress, not a way of avoiding it.

God, you are the source of all real relief. Help me to trust in you that I may be refreshed, grow and bear fruit.

Mark Neilsen

Go To The Stream Of Grace

■ **As the deer longs for streams of water, so my soul longs for you, O God.** Psalm 42:2

The psalmist tells us that to "thirst for God" is like a deer yearning for water. Some readers have probably been lucky enough to have seen a deer in the morning or early evening peacefully drinking at a stream. Twice a day, in no hurry (unless disturbed by other creatures), they leisurely savor life-sustaining water. What can we learn from this image? We can develop a thirst for God if we go to the stream of grace twice a day—and do so leisurely, not rushed. Before the busyness of the day has captured our attention, we can pause in prayer and unite with God. We open ourselves up to be filled, perhaps with our arms open in a receptive posture. We drink in this light and love, savoring silently, gratefully. Then, when the time is right, we move on into our day. Similarly, at the end of the day, we can return to the stream of grace, to drink again of God's loving Spirit, to carry us into the evening and/or into sleep. When such savoring prayer becomes part of our daily routine, we will probably find that we can't live without it. Our spirit begins to thirst for God every bit as much as the deer yearns for the running stream. And that communion is a foretaste of heaven, waiting for us every day.

James McGinnis

Learning To Trust

■ **Jesus said to him, "You may go; your son will live."
The man believed what Jesus said to him and left.**

John 4:50

Trusting the words of Jesus seems so natural in this story. I rarely find it so clear and simple! Usually, I am either very unsure about what to do or I discount what might happen. I want certainty about the situation! Yet the direction for my life is usually not that precise or apparent. This Gospel story reminds me to listen closely to life because God speaks through people, events, and many situations besides my own meditation. I need to trust that God is with me. I am often not sure what I "hear" at first, so I need to be patient and to ponder it a while. I also have to trust my prayer, my intuition, and the promises in Scripture which assure me of God's guidance.

I am always re-learning trust in God. Last year I was searching for a place to live. I fretted and stewed. Finally, I just let go and stopped being anxious, placing my confidence in God's guidance to help. So after this, a friend of mine unexpectedly helped me find a place that was much more wonderful than anything I had envisioned. How much worry and anxiety I could have avoided had I trusted God and believed much sooner that all would be well!

Sr. Joyce Rupp, O.S.M.

The Fear Of Death—And Life

■ **O my people, I will open your graves and have you rise from them.** Ezekiel 37:12

Although the fear of death is universal, an even more sobering reality is the possibility of never learning to live. Often, those who are most afraid of dying have invested the least in life. Incapable of real commitments, they stand on the sidelines as observers—watching without participating, applauding without making any effort to achieve anything themselves, criticizing without offering either constructive suggestions or any help. Their policy is "not to get involved." They avoid intimacy at all costs and seldom put themselves in any situation where they can be taken advantage of. But perhaps because they have a vague sense of having missed out on something, they have a hard time "letting go" when death draws near.

God is passionate when it comes to opening graves. Those who need to be "raised" are not just the physically dead but the spiritually dead. When people—whether "living" or deceased—are no longer animated by the divine life, they are equally in need of having the tombstones rolled away.

Breathe your life into us, O Creator God, that we may live.

Elizabeth-Anne Vanek

A Hunger For Truth

■ **Jesus then said to those Jews who believed in him, "If you remain in my word, you will truly be my disciples, and you will know the truth, and the truth will set you free."** John 8:31-32

Perhaps you have seen the poster that reads, "The truth shall make you free . . . but first it will make you miserable!"

The truth does sometimes make us miserable, all the more as we cling to the convenient lie, the alluring myth or the cherished illusion. Jesus offers his disciples not perpetual bliss, but freedom, especially freedom from sin.

But some who heard Jesus preferred to cling to their own notions of who the Messiah was, what the Kingdom would be like and how the Law of Moses was to be interpreted. And don't we all, sometimes, hold on to habits, ideas, ways of relating long after we have recognized that these are not good for us?

Over and over Jesus offers us truth and freedom. And because we have been created with an unquenchable desire for more and more truth and greater freedom, we listen. Let us be grateful that someone who knows the truth offers it to us and that from time to time, we can accept it and grow.

Mark Neilsen

Trusting God In The Darkness

■ **I will turn their mourning into joy; I will console and gladden them after their sorrows.** Jeremiah 31:13

I once took a six-month leave of absence from my Franciscan community. I could no longer see my way, and I needed time to go apart and rest.

I spent part of that leave at a monastery in Michigan, where silence and solitude nourished my spirit and helped to clear my vision. But the turning point came during a long auto trip—a big U-turn from Detroit to Phoenix and back. Suddenly, as I was driving through Colorado, lost in prayer, a paraphrase of the words of Jeremiah hit me forcefully— "I will turn **your** mourning into joy . . ." It was the answer and experience I had been seeking. My questions faded, and I gladly returned to my community.

No doubt you have had a similar experience. The darkness that you wrestled with for days or months suddenly was lifted. Yet sometimes in our journey of faith, we need to stay with the darkness, feel its pain and let it teach us. We need to trust that God—in his time and in his way—will bring light out of the darkness and joy out of mourning. As St. Teresa said: "Let nothing disturb you, nothing afright you. All things are passing. God alone suffices."

Fr. Kieran Kay, O.F.M.Conv.

Jesus Calms Our Storms

■ **Jesus got into the boat with them and the wind died down. They were completely astounded.** Mark 6:51

Jesus walks on the water in the midst of a wild storm, and when he gets into the boat with his disciples, the storm yields to calm and stillness. Does this remind you of your own life? It certainly reminds me of mine, especially when I find myself pressed and overwhelmed with too much to do. Many a time I have reached the point of thinking I am going to be crunched by the "storm" of my busyness, and then I remember to pray. I mean *really pray.* I stop everything, close my eyes, and turn my total attention to the deep part of me where God dwells. I sit there a while and unite with God. As I do this, I discover again that I can't manage my life without God's grace working in me. I remember who it is that has the true power and the vital energy.

It's quite amazing what happens when I deliberately invite God into the boat of my life. The wild winds of my inner self become calmer. My work goes better. I lose my panic and anxiety. I feel better about myself, and I recover my peace.

Thank you, Jesus, for getting into the boat with me, for calming the storms in my life, and for teaching me what a difference your presence makes in my life.

Sr. Joyce Rupp, O.S.M.

We Are Made For Worship

■ **Enter, let us bow down in worship; let us kneel before the Lord who made us.** Psalm 95:6

Worship requires that we should bow down and shut up. But is such behavior worthy of a human being? Is it really worthy of God?

Worship does indeed entail for creatures an element of radical humiliation, of making oneself small, of surrendering. Worship always entails an element of sacrifice, of giving something up. This is precisely what attests that God is God and that nothing and no one has the right to exist before him, save by his grace. With worship we give up, we sacrifice our very self, our own glory, our own self-sufficiency . . . By worshipping, we become genuine in the deepest meaning of the word. In worship, we anticipate the return of all things to God. We surrender ourselves to the meaning and flow of existence. As water finds its peace in gliding towards the sea, and the bird its joy in following the wind, so the worshipper in worshipping. Worshipping God is not therefore so much a duty or an obligation as a privilege, even a need. We need something majestic to love and worship! We are made for this. So God is not the one who needs to be worshipped, we are the ones who need to do it.

Fr. Raniero Cantalamessa, O.F.M. Cap.
The Ascent Of Mount Sinai

Sin: A Source Of Divine Grief

■ **Looking around at them with anger and grieved at their hardness of heart . . .** Mark 3:5

When Christ came to earth, the greatest problem he encountered was not sin, but rather humanity's refusal to be redeemed from sin. In today's Gospel, Jesus becomes angry—not just a little ruffled, but wrought up—because a good deed is being obstructed. One would expect such a reaction from an all-holy God. What tore Christ apart was the hardness of those trying to interfere with goodness. It was too much for him. He wanted to win these people over, to help them, and they would have nothing to do with him. And because of that, he grieved. The Son of God grieved!

Sadness or sorrow is one thing, but to grieve is a far more profound experience. Think of how we grieve at the death of a loved one. How deep and lasting the pain! Yet that is how Christ is affected when he finds himself unable to reach our hearts because we have decided against him. What a staggering thought—I have it in my power to reject Christ's compassionate advances—as if he and I were two equals pitting our wills against each other.

O Lord, save me from misusing the free will with which you have gifted me.

Sr. Mary Terese Donze, A.S.C.

Small Steps Toward Holiness

■ **For by one offering Christ has made perfect forever those who are being consecrated.** Hebrews 10:14

I confess a weakness for bumper-sticker theology like, "Christians aren't perfect, just forgiven." But how does that fit with this passage from the Letter to the Hebrews? It appears that the sacrifice of Jesus has insured our perfection, but it is still a long way off.

Meanwhile, we are "being consecrated," made into the image of our Savior. In the economy of Divine Providence, the sacrifice of Jesus not only insures that we are forgiven once and for all time, but that we are being transformed into the image of God's own perfection.

Forgiveness does seem to have a transforming effect on me. When I can really accept it—which means first accepting my need for it—I can discard a load of guilt and fear. Perhaps the lightheartedness following such an experience is one small step on the road to holiness.

Most of the time, however, the transformation into perfection seems a long, long way off. During those times, I console myself with this little bit of wisdom: "Be patient! God isn't finished with me yet."

Mark Neilsen

A Life Of Faith Isn't 'Peachy'

■ **Let us rid ourselves of every burden and sin that clings to us and persevere in running the race that lies before us . . . In your struggle against sin you have not yet resisted to the point of shedding blood.** Hebrews 12:1, 4

Holiness is a long pilgrimage—a very long one. To understand that trip best is to understand that the life of a Christian is a battle, a spiritual combat. Contemporary theology often leads us to believe that everything has to be "peachy." Haven't you heard those sermons about "positive thinking" and "creation spirituality"? The preacher promises everything will be wonderful. As soon as you get rid of your inhibitions, repressions, and neurotic defense mechanisms, you'll absolutely glow in the dark! You won't hear that from me. What I'm going to tell you about is a perilous spiritual warfare that goes on in the soul with countless enemies from the world, the flesh, and the devil . . . though . . . the most persistent enemy is always self, that dangerous Trojan horse within. Have you ever tried the "geographic cure" for some chronic problem like alcoholism or depression—changing jobs or moving to another city? The problem is, you have to take yourself along with you. You can never escape yourself; you can only change yourself.

Fr. Benedict J. Groeschel, C.F.R.
Healing The Original Wound

God Reaches Us In Simple Ways

■ **Naaman went away angry, saying, "I thought that he would surely come out and stand there to invoke the Lord his God, and would move his hand over the spot, and thus cure the leprosy."** 2 Kings 5:11

Not only did Naaman know what he wanted— cure of his leprosy—he also knew how he expected it to be done. His healing, Naaman thought, would be extraordinary and dramatic. To be told to wash seven times in the Jordan was as unspectacular as the river water itself. No spectators, no prophet, no special words and gestures. Naaman was so angry he was about to leave uncured when his servants convinced him to follow Elisha's directions.

Isn't this our story sometimes as well? When we pray, we know exactly what we want from God— healing, direction, protection, inspiration—and we want it pain-free, obvious, immediate. How little leeway we allow God! No wonder we are frequently disappointed.

God's will and purpose in our lives will be worked out for the most part in common daily circumstances, through ordinary people near at hand, in familiar signs and symbols. Part of the message of the Incarnation is that God desires to reach us through what is human, simple, and earthy.

Lord, help me see and take advantage of the simple ways by which you may be trying to heal me.

Nancy F. Summers

Name—Don't Count—Blessings

■ **How can I repay the Lord for all the good done for me?**

Psalm 116:12

Wanting to compensate others for favors received is a common human trait.

The desire to return good for good is natural in our relationship to God as well. Of course, we can never really repay God for what we have received, and we certainly don't earn future blessings by present good works. Instead, our desire to give to God flows, not out of our emptiness, but out of a sense of having received abundantly.

This means that we spend time occasionally counting our blessings. We need to know and honor the specific concrete ways that God has blessed and gifted us. Actually writing these down in a list or prayer journal might prove helpful. To have a vague sense of having received graces is one thing; to name these one after another is quite another. When we regularly review how blessed we are, our lives become grounded in gratitude, our actions the joyful overflowing of God's abundant life in us.

Lord, I will open my eyes today to each and every blessing you have bestowed on me.

Nancy F. Summers

The Spirit Of The Gospel

■ **How can you believe, when you accept praise from one another and do not seek the praise that comes from the only God?** John 5:44

No matter how tenaciously we may cling to an image of Jesus as "meek and mild," words like these shake us up. This is a Jesus who demands a reckoning. We live in a culture that places high value on gaining praise from other people. Indeed, fads are what govern much of our life. What's "in" is what matters. How we dress, the cars we drive, the ways we spend our leisure time, the "in" language we use—all these make us seem more clever and witty to other people. And what others think of us, we seem to believe, is what counts.

One difference between a child and an adult is the freedom to act, not according to fads, but according to who we really are. What distinguishes a child from an adult is the capacity to be guided by the spirit of the Gospel, not the spirit of the age.

Lord Jesus, help me to care little for the praise of others and to seek only "the praise that comes from the only God."

Mitch Finley

The Need For Cleansing

■ **Unless I wash you, you will have no inheritance with me.** John 13:8

When I imagine Jesus preparing to wash *my* feet, I immediately wonder, "Are they clean enough?" I am uncomfortable, almost to the point of panic, deeply afraid that, once my socks are removed, my feet might smell in the presence of the Lord. Like Peter, I don't want this to happen at all.

Why? On the one hand, I don't want to admit the need for such cleansing: the dirt, the bodily sweat and oils remind us that neither our world nor ourselves are perfect. And if anyone is going to wash my feet and encounter that imperfection, I'd rather it were myself; then I would avoid the vulnerability that comes with admitting neediness.

On the other hand, I would in some ways prefer a God who does not stoop to such service and then remind me that I must do the same. Often it would be more convenient to have a remote and powerful deity who magically obliterated the world's dirt and ugliness without getting his—or my—hands dirty.

But Jesus says this washing is necessary if we are to know him and enter his Kingdom. Let us pray, then, that we might joyfully receive this cleansing and follow the example of Jesus in serving others.

Mark Neilsen

When The Spirit Says "No"

■ **[Paul and Timothy] . . . had been prevented by the Holy Spirit from preaching the message in the province of Asia. When they came to Mysia, they tried to go on into Bithynia, but the Spirit of Jesus did not allow them.**

Acts 16:6-7

At first glance these two divinely inspired "Nos" to Paul and Timothy seem startling. The two were traveling in Asia Minor with the goal of preaching the Gospel. What could more clearly and evidently be the will of God than to preach the Gospel at the next place on one's itinerary? Surely the answer would be "Yes." Instead, they were told "No" by the Holy Spirit. St. Luke, the writer of Acts, never says exactly how these messages from the Holy Spirit are given, but in other places Luke notes that the Spirit uses prayer, visions, dreams—even throwing dice.

How they were told "No" to their plans isn't as important as the fact that it happened at all. Is there a message here for us? We need to be aware that the Holy Spirit can and does say "No" at times to our cherished plans—not just our neutral or selfish plans but even our plans to do good and noble things. But if the answer is "No" to one approach, we must do what Paul and Timothy did. Instead of going home in a huff, they remained open to the Holy Spirit and that very night got new directions.

May I remain open each day to the Holy Spirit.

James E. Adams

Open Our Eyes, O Lord

■ **The disciple whom Jesus loved said to Peter, "It is the Lord!"** John 21:7

When we try to understand who you are, Lord, we always think too small. Our imaginations aren't big enough to take in more than a fraction of your reality.

Like the disciples, we need a dramatic event to challenge us to think "bigger"—a miraculous catch, perhaps, or some other sign of abundance.

Help us in our disbelief, even when there are no signs to startle us into recognizing your presence.

Stretch our imaginations and our hearts so that we can make more room for you.

Open our eyes so that we may see the many gifts you have lavished upon us—especially the gift of your friendship.

Then, made bold by this new way of seeing, we will find the courage to do your work in the world.

Then, empowered by your presence, we will reveal your love to those who do not know you.

Then, filled with your compassion, we will nurture those you have entrusted to us.

Elizabeth-Anne Vanek

A Gentle Stirring

■ **My sheep hear my voice; I know them, and they follow
me.** John 10:27

Hollywood falls comically short as it tries to
portray how God usually communicates with us.
There are no words echoing from storm clouds or
rumbling out of whirlwinds or earthquakes. Nor are
there normally miraculous wonders or angelic messengers.

Instead, the voice we hear is barely audible, and
seldom dramatic. Drowned out by noise, obscured by
our frenetic lifestyles, this voice is often nothing
more than a faint whisper, a gentle stirring within.
It demands a trained ear and a willing spirit so that
we may hear and respond. Without grace and desire,
we would hear nothing.

When we are attuned to this voice, Jesus' call,
"Follow me," resounds in our hearts, not as a command, but an invitation to the fullness of life. We
respond not from "herd instinct," but because we
recognize that in following Christ, we can become
uniquely ourselves—gifted women and men who use
our talents for God's glory and our own delight.

*Help me learn to quiet me soul so that I may hear
the gentle stirrings of God.*

Elizabeth-Anne Vanek

The Christian 'Faithful'

■ **It was in Antioch that the disciples were first called Christians.** Acts 11:26

The Christian "faithful" are reliable, dependable, trustworthy.

And they also are faith-full, full of faith. They can be trusted completely because they have entrusted themselves completely—to God and Christ, to God's people, to God's creation.

Today, however, "faithful" no longer is a parlor word. Dogs are faithful. Federal Express is faithful. U.S. Marines are "always faithful."

But much of Western society is uncomfortable with it, from coaches to spouses. And yet, this is the distinguished title you and I bear. We are the Christian faithful. This perhaps more than any other single word sums up who we are as Christians. We are men and women who are full of faith and who keep faith. The term tells who we are, because the term tells who we love.

We are Christian faithful because we are committed to Christ. No commitment may take precedence over that. In baptism God "put his seal on us," the seal of the Spirit. Somewhat as a Roman soldier was branded with the seal of the emperor . . . so Christians are stamped with the seal of the Spirit. We belong to Christ.

Forgive me, Lord, when I am less than faithful.
Fr. Walter J. Burghardt, S.J.
To Christ I Look

A Friend In Jesus

■ **I have called you friends, because I have told you everything I have heard from my Father.** John 15:15

"Friend" may not be the first word that comes to your mind when you think of Jesus Christ. Lord, perhaps, Redeemer, Son of God, or any number of other titles that so rightly honor Christ. But *friend?*

Friendships are made of secrets revealed, burdens eased, and masks removed. A friend is someone who chooses to be with us, not out of obligation but preference. With a friend there is mutual acceptance, an easy camaraderie in which there is nothing to prove. We turn to our friends especially when we have something to share: good news, bad news, a joke, a meal, a dilemma. Even when we have none of these, we seek them yet, just for the pleasure of their companionship.

Those of us trained in rigid servanthood or fearful obedience may find friendship a much too casual or presumptive way of relating to our Lord. In spite of our initial shock or reluctance or sense of unworthiness, Jesus comes to each of us, calling, "Friend." This is what he offers to us; this is what he desires from us.

Jesus, help me to realize the awesome truth that you want to be my friend.

Nancy F. Summers

In Praise Of Praise

■ **They strengthened the spirits of the disciples and exhorted them to persevere in the faith . . .** Acts 14:22

Everybody needs some encouragement and recognition . . . but some people think that praising others is beneath them . . . that it is just blarney or flattery . . . insincere.

No question that some praise is insincere, because it is a lie told to get something out of the other. But what about the honest recognition and appraisal of another's talents and achievements? To do this, one must be attentive to what others are doing. One must see the small developments and little victories . . . What a pity to be so small-minded that we are loathe to give credit where it is due. The hunger for a little assurance these days is so great that the receiving of it causes unusual joy. Everyone needs encouragement in order to grow toward the vision they have of themselves. To recognize this we must take our eyes off superstars . . . and look rather at the everyday behavior of the people around us.

To be Christian is to love; to wipe away the tears; to rejoice in others' growth. It is a measure of our personal greatness to excel in noticing, upholding and celebrating the greatness of our neighbor.

Fr. Alfred McBride, O.Praem.
Year Of The Lord

The Pain Of Rejection

■ **It was not you who chose me, but I who chose you and appointed you to go and bear fruit that will remain.**

John 15:16

Rejection, especially by someone we love or whose approval has been our support, is one of the sharpest pains the human heart can experience. To be unwanted, to be passed over as of no account, to be deliberately ignored—these things wound us at the core of our being. As with the small boy who sits apart and alone because nobody chose him to be on either side of the school ball team, something in us is annihilated, killed by rejection.

Jesus knew the anguish and loneliness of rejection. And in our own rejections, he would have us remember that we count in his eyes. From all eternity, we were chosen as part of the divine plan of creation. We are not just one of many—as a single grain is in a handful of sand. Rather, through a deliberate act of divine love, God chose each one of us, singled us out by name, and willed us into human existence.

No matter how low or how left out of things we feel, we can raise our broken hearts to God and say, "You chose me. I am special to you. Support me now that the help of those about me has failed."

Sr. Mary Terese Donze, A.S.C.

Up To The Challenge

■ **The Advocate, the Holy Spirit that the Father will send in my name—he will teach you everything and remind you of all that I told you.** John 14:26

In the Hebrew scriptures, there are several stories in which the response to God's call is "Who? *Me?* I am a poor speaker! I am too old! I am too young! I am a simple shepherd! I am afraid! . . . " Those who protested knew their own strength would be inadequate for the great task ahead. Only with God's strength would they succeed in accomplishing their work. In the Christian scripture, particularly in the Acts of the Apostles, we see simple folk preaching eloquently, transforming the world around them. They too had to turn to God as the source of their ministry.

There are times when the tasks facing us far exceed our skills, training or energy levels. We find ourselves in situations in which we might well say, "Who? *Me?* Impossible!"

And yet, in spite of our deficiencies, we are able to accomplish the tasks at hand. We may find the right words to comfort someone who is grieving. We may complete a difficult assignment on time. We may find the wisdom to resolve a painful conflict. When we allow God's spirit to work in us, then we can indeed rise above our limitations.

Elizabeth-Anne Vanek

God's Not Finished With Me

■ **The Lord will complete what he has done for me.**

Psalm 138:8

Do you have any partially completed projects? Maybe a craft, a task, a goal that hovers somewhere between the moment the idea was conceived and the finished product? Most of us do. If we allow ourselves to, we can look upon that project, not as something inadequate and flawed or a burdensome thing we wish we never started, but rather as a delightful reminder of what has already been accomplished and an encouraging vision of its future completion.

We are God's projects-in-process. We are not mistakes or doomed experiments. Rather, we are the partial representations of the beautiful wholeness we are destined to become. It can be awkward and embarrassing to exist in a state of incompletion. No less frustrating is the fact that we must live in community with other unfinished projects. For ourselves and others, we would prefer perfection to the messiness of gradual growth. Let us strive to make peace with the process, remembering that the Lord is no dabbler. What God has begun, God will bring to glorious completion.

Nancy F. Summers

Let Troubling Questions Go

■ **On that day you will not question me about anything.**
John 16:23

Two-year-olds have a well deserved reputation for questioning everything.

Day in and day out, they issue a continual stream of "what? why? and how?" As an adult, I find that I am not so different from these tots. Given the opportunity to talk to Jesus, I would certainly not be at a loss for questions. I have cosmic questions, personal questions, and smoldering questions about injustice, suffering and evil. It is difficult to imagine a day I wouldn't have questions—it would probably be the day that I had all the answers.

But perhaps the day of not questioning Jesus will be the time when I don't *need* any answers. Knowing that the universe is in the hands of a good God may one day be enough for me. Then I will receive a peace that comes not from receiving answers, but from letting go of the questions themselves. I will really trust that the loving God knows all, and that this is all that really matters.

Jesus, you have predicted that one day we will have no questions. May that day come soon.
Nancy F. Summers

Overcoming Troubles

■ **I have told you this so that you might have peace in me. In the world you will have trouble, but take courage, I have conquered the world.** John 16:33

We all have a tendency to bargain with God for protection from the dangers of living in an uncertain world. Our hearts are filled with these unspoken deals: "If I live this way, perform these religious rituals, give enough to charity, then God will keep me and my loved ones safe from disease, crime, poverty," and so on. Although this is a very human tendency, it is not Christianity.

Jesus never promises his followers that they will avoid life's difficulties if they seek the Kingdom of God. And isn't this our actual experience? Even as we try most earnestly to live out the Gospel, we find ourselves having to confront the typical "troubles" of mind, soul and body of human life.

Jesus never promises that we can avoid such problems, but he does tell us to take courage and find peace in him. Christ has overcome the world and through him we, too, can overcome—not avoid—the troubles of our lives.

Jesus, help me to trust in your word alone, not in some deal I have made up.

Mark Neilsen

Ready For God?

■ **Then the Lord said, "Go outside and stand on the mountain before the Lord; the Lord will be passing by."**
1 Kings 19:11

Where shall we stand, what position shall we take to observe God's passing by? In some parts of Asia, the location of buildings, doorways and even furniture is determined by "geomancy"—the art of determining future events by means of geographic features. Believers in this art think that one can take advantage of an energy, a life-force, that exists in the earth by finding the proper location and facing in the right direction. Hotels, banks and businesses of all kinds consult experts in order to locate themselves to insure prosperity and success.

As Christians, we also want to place ourselves in the best position in order to receive the graces that God has in store for us. Elijah kept alert so that he could catch the passing of God. He discovered that God speaks softly and walks quietly. God is eternally passing by in the quiet of each moment, hoping that we will notice.

God, help me to watch and listen for your passing today.

Sr. Ruth Marlene Fox, O.S.B.

The Power Of The Spirit

■ ... the love of God has been poured out into our hearts through the Holy Spirit that has been given to us.

Romans 5:5

We are made by Love and for Love.

Sometimes, however, we fall short in terms of our *ability* to love. Fatigue, stress, disappointment and ill health are only a few of the factors which can wear us down, preventing us from reaching out to others. At times, I have been so over-extended that even the sound of the telephone has caused me to tense: "Who is it this time?" I ask myself. "A student in distress? A colleague needing help with a project? A friend who wants to chat?" For me, a hectic schedule can drastically decrease any generosity of spirit I might have.

But even if my initial response is limited, I am usually able to move beyond this—not through any strength of my own, but because God's grace opens my heart to the reality of the other person. Instead of focusing on my own needs, I find myself gradually drawn into an awareness of the one making demands on my time. Through grace, I find the compassion to love whomever God wants me to love in that given moment. This, I know, is nothing less than the power of the Spirit at work.

Elizabeth-Anne Vanek

Disciples Must Not Retaliate

■ **You have heard that it was said, "An eye for an eye and a tooth for a tooth." But I say to you, offer no resistance to one who is evil.** Matthew 5:38-39

Why is it that most Christians don't take these words of Jesus seriously? Even many who believe in the "literal truth" of the Bible can find reason upon reason why Jesus didn't *really* command his followers to forsake retaliation. Why do we try to insist that Jesus either supports us or looks the other way when we attack our enemies or "get back" at those who have done us harm? His words are so clear.

I know I don't always live up to the standard Jesus sets for me in this passage and the one that follows it, requiring us to love our enemies. I doubt that I can always "turn the other cheek" or offer sincere prayer for those who are making my life miserable. And I, too, can come up with reason after reason why, this time, in this case, retaliation is called for and violence is justified.

But when I rationalize like that, I make a mistake. It is one thing to be momentarily unable to live according to God's command; it is quite another to pretend it wasn't a command at all.

Mark Neilsen

The Gate That Leads To Life

■ **How narrow the gate and constricted the road that leads to life. And those who find it are few.** Matthew 7:14

Turning to Christ each day is more than turning from temptation and sin. What was given you in baptism was life, a sharing in God's own life. From that moment, aware of it or not, you were a fresh creation, alive with the life of the risen Christ, empowered to know the living God and to love him, empowered to hope against hope for a life that will never end . . .

To come alive and to stay alive in Christ, you must grow, for when you cease to grow, you begin to die. And how do you grow into Christ? Get to know him. Not a catechism Christ whom you memorize. Not simply the Christ of theology, revealed and concealed in concepts. Let him get inside of you. Listen to him fervently as he speaks to you in his book and in his life, through his community and from his cross. Let him shake you and shiver you, tear you and strip you naked.

Whatever you do, don't exile him to the edge of your existence, a shadow stalking your steps, the phantom of your opera. Turn to Christ each day, if only to pray . . . "I believe; help my unbelief!"

Fr. Walter J. Burghardt, S.J.
To Christ I Look

Rejoice, Repentant Sinners!

■ **There will be more joy in heaven over one sinner who repents than over ninety-nine righteous people who have no need of repentance.** Luke 15:7

Here is another characteristic of the Christian God as opposed to the God of reason, a characteristic of the good news that Jesus preached . . . *For Jesus, even though to sin is the greatest conceivable evil, to be a sinner is a value.*

Hate sin with all your heart and avoid it. But if you have sinned and—this is important—repented, then you have reason to rejoice, because there is greater joy in heaven over the sinner who repents than over ninety-nine who have no need of repentance. Who can understand this kind of madness? The kind of madness that seizes the Church when, on the vigil of Easter, she speaks of the sin of Adam as a "necessary evil," as a "happy fault," because it brought us our savior Jesus Christ . . .

If you have sinned and repented, consider yourself very lucky indeed because grace is going to be poured into you in superabundant measure. The repentant sinner (the sinner who returns to God in love) draws God to himself with greater force than a magnet. God finds him not loathsome, but irresistible.

Fr. Anthony de Mello, S.J.
Contact With God

God Is Hidden In Difficulties

■ **Suddenly a violent storm came up on the sea, so that the boat was being swamped by waves; but he was asleep. They came and woke him, saying, "Lord, save us! We are lost!"** Matthew 8:24-25

Trials always *look* like impossible situations. We try to accept them but things get too tough. Our faith and trust wither and we begin to sink. We call for help and Jesus rescues us. There is a brief calm. If we continue the journey, the wind and the waves start up again. Again we try to find Jesus in the particular difficulty; again we start to drown; he saves us. This is the story of everyone's spiritual journey. The only mistake is to go down—and not yell for help . . .

God is hidden in difficulties. If we can find him there, we will never lose him. Without difficulties, we do not know the power of God's mercy and the incredible destiny he has for each of us. We must be patient with our failures. There is always another opportunity unless we go ashore and stay there. A no-risk situation is the biggest danger there is. To encounter the wind and the waves is not a sign of defeat. It is a training in the art of living, which is the art of yielding to God's action and believing in his love no matter what happens.

Fr. Thomas Keating, O.C.S.O.
Awakenings

Reclaiming Your Chosenness

▣ **Here is my servant whom I uphold, my chosen one with whom I am pleased, upon whom I have put my spirit.**

Isaiah 42:1

We have to dare to reclaim the truth that we are God's chosen ones . . .

The great spiritual battle begins—and never ends—with the reclaiming of our chosenness. Long before anyone else saw us, we are seen by God's loving eyes. Long before anyone heard us cry or laugh, we are heard by our God who is all ears for us. Long before any person spoke to us in this world, we are spoken to by the voice of eternal love. Our preciousness, uniqueness and individuality are not given to us by those who meet us in clock-time—our brief chronological existence—but by the One who has chosen us with an everlasting love, a love that existed from all eternity and will last through all eternity . . .

One thing you must do is to celebrate your chosenness constantly. This means saying "thank you" to God for having chosen you, and "thank you" to all who remind you of your chosenness.

Gratitude is the most fruitful way of deepening your consciousness that you are not an "accident," but a divine choice.

Fr. Henri J.M. Nouwen
Life Of The Beloved

The Tragedy Of Judas

■ **Amen, I say to you, one of you will betray me.**

Matthew 26:21

The most tragic figure in the Passion is Judas. Tragically, the event that never took place—as far as we know—was the conversion of Judas. Can you picture it? Judas would have knelt down at the cross, at the feet of Jesus, and he would have said, "Forgive me, forgive me!" Would he have been forgiven? O yes!

Fra Angelico, Michaelangelo, Leonardo—all the great Christian artists would have painted the scene of that conversion! In this city—and in every city in the world—there would have been a church named "St. Judas the Penitent." But it didn't happen.

I have always felt sorry for Judas. I've always prayed—I pray to this day—that in those final moments before he took his life, Judas converted. Yes, I pray for that. Absolutely. And I suppose I have a very good reason for praying for that. It is this: I know that without the grace of God, I would do the same thing. If God took his grace away today, I would betray him before the sunrise.

Jesus my savior, may all who have turned from you in despair and hate be given another chance.

Fr. Benedict J. Groeschel, C.F.R.
Five Figures Of The Passion

Jesus Loved All—And So Must I

■ **Then he . . . began to wash the disciples' feet and dry them with the towel around his waist.** John 13:5

When Jesus washed the feet of the disciples, he didn't look up. Whether the feet of Peter, of John, or of Judas, he didn't want to know. He just wanted everybody to know that his love went out to them all, whether they were the scum of the earth or princes.

He did not want to see whether the face was beautiful or ugly; whether the face had virtue or vice written on it; whether the face was noble with dignity or sodden with drink and drugs; whether the face was upon a virtuous body or one that had gone through every house and every indecency in town. He did not know, or want to know, whether the face was black or white or red or yellow; whether of a man or a woman; slave or free, master or servant, Jew or Gentile.

And we, his followers, must do as he did. "This is my body given for all of you. This is my blood shed for all. And I wash humankind's feet of its grime in sin, its indignity. I will not look up to make preferences..." This is the summation of the Gospel: to serve all. If we would aspire to be the greatest, then we get on our knees and wash the feet of all manner of people.

Fr. William J. Bausch
Timely Homilies

Inviting Jesus Into Our Lives

■ **But they urged him, "Stay with us, for it is nearly evening and the day is almost over."** Luke 24:29

Most of us know the Emmaus story by heart. Yet we may gain new insight from it if we imagine it in a second way that didn't happen, but easily could have.

As the disciple Cleophas and his companion reached the Emmaus turnoff, the stranger who had joined them made as if he were going on. They thought, "He shouldn't be traveling this robber-infested road alone so late. But if we invite him to join us, we may have to pay for his lodgings, and we're pretty tight for money." So they bid the stranger good-bye—and went on to eat their supper alone. The Gospel certainly implies that this would have happened if the two had not pressed him to share their food and shelter.

We should think that over. Christ said, "What you do to others you do to me." If we do not invite Christ into our lives daily by kindness to the persons with whom we live and associate, we will be living this second and sad version of the Emmaus story. We may go to Mass and receive Christ in the Eucharist, but we will not really be inviting him into our lives.

Fr. Herbert F. Smith, S.J.
Sunday Homilies

Jesus Rebukes Out Of Love

■ **Later, as the eleven were at table, he appeared to them and rebuked them for their unbelief and hardness of heart because they had not believed those who saw him after he had been raised.** Mark 16:14

Imagine standing there right in front of Jesus, the Risen Savior, and being rebuked by him for your lack of belief and the "hardness" of your heart! Perhaps that is what purgatory is all about—looking into the face of God with no excuses, no false pretenses, no make-believe to shield you from the gaze of Love.

After all, it was love that made Jesus seek out these disciples, weak of faith and hard of heart though they were. He knew the truth about each one of them; he just wanted them to know it, too. Out of love, he rebuked them to set them free to believe in him and to proclaim the Good News of salvation to the whole world.

If your conscience sometimes rebukes you for your lack of faith and the hardness of your heart, I hope you are not discouraged. Remember the Risen Savior, the One who longs to set you free to believe and to carry the Good News to a world that is in desperate need of hope.

Mark Neilsen

Sharing Our Gifts

■ **Of everything you give me, I will faithfully return a tenth part to you.** Genesis 28:22

How we cling to what we have—our privileges, our position, our power, our possessions! How hard it is for many of us to give away anything except what is clearly unneeded surplus! Yet God calls us to a radically different way of living: sufficiency and sharing. Jacob promised 10% of everything God gave him, not 10% of what was left after he purchased everything he wanted.

Why should we be called to share what we have in this way? Because all that we have is a gift from God in the first place! The talents we were born with, the money and other goods we have been able to get are not generated by our own unaided efforts. Rather, they are gifts of God and the fruit of an enormous investment by many people, beginning with family, teachers and others who helped us.

All we are and have is ultimately gift. If we can see it that way, how could we not share at least of tenth of it with others in need?

Jesus, thank you for your abundant gifts in my life. Help me to be more willing to share them.

James McGinnis

Good Things Can't Be Rushed

■ **Wait for the Lord with courage; be stouthearted, and wait for the Lord.** Psalm 27:14

In this day of "instant everything," to wait patiently for *anything* is almost counter-cultural. What courage it takes to wait for the Lord, especially when he is long in coming! Sometimes, when everyone else is impatient for action, we have to try to be patient with waiting. We may have to stand up to our relatives, friends and even "the experts" who want us to give up on the Lord when no answer seems forthcoming.

Our society's understanding and use of time may have changed considerably in the last few decades, but God's hasn't. God knows that great works take patience, concern for the smallest of details and time to come to fruition.

Our world cries out for renewal, but we cannot hurry the Lord's great works of creation and re-creation in our lives. We must stand firm in our belief in God's great love and care for us. We must be stouthearted, and wait for the Lord.

Lord, give me the courage to wait and the wisdom to discern your will for me.

Jean Royer

Jesus' Seal Of Authenticity

■ **They asked him, "What sign are you going to perform for us to see?"** John 6:30

We seem to be attracted to the idea of "something for nothing." Even when we say we realize that there is no such thing, we still easily get caught in such schemes. Some weeks after entering a mail-order contest, I received a confidential announcement that I had won a fine diamond, which could be mine for a small price. A convincing "certificate of authenticity" was included. But the small print revealed that the jewel was a genuine diamond *simulant*. In other words, I had a certificate for a genuine fake diamond.

The people in St. John's Gospel in today's reading wanted a certificate of authenticity from Jesus. They were trying to verify the truth of Jesus' claims before they risked putting their faith in him. They wanted a sign that would assure them Jesus was authentic. Today we also look for such assuring signs from Jesus. But the sign has been given—Jesus' life, death and resurrection. The Scripture gives us Jesus' certificate of authenticity. We have been given no fake; we have been given the true bread from heaven.

Lord, when I am tempted to want "signs," help me to know you better through Holy Scripture.

Sr. Ruth Marlene Fox, O.S.B.

When Our Paths Cross

■ **The Spirit said to Philip, "Go and catch up with that carriage."** Acts 8:29

Philip was walking the road south from Jerusalem, minding his own business, probably mulling over in his mind the recent events in Jerusalem—Jesus' death and resurrection. Meanwhile, a court official of the queen of Ethiopia was also going south, riding comfortably in a chariot, also minding his own business. Here were two people, traveling parallel journeys—unaware of each other. Then the Spirit of God enters the scene, the lives of the two men cross, and they are both changed. The official asks to be baptized and Philip is energized for evangelizing.

We never know when the Spirit will gift us with the crossing of our life with that of another. By what accident, by what simple word by what inconsequential action, have you met a person, whose life you touched or who touched yours in a meaningful way? Like Philip, we can always be open to listening to that voice of the Spirit inviting us to take the initiative to respond to another's need. We never know what gift is waiting for us or for the other person.

Holy Spirit, may I always be open to your direction when you are leading me to interact with others.

Sr. Ruth Marlene Fox, O.S.B.

Better Praise Than Complaints

■ **The favors of the Lord I will sing forever.** Psalm 89:2

During the Easter season, there are many comforting stories about the appearances of the risen Christ and of healings which came about through Christ's name. I, too, rejoice in the Lord's blessings in my life, but some "favors," some "opportunities" are more difficult to recognize. At times I fail to see them—much less take advantage of them.

I was sitting in a health clinic recently waiting to be called. The room was filled with people, and it was getting hot and stuffy. All of us had been waiting for a long time. Then we began to complain. Finally, a woman near me said in anger, "What a waste of time! Think of all the things I could be doing!"

All of a sudden it hit me, and I thought, "Yes, indeed, think of all the things *I* could be doing right here and how. I could be thanking God for my eyes, my ears, my tongue, my hands, my feet. I could pray for each troubled person in this waiting room—including myself." Then my name was called. I had wasted the hour complaining.

O Jesus, gentle and patient, help me to use the unexpected free time you give me to praise and thank you for so many favors received.

                                      Sr. Marguerite Zralek, O.P.

God Wants To Draw Near

■ **Whoever loves me will keep my word, and my Father will love him, and we will come to him and make our dwelling with him.** John 14:23

What an incredible promise—that God and Jesus will actually come to us and make their dwelling with us! They want to move in with us. Not only do they want to live in the same space; they want to inhabit our very heart! In the Eucharist Jesus becomes our food. Through his Spirit, Jesus penetrates our spirit. Jesus wants to walk with us every moment of every day. There is no place we can go that God isn't there. Not just there—but there *for us*. The God who created the entire universe is the same God who knew us in our mothers' wombs, who calls us each by name, who loves us so tenderly, and who invites us to keep the word of Jesus so that in Jesus and his Spirit God can actually dwell within us.

What is this word of Jesus we are to keep? It is as clear as it is challenging: "Love one another as I have loved you." Every time we think of others first, sacrifice for others or walk the extra mile, we make it possible for Jesus and God to make their home in us. What a partnership! With God in us, there is nothing for us to fear.

James McGinnis

God's Bittersweet Pruning

■ **I am the true vine, and my Father is the vine grower. He takes away every branch in me that does not bear fruit, and everyone that does he prunes so that it bears more fruit.** John 15:1-2

One of my favorite jaunts is a walk through row upon row of grapes in our nearby vineyard. One day, to my horror, the vines seemed naked! Piled high near the vines lay perfectly healthy leaves and branches that had been cut away. "What are you doing?" I demanded of the gardener. "There's nothing left but the vine itself and clusters of green grapes." As his pruning continued, the gardener patiently explained that the trimming of healthy leaves and branches would help the vine bear more fruit.

"That's it!" I thought. When God strips from my life something I deemed essential, something perfectly good in itself—when a best friend moves away, when the only person I could really talk to dies of a heart attack, when I lose my job, when all I have left in life is God—that's it! "Stop!" I tell God. "Do you know what you're doing? There's nothing left but me—and you!" And God goes on pruning, gently explaining that I, too, will bear more fruit.

Sr. Mary Charleen Hug, S.N.D.

Taste And See

■ **Taste and see how good the Lord is.** Psalm 34:9

What does it mean to "taste and see that God is good"? Many would think of the Eucharist. This is most surely a wondrous way of tasting God's goodness, but there are many other ways as well.

We can feed on our good memories and remember how we have been blessed with God's love. We can be nourished by a moment of wonder and beauty and be fed by God's creation. We can experience the bounty of another's care and concern and taste the compassion of God.

The Easter season calls us to celebrate the Risen Life of Jesus. It is also an invitation to welcome life in a springtime world, to see the stirrings and marvels of death being overtaken by life.

It is all too easy to be preoccupied with work and worries and forget to "taste and see." What will you "taste and see" today? How will you enjoy God's goodness?

Risen Jesus, our Easter world is filled with many spiritual and material gifts. Slow us down today and guide us to taste the wonders of your goodness.

Sr. Joyce Rupp, O.S.M.

We Are Not Alone

■ **I will not leave you orphaned; I will come back to you.**
John 14:18

Being orphaned is, sadly, a fact of life the world over. War, drought, natural disasters and accidents account for the literal "orphaning" of millions. And there also are those who lose their parents to alcoholism, workaholism, drug addiction or indifference; some parents are, in effect, absent.

To be orphaned is to be alone. It is to be without resources and without comfort, without guidance and without meaningful companionship. Whether one is living with parents or not, whether one is living in a home or not, one can nonetheless be orphaned. Whatever one's age, whatever the circumstances, the state of being utterly abandoned is devastating.

Jesus knew that the shock of his death would leave his friends feeling orphaned, and that in their grief and disappointment, they would be inconsolable. To them, therefore, his parting gift was the promise of the Spirit. To us, Jesus makes the same promise. In our moments of radical aloneness, he is with us as he said he would be.

Elizabeth-Anne Vanek

Groping For God

■ ... so that people might seek God, even perhaps grope for him and find him, though indeed he is not far from any one of us. Acts 17:27

I can honestly say that I seek God in my life. I try. Sometimes I try harder than others. But when was the last time I "groped" for him?

"Grope" is such a strong word because it conjures up images of desperation and passion. The intensity of my reaching out for God has a lot to do with how much I think I need God at the moment.

When my mother was dying of cancer, I know I groped for God. I clawed my way to God. I shed tears that were prayers of desperation to God. When my children were born I groped for God, wanting to thank my Lord personally for the beautiful gifts of life that had been given us.

But in my everyday life—where I know I need God—I'm afraid my groping is not so intense and passionate. Sometimes I halfheartedly reach out, but I long for the perseverance and sense of hope that comes from fighting my way to God.

Lord, give me the grace to grope for you every day— and the grace to find you.

Steve Givens

Re-dedication

■ **Peter was distressed that he had said to him a third time, "Do you love me?" and he said to him, "Lord, you know everything; you know that I love you."** John 21:17

Jesus knew what Peter didn't—that Peter needed to declare his love in a strong dramatic way. This was not only to compensate for his earlier denials, but also to inaugurate Peter as the leader of the early Christian church. Peter's declaration was not a matter of informing Jesus of a previously unknown fact; rather, it was an opportunity to re-dedicate himself to a relationship with Jesus.

We who have been dedicated to Christ through baptism and confirmation will need from time to time to make a renewal of our commitment. We may have drifted for a while and now wish to proclaim a new resolve. Maybe we are being called to a different kind or level of service. Perhaps we have recently experienced God in a new way and feel impelled to declare our love with fresh fervor.

It is important for us to find ways of enacting our re-dedication to Christ. These may be public rituals or private practices, but, either way, they should be creative ways of pledging ourselves anew. Then we will be prepared and able to respond to that haunting question asked of us also, "Do you love me?"

Nancy F. Summers

Love Yourself

■ **You shall love your neighbor as yourself.** Mark 12:31

This second commandment which Jesus proclaimed is a challenge not only to love others, but
also to love myself well. After all, I am to treat others
as I treat myself, and sometimes I treat myself
rather shabbily. I do this when I do not allow myself
enough sleep, fill my body with unhealthy food, over-
work and get stressed, omit play and prayer in my
day, forget to affirm and be grateful for my personal
gifts . . . the list could go on and on. Jesus' commandment assumes that I love myself and that I am good
to myself. On this basis, I am then to be good to
others.

I believe there are false messages in the back of
our minds that keep us from living the second commandment. One message says that we aren't supposed to think kindly of ourselves because that would
be pride. Another tells us that we should not give
ourselves much attention because that would be
selfish. Yet if we are not kind and considerate of our
own persons, how can we be this way with others?

*Jesus, help me to be kind to myself so that I will
then treat my neighbors in like manner.*

Sr. Joyce Rupp, O.S.M.

The Bread That Satisfies

■ **I myself am the living bread come down from heaven.**
John 6:51

By participating in the Eucharist we discover that bread alone will not satisfy us. The bread of life teaches us that our core hunger lies deeper than our cravings for material satisfaction; it reminds us that the empty spaces inside us will never be filled by cramming ourselves with food and drink, possessions and relationships. We learn that the more we gorge, the hungrier we become. Our appetite seems insatiable.

Through Eucharist, we are put in touch with our deepest desires. We discover that we don't need to *have* more, but to experience intimacy and belonging. We find that we don't need to *do* more, but to live more intensely and more intentionally. The bread we receive awakens in us the memory of our spiritual needs. Through it, we taste the very presence of God—a presence that is warm, comforting, inviting, a presence which gently takes the edge off all our other wants. Through the ritual actions of eating and drinking, we share in the life of Jesus. In us, heaven and earth can meet, for we, too, are transformed into living bread—the body of Christ.

Elizabeth-Anne Vanek

Just Keep On Keeping On

■ ... in everything we commend ourselves as ministers of God, through much endurance, in afflictions, hardships, constraints, beatings, imprisonments, riots, labors, vigils, fasts ... 2 Corinthians 6:4-5

Sometimes you will be tired, sometimes you will feel emotionally drained. We are all human, but we go on in spite of this. You can have no mental agony that will ever equal that of Christ in Gethsemane or that of his Blessed Mother under the cross. No one will ever be as tired as Christ was on that cross. So what are you excited about? You feel lousy? Fine. Keep going. You are an apostle—a man or woman in love with God and totally dedicated to him in this world.

Stop taking your psychiatric pulse. Stop worrying about your aches and pains, your little tensions and fatigue. Keep going! You've been told you are on your way to the cross, so set your feet at a hundred miles an hour to get there. Physically you are well-taken care of. All your legitimate needs are being met. You are loved and cared for, so what's the problem? Christ is waiting ...

You have problems? ... Nagging fears? Christ must have had fears too. Unite yourself with him and his passion and *keep on going*!

Catherine de Hueck Doherty
Grace In Every Season

A Reason For Trust

■ **The one who supplies seed to the sower and bread for food will supply and multiply your seed and increase the harvest of your righteousness.** 2 Corinthians 9:10

Scripture tells us in many places that we ought to share what we have with others, but in this passage, St. Paul explains why we can do so with confidence. This is a particularly good message today in view of the concern for future economic security that so many of us have.

That concern is understandable: the cost of basic needs like housing and health care keep going up, and changes in the global economy seem to happen so quickly that no one's job appears really safe. How can we be sure that we will have enough for the future?

Of course, we need to trust in God, but St. Paul suggests why it is reasonable to have that trust. Everything we have now is the result of what God has given us: human creativity and social instincts, productive soil, the ability to communicate, and more. We talk of the wonders of science, but aren't they really the wonders of the God who created both the universe and our ability to understand it?

Give abundantly, says St. Paul, for the One who has supplied your need will continue to do so.

Mark Neilsen

Mother Bird

■ **So do not be afraid; you are worth more than many sparrows.** Matthew 10:31

To think of an omniscient God counting the hairs on our heads or being aware of each little sparrow is too overwhelming to be comforting. I prefer to think of God on a smaller scale—perhaps as the Mother Bird who presides over my backyard. Over the years, this Mother Bird has cherished all the birds that have visited, nested, learned to fly, dug for worms or splashed in puddles. She saw the neighbor's cat get the blue jays and she grieved over the sparrow which succumbed to the whiskey we hoped would revive it following another feline attack. She has rejoiced when eggs hatched and when fledglings took wing. She has adopted forlorn hatchlings left fluttering in fright under the hedges, beckoning them to a tender dance of acquaintanceship and a lesson or two in flying.

God, like this Mother Bird, hovers over all of us, noticing our fear of flight, our tug with gravity. God, like this Mother Bird, shelters us beneath comforting wings when we need to be sheltered, always knowing when to send us on our way. God, like this Mother Bird, holds each of us in heart and in thought.

Elizabeth-Anne Vanek

Brave Enough To Trust God

■ **"Lord, if you wish, you can make me clean."**

Matthew 8:2

When Jesus came down the mountain, large crowds followed him. Among this huge throng of people was a leper who stepped out and asked Jesus to heal him. The power of Jesus was evident as he stretched out his hand and touched the leper. The "leprosy was cleansed immediately" (Matthew 8:3).

What was it like for the leper to make this request? Was it fearsome and overwhelming? Did he feel a tremendous vulnerability? Did he wonder whether Jesus would say "no" or push him aside? Was he mindful of the crowd's ability to beat or berate him? Many such emotions must have accompanied the leper's decision to step forward.

Would I have been so brave? Could I step out from the crowd to ask Jesus to share his power with me? Would I have had the leper's faith that Jesus could heal me? Do I worry too much about what the crowd might think? Can I overcome my doubts and fears and have faith that God will take care of me?

God's goodness and power are here for me. I must do my part and be receptive, trusting and open to receive.

Sr. Joyce Rupp, O.S.M.

Trusting God To Help Us

■ "Amen, I say to you, in no one in Israel have I found such faith . . . You may go; as you have believed, let it be done for you." At that very hour his servant was healed.

Matthew 8:10,13

Trust is a beautiful but very delicate virtue. It is a gentle offshoot of faith. Trust begins when "reason" as we understand it—the intellect and what have you—folds its wings and allows the wings of faith to open up. For trust cannot exist without faith.

If I have faith in a person, an institution, a community, a family, I will trust! Wherever there is faith, there is trust.

The first one we must trust is God—the Trinity. Do we really do that? Most of the time we either question the existence of God or, more likely, if we believe that he does exist, we question his ability to help us. We think that our everyday problems are our own to solve, and that we needn't have faith or trust in God to solve them. If possible, we would prefer to solve our own problems all the time! It gives us a sense of power, of being our own master. We are willing to have God around and to rely on him only when it becomes quite clear we cannot solve things ourselves.

Catherine de Hueck Doherty
Grace In Every Season

Aspire To A Living Faith

■ **You must consider yourself dead to sin but alive for God in Christ Jesus.** Romans 6:11

I am inclined to mistrust religiosity without heart, piety without humor and ethical righteousness without compassion. Every now and again, I run into people who outwardly conform to all that their religious tradition demands but they lack basic vitality. They know all the correct words and gestures, but have somehow missed the meaning along the way. Instead of exuding energy and enthusiasm, they seem habitually gloomy, cynical and lifeless. Sadly enough, neither their prayers, religious observances nor spiritual reading seem to have made an impact on them.

Being alive in God is, perhaps, more difficult than dying to sin. We tend to have more strategies for avoiding the power of darkness than we do for tapping into the inner life, that life which is God's own creative breath. We resist letting that breath dance and frolic within us; we resist letting that breath awaken us to the deepest desires of our hearts; we resist letting that breath arouse in us the spirit of hospitality. Let us indeed die to sin, but let us also be fully alive—for God's sake and ours!

Elizabeth-Anne Vanek

God Will Never Forget Me

■ **The Lord has remembered faithful love toward the house of Israel.** Psalm 98:3

The local parish sponsored an evening program, and a carload of us went. After the program and social hour, the crowd began to disappear and I started to look for the people with whom I came. They were all gone! They had forgotten me. As almost the only person left in the room, I had a terrible sinking feeling in my heart which collected tears from similar past experiences of being forgotten. Later, after catching a ride home, I realized that even though people may forget me, God never forgets me.

Today's psalm holds great consolation. God remembers me with steadfast kindness and faithfulness. God will never forget me, for God's memory is foolproof. Even when I feel alone, hurt, rejected and abandoned—perhaps *especially* then—God remembers me and embraces me in love and faithfulness. At those times, I need only to remember that God remembers me.

Sr. Ruth Marlene Fox, O.S.B.

The Fruit We Bear

■ I am the vine, you are the branches. John 15:5

A vine may be worth more than the sum total of its branches, but it is the branches that bear the fruit. "Where would the grapes be if there were no branches?" we might ask. "Where would the branches be if there were no vine?" we might ask, conversely. Jesus' image of the interdependency of trunk and branches suggests that a rich harvest is the product of both—that is, of both *his* life and *our* responses.

Too often we limit our understanding of the "harvest" to the works we do for the sake of Jesus' name. We limit it to the ministries of peace and justice, education, healing, social care and worship. Or to time spent performing what were once commonly called "corporal works of mercy." But there is more to the harvest than the labor of our hands. The fruit we bear is nothing less than the fruit of God's love—our total self-giving which allows God to be all things to us and to work great wonders through us. This love—greater than anything else we can offer—makes no distinction between God's love and ours, between God's heart and our hearts, between God's delight and our own. And it is this self-giving which gives God more glory than anything else we can do.

Elizabeth-Anne Vanek

Look Up For Inspiration

■ **The heavens declare the glory of God; the sky proclaims its builder's craft.** Psalm 19:1

The ancient people viewed the heavens, and they were very impressed. The daytime sky, with fluffy white clouds against a blue background and brilliant sun, was a reminder of the Lord. The night scene, with its gentle moon and sparkling stars, was equally impressive. It was all so beautiful that they called it "the glory of God."

Today, our advanced astronomy and space travel have defused many of the ancient, poetic concepts about the heavens. At the same time, modern knowledge has made us much more aware of the mysteries of the planets and stars. Science, satellites and space travel have provided many answers but raised many more questions. The new scientific picture is far more exciting than the old poetic one.

Is there any limit to space, or is it like the limitless God? Is the gigantic order operating in the universe too immense and fantastic for the human mind to grasp? The God of the universe remains hidden in the deep recesses of space. When we view and explore the brilliant face of the sky, we acknowledge, with 20th century confidence, that "the heavens declare the glory of God."

Fr. James McKarns

Whole-hearted Submission

■ **I am the true vine, and my Father is the vine grower. He takes away every branch in me that does not bear fruit, and everyone that does, he prunes so that it bears more fruit.** John 15:1-2

Allow God to act, and give yourself completely to him. Let the chisel perform its task, the sharp needle do its work. Let the brush of the artist cover the canvas with many tints which only appear to smear your canvas. Cooperate with all these divine operations by a whole-hearted, steady submission, forgetting yourself and enthusiastically giving yourself to duty. Continue in this way in your own allotted path without trying to know all your surroundings or the particular details of landscape. Proceed on this path without being able to see ahead of you, and you will be shown step by step how to go. Seek first the kingdom of God and his righteousness by love and obedience, and all the rest will be added to you.

. . . remain peacefully united to God by love, follow the clear straight path of duty without looking ahead. The angels are beside you during this time of darkness, and they will bear you up. If God asks more of you, he will make it known to you by his inspirations.

Fr. Jean-Pierre de Caussade, S.J.
The Joy Of Full Surrender

Thanks To Divine Providence

■ **God has overlooked the times of ignorance.** Acts 17:30

It's a good thing, too, that God overlooks such times!

Have you ever driven somewhere early in the morning, arrived at your destination and then, thinking back, could not recall the trip? You can remember, perhaps, backing out of the driveway and turning onto the first street, but from there on your mind is a blank. What happened during the ride? You can only assume that you looked before you turned and somehow you didn't greatly exceed the speed limit.

Often when I stop to pray and reflect, what I find is that I spend much more time ignoring God than being aware of God. It's even easy for me to do so, because God does not cry out for my attention like all the other things in my life do. God waits patiently for me to return. And when I come back, God is there with forgiveness and love. And, thankfully, just as God overlooks our times of ignorance, God watches over us during our times of ignoring. So not only do I arrive back in God's care, I arrive back safely. Somehow, God helped me through the journey, even though I didn't stop to ask directions.

Praise to you, Lord, for the times you watch over us—even when we don't realize it.

Steve Givens

Celebrating Easter Daily

■ **Amen, amen, I say to you, you will weep and mourn, while the world rejoices; you will grieve, but your grief will become joy.** John 16:20

Remember the times you thought you couldn't endure the pain or the loss any longer? It seemed too much to bear. Maybe you are in a situation like that now. At such times it's difficult to believe that grief will be turned into joy. Others can assure us that the pain will pass with time, but usually everything in us doubts this. That's why we need to celebrate Easter continually. We need to recall and welcome the Easter story much more than just once a year. We celebrate Easter every time we look closely at the little surprises of joy in our lives. Each time we announce these joys to ourselves or to others, we are like the angels at the empty tomb announcing resurrection.

I know a woman who is never without the pain of four metal rods pressing in her back. Yet she has found joy beyond her daily pain. She relishes happiness in her relationship with her spouse, delights in her grandchildren, enjoys the beauty of the changing seasons. She is an Easter person who daily chooses to believe that she does not have to stay in the tomb of discontent and discouragement.

Sr. Joyce Rupp, O.S.M.

The 'Blessedness' Of Suffering

■ **Blessed are they who mourn, for they will be comforted.**
Matthew 5:4

Is there a sense in which the sorrowing are blessed because only they *can* receive comfort, only *they* are able to receive true consolation? . . . Leon Bloy once said, "There are places in our hearts which do not yet exist, and it is necessary for suffering to penetrate there in order that they may come into being." This, I think, is the key to the blessedness of suffering and sorrow. True sorrow opens our being, breaks through the smooth veneer of routine and regularity and exposes our inner selves. In sorrow, the depths of our hearts are touched, are carved out . . . carved out to leave space for a receptivity to God. For it is in the depths of our hearts that God is found. It is when our hearts are truly emptied out, wounded, made vulnerable, that we are able to receive the true comfort which comes from God, from his loving presence . . . This beatitude suggests that we should not be so eager to whisk away sorrow with an artificially contrived comfort, with pious platitudes or religious posturing. Rather we should wait in our sorrow for that authentic comfort which comes from God alone and which is revealed to us in sorrow's own space.

Luke Timothy Johnson
Some Hard Blessings

A Little Light Goes A Long Way

■ **You are the light of the world . . . your light must shine before others.** Matthew 5:14,16

What a powerful affirmation—to be assured that we have this light within us that is meant to be shared. How many people believe that they are filled with the wondrous light of God? Like one tiny candle shining in a dark room, the light within can make a profound difference. When the light within one person is shared, it brings what the heart needs most.

Recently, I received such a light through a visit of two widowers whom I had only met through letters. They were vacationing in the area and called to invite me to lunch. The light came to me through their openness, graciousness, hospitality and delightful sense of humor. I had been caught up in my own small world of busyness and studies. I didn't think that I could "fit" two more people into my life that day. Because I met them, however, I found a clearing space in my heart. I found communion in the simple and unpretentious humanness shining through the life of two caring strangers. They gave me joy and they expected nothing in return. The light they shared with me was truly the light of God.

Thank you for the gift of your light within me.

Sr. Joyce Rupp, O.S.M.

A Listening And Sensitive Heart

■ **Give me discernment, that I may observe your law and keep it with all my heart.** Psalm 119:34

Authentic discernment is possible only when one has the graced ability to listen in love to the deepest impulses, urges and longings of the human heart with great care and exquisite respect . . .

The sunflower delights both our eye and imagination. In the morning the golden flower faces the east, awaiting the dawn; by evening it gazes to the west as though pursuing a god. Two qualities are evident in this docile plant: a "listening" power that enables it to take in the sun's warm rays, and its ability to respond to the brilliance of the sun's light. This image highlights the importance of sensitivity in the discernment process. The slightest impulse, urging or prompting must be absorbed and processed to see whether or not it comes from the Master. That listening and processing is grounded in love. Love pulls us out of self-preoccupation and the narrow confines of our parochialism. The sunflower illustrates a type of listening and love characteristic of a discerning heart. Would that the simplicity, spontaneity, docility and flexibility of the sunflower were ours!

Bishop Robert F. Morneau
Spiritual Direction

Jesus Is Present In All Storms

■ **They came and woke him, saying, "Lord, save us! We are perishing!"** Matthew 8:25

Was it necessary to wake Jesus up? It would seem not, because Jesus immediately asked, "Why were you terrified?"

Through events, other people, and our experience of prayer, such questions are directed to us . . . We go through periods of turmoil, get frightened, wake Jesus up, experience the wonderful calm he bestows, and are reassured. Suppose we hadn't woke him up? Would we have been protected? Of course! That is the point of the story. Jesus is present in every storm.

Once we believe that God is present in the storm and is protecting us, we know we have all the help we need. God never goes anywhere; he just seems to. Sometimes God takes a lengthy snooze and seems quite content to sleep on and leave us in our anxiety. The purpose of God's sleeping is to make us realize that he has not left us at all, but is assisting us more than ever at a deeper, more subtle level. This is the level of pure faith. The conviction grows that whatever we may think or feel, Jesus is in our little boat and is giving us all the help we need; we can just relax and let go of all fear.

Fr. Thomas Keating, O.C.S.O.
Reawakenings

'Prayer By The Church'

■ **Peter was being kept in prison, but prayer by the church was fervently being made to God on his behalf.**

Acts 12:5

"Prayer by the church." What a powerful event when many believers unite in prayer on someone's behalf! To be the person that the church is praying for or about is almost too much of a blessing to accept. What a sense of gratitude and determination to pray is engendered in me! Joined with all the church—the people in my local parish, the people in the diocese, the faithful all over the world and the church in heaven—is my humble, simple and solitary prayer. And so it is increased to become a mighty force . . . like the trickle of an upriver streamlet joining the thunderous waters of Niagara Falls.

I do not know specifically what help in the lives of others has been brought about through my prayers and acts. Nor do I know exactly what help I have received through prayer. But I know and firmly believe in the "communion of saints" and in the power unleashed by the unified prayer of the church. And I am profoundly grateful for it.

O Lord, let my life be a prayer for others.

Jean Royer

Living By Faith

■ **When Jesus saw their faith, he said to the paralytic, "Courage, child, your sins are forgiven."** Matthew 9:2

If we are to bring the Gospel message into everyday life . . . we must put aside all nonessentials, stop all word games and all the useless discussions. Yes, we must now come to the essence of things!

The essence of things is this: we must begin to live by *faith* and not by mere "religion." We must have an encounter with God and allow God to enter our very depths. We must remember that God loved us *first*, and that our religion is truly a love affair between God and us, us and God. It is not merely a system of morals and dogmas.

We must love God back passionately! Through others. We must love our neighbor, not only as ourselves but with the heart of God . . .

The father of love is faith. We must begin to *live by faith*, of which the outward signs of religion are but handmaidens, and of which the sacraments are the visible signs. When we do, the world will change.

Catherine de Hueck Doherty
Grace In Every Season

Rock-solid Faith

■ **I love you, O Lord, my strength, O Lord, my rock.**
Psalm 18:2-3

I enjoy collecting rocks—all sizes, all shapes. Our motherhouse is in Wisconsin in what was once Native American Indian territory. I once found a bulky, yellow-tinted rock with a curious shape. I have kept it as a paperweight, and it reminds me of some of my origins near the Mississippi River in Wisconsin.

Another experience, however, is the one that most reminds me of the strength of rock. My father used to take us children to the shore of Lake Michigan on a late winter or early spring afternoon. We walked around a point of land that juts out into the lake. As a small child, I had the feeling that I was surrounded by water, wind and sky. The wind would lash at the rocks on which we stood. The waves seemed huge and sprayed us with cold darts of water. Somehow I wasn't afraid because the rocks seemed so solid.

I can pray as the psalmist, " I love you, O Lord, my strength, O Lord, my rock," because I, too, have experienced God as a solid presence in joy and in sorrow, always there to support me.

Sr. Marguerite Zralek, O. P.

Be A Willing Messenger

■ **The Lord God has given me a well-trained tongue, that I might know how to speak to the weary a word that will rouse them. Morning after morning, he opens my ear that I may hear.** Isaiah 50:4

Some guests on television talk shows work with public speaking consultants to learn how to get their message across in a short time. Often in our lives we would like to have such a consultant. God inspires us with a message to give to someone. We want to deliver it but we just don't know how to say it. Or we are afraid to speak up. Words of encouragement, advice, condolence, anger, even love sometimes get bottled up inside. What are we to do? Follow the example of the best talk show guests. They get their message across by being themselves. Instead of fretting over delivering a specific message, they approach their time on camera as an everyday conversation and so they are relaxed. Often it is this way with us. Our ordinary conversations or our everyday actions deliver God's messages to others. Many times it happens without our even being aware of it. God asks not that we be eloquent but simply that we be willing messengers. God will put the right words on our tongues at the right time. We just need to relax and be ourselves so that the Spirit may act through us.

Charlotte A. Rancilio

The Hidden Ways Of Grace

■ **But at daybreak on the first day of the week they took the spices they had prepared and went to the tomb.**

Luke 24:1

Any grave is unnerving enough, but there is something especially forbidding about the cellar-black slots cut in cold rock under the Church of the Holy Sepulcher in Jerusalem.

"In just such a hole as this," a Holy Land guide says, "Jesus Christ was buried." You peer into that hole and realize how precious a gift is your Christian faith—and how improbable. Not in a millennium would you imagine that out of such a desolate hole emerged the Redemption of the world!

Those black burial niches in Jerusalem provide you a new appreciation of the hiddenness of grace, of the mysterious workings of redemption, much of which takes place in tomb-like darkness beyond our earthly vision. Catholic tradition holds that even while in his tomb, Jesus descended into the realm of the dead to proclaim redemption there. Jesus-in-the-tomb richly symbolizes the mostly hidden way that redemption will unfold until the Second Coming. We cannot always see the workings of grace.

While it may at times seem that God has abandoned the world, we know through faith that God is working always and everywhere.

Lord, I believe. Help me overcome my doubt.

James E. Adams

Love That Means Something

■ **For God so loved the world that he gave his only Son.**
John 3:16

So carelessly is the word "love" used that it has practically lost its force. People say they "love" their children, their dog—and Monday night football!

Actually, "love" is a precious word which we ought to use precisely and with meaning, never carelessly or cheaply. We should be prepared to back up the use of this word with action. God uses the word wisely and well, never in a shallow sense, never lightly, as we might when we say we "love" a good steak. God tells us that he loves us—and he means what is said.

One characteristic of true love is generosity, a generosity which knows no limit. Love and giving, when understood properly, are synonymous. How much does God love us? The answer is in today's Gospel: "God so loved the world that he gave his only Son." God simply had no gift to give more precious than his only Son. Nor is the gift merely precious and actually useless—as is a diamond which a man gives to his wife. God's gift is both immeasurably precious and eminently practical. The Gospel goes on to say that God gave his only Son that whoever believes in him may not die but may have eternal life.

Lord, help me to be generous and loving.

Fr. Charles E. Miller, C.M.
Opening The Treasures

Don't Fear Faith's Demands

■ **The Lord is my light and my salvation; whom do I fear? The Lord is my life's refuge; of whom am I afraid?**
Psalm 27:1

Contemporary man, to a degree, finds it hard to return to faith because he is afraid of the moral demands that faith makes upon him. *The Gospel is certainly demanding.* Christ never permitted his disciples and those who listened to him to entertain any illusions about this. He spared no effort in preparing them for every type of internal or external difficulty, always aware that they might decide to abandon him. So if he said, "Be not afraid!" he certainly does not say it in order to nullify in some way that which he has required. Rather, by these words he confirms the entire truth of the Gospel and all the demands it contains. But he reveals that his demands never exceed man's abilities. If man accepts these demands with an attitude of faith, he will also find in the grace that God never fails to give him the necessary strengths to meet those demands. The world is full of proof of the saving and redemptive power that the Gospels proclaim . . . How many people there are in the world whose daily lives attest to the possibility of living out the morality of the Gospel!

Pope John Paul II
Crossing The Threshold Of Hope

The Message & The Messenger

■ **Through all the earth their voice resounds, and to the ends of the world, their message.** Psalm 19:5

When the Lord asked Moses to be his spokesman, Moses reminded God of his speech impediment. Yet through him God's chosen people were freed from tyranny. When the Lord asked him to become a prophet, Jeremiah claimed he was too young. Yet God's word became a fire within him. The Apostles were poor, unlettered fishermen, yet through them Christianity grew worldwide.

God is forever showing his people that it isn't the messenger that is important. It's the message. "God loves you personally. God died for you. Right now this very God is preparing a place just for you so you can spend all eternity with him." Wouldn't you think a message so soul-searing, so compelling could stand on its own? But even God's Good News needs a messenger. That messenger is YOU.

Age doesn't matter, nor occupation, nor handicap. Once it burns its way through your bones, just being the "you" God created you to become is sufficient for this message to be proclaimed. It takes on your personality, your temperament, your vision. What a compliment our loving God pays us! His message follows us as we live out our days. How will *you* proclaim it?

Sr. Mary Charleen Hug, S.N.D.

The Door To Our Hearts

■ **I am the door.** John 10:9

Sometimes I feel I am living outside my heart and trying to find my way back in. At such times I recall that famous painting of Jesus standing at a door. There is no knob, suggesting that the door must be opened from the inside. Jesus waits at the door, yet never forces it.

Jesus does more than wait at the door. He *is* the door! And for those of us who need more space, Jesus is even the gate. He is the way back into your heart.

What are the ways I block or deny entrance to my heart? What do I pile up on the other side of the door, hesitant to reach out for the door knob—forgetting I am the one who must open the door? Behind the walls of my excuses and the heap of my denials Christ waits with infinite patience. Then one day in my self-made wilderness a glimmer of light shining through a crack in the door gives me courage. I cautiously open the door and recognize the voice of the One who was waiting for me. Having opened the door I am free to come in and go out and find pasture.

May there always be a little light shining through a crack in your excuses and denials.

Sr. Macrina Wiederkehr, O.S.B.

God's Welcoming Presence

■ **In all truth I tell you whoever welcomes the one I send welcomes me. And whoever welcomes me, welcomes the one who sent me.** John 13:20

Has it ever occurred to you that the people who surround you have, in some way, been sent to you from God?

How can you be a *welcoming presence* for those at your side so that the Christ-Bond between you and among you will become a constant blessing? Do you recognize the daily footwashing that goes on in your own household of faith?

Take some time today to pray for the people in your life whom you may have taken for granted. Make a list of names of specific persons in your life. Look at each person on your list with a loving glance. Say aloud to each person. "To come into your presence is like coming into the presence of God."

If you pray these words often your attitude about some people may undergo a profound change.

Sr. Macrina Wiederkehr, O.S.B.

Don't Give In

■ **Do not let your hearts be troubled. You have faith in God; have faith also in me. In my Father's house there are many dwelling places. If there were not, would I have told you that I am going to prepare a place for you?**

John 14:1-2

Can Jesus be trusted? I want very much to believe that he can be, and not simply because I hope to some day dwell in the Father's house. I also want to believe so that my heart does not have to be troubled.

At the same time, I know that faith itself can be a struggle. Jesus knew what it was to be troubled, too, when Lazarus died or when Jerusalem failed to believe his message or when he prayed in Gethsemane. Each one of us knows times of doubt about whether or not our beliefs, even our religion itself, are true. Each of us experiences times of darkness in which we cannot seem to find any consolation in our most cherished beliefs. Such times may come, but we don't have to *let* our hearts be troubled, we don't have to give in to the darkness or accept it.

That is our part: refusing to give in to the troubles of our hearts. Jesus will do the rest by strengthening our faith.

Merciful God, strengthen our faith even when our hearts are troubled.

Mark Neilsen

Give As Much As Others Need

■ **Such as my love has been for you, so must your love be for each other.** John 13:34

The duty of loving one's neighbor is not exclusive to Christianity. Jews and Muslims also have preached love of neighbor. Many people who profess to be atheists or agnostics are generous and compassionate. What, then, is different about the Christian call to love? What was the love Jesus modelled for us?

The standard of love to which Jesus calls us involves more than extending alms and befriending the widow and orphan. His example was a complete emptying of self, an unrestrained pouring out of love—without motives, without calculation of cost. His love was not measured by percentages (for example, tithing) or by legal requirements. Rather, he gave according to the need each person presented, making himself fully available to everyone he encountered, even if this meant breaking laws of ritual purity or breaking the Sabbath in order to heal. To love as Jesus loved is to *become* love. It is a decision which comes from the experience of God's love and from the desire to share this love with others. It comes from a willingness to die to self, so that God's love can be present.

Lord, let your love be the love we offer the world.
Elizabeth-Anne Vanek

A God So Near

■ **The Lord is near to all who call upon him.** Psalm 145:18

Well-intentioned and spiritually hungry people have tried for thousands of years to find God. Some have traveled to distant lands, searching for God in ancient religions or contemporary cults. Others have become pilgrims, visiting medieval shrines and seeking wisdom through sacred relics. They are not necessarily obstinate to seek God in these places, for surely God is everywhere. But the search for God can be confusing and perhaps endless if you don't know where or how to look.

God has given us some directions in the Psalms. All it takes to reach God is a short trip from standing on our own to kneeling before our maker. When we can surrender ourselves in prayer to God, then we can find God. Only then can we bare our souls, open our hearts, and find God waiting, always waiting close by. God remains hidden from our earthly eyes, but God is near though faith. God is one short call away, and is close enough to hear us even if we whisper.

Thank you, Lord, for being near to us, always ready to respond to our call.

Steve Givens

Trust Your Shepherd

■ **Know that the Lord is God, our maker to whom we belong, whose people we are, God's well-tended flock.**

Psalm 100:3

God has determined, unless I interfere with His plan, that I should reach that which will be my greatest happiness. He looks on me individually, He calls me by my name, He knows what I can do, what I can best be, what is my greatest happiness, and He means to give it to me.

God knows what is my greatest happiness, but I do not. There is no rule about what is happy and good; what suits one would not suit another. And the ways by which perfection is reached vary very much. The medicines necessary for our souls are very different from each other. Thus God leads us by strange ways. We know He wills our happiness, but we neither know what our happiness is nor the way. We are blind. Left to ourselves we would take the wrong way. We must leave it to Him.

Let us put ourselves into His hands, and not be startled though He leads us by a strange way. . . . Let us be sure He will lead us aright, that He will bring us to that which is, not indeed what *we* think best, not what is best for another, but what is best for us.

John Henry Newman
Lead, Kindly Light

Fear Of Rejection

■ **The stone that the builders rejected has become the cornerstone.** Mark 12:10

Late one evening a pastor I know quite well called me. He is a kind-hearted, generous man who cares deeply about the welfare of his parishioners. His voice that night was tense, sad, angry. He said he had just come home from a parish meeting in which a small but very loud group of people openly opposed his theology and his style of leadership. This group had hassled him for two years, and he had decided he had had enough. He told me he was resigning.

As I listened to him I thought of my own tendency to want to run away from those who reject me or my message, especially when these people are not open to change. It is ironic, though, that we who profess to follow in Jesus' footsteps never want to do so when it means experiencing the rejection which Jesus experienced. I think that the true disciple does not give up easily. The one who follows Jesus and speaks his message will have some rejection because the message of the gospel is not an easy one to hear or accept.

Jesus, be our strength and courage when we want to give up in the face of rejection. Guide us to know when to "hang in there" and when to say "enough."

Sr. Joyce Rupp, O.S.M.

The Pursuit Of Happiness

■ **Happy are those who fear the Lord, who greatly delight in God's commands.** Psalm 112:1

"In Hollywood, if you don't have happiness, you send out for it." Put that way we see the outrageousness of the idea that happiness is some kind of object or service that is for sale, such as a cheeseburger, a fur coat, a car, new suit or airline ticket . . .

Not only is happiness not an object, it is also not something we can directly seek in any sense. . . . Rather than being concerned about the pursuit of happiness, we are told by Scripture to seek goodness, honesty, respect for others and for our world, concern for others, healing and caring, service, work that needs doing. Doing our work well, serving the needs of those around us, being grateful for the gifts given us and using them well, all this easily brings with it a sense of worth, of legitimate satisfaction, a sense that my days and hours are not just dragging by. We experience a certain glow that we call happiness . . .

The emphasis is not on me and my needs, but on others, on matters beyond and outside myself. Happiness comes from giving ourselves to these matters, these persons, not in trying somehow to gild and polish this little self.

Fr. Don Talafous, O.S.B.
A Word For The Day

Patient Persistence In Prayer

■ **Your ways, O Lord, make known to me; teach me your paths.** Psalm 25:4

I once I asked a large gathering of retreatants to write down some of their questions regarding prayer.

Quite a few wanted to know how they could tell if they were doing God's will. Others wanted to know if they were on "the right path." Psalm 25 suggests that we need to ask God for guidance if we are going to be living the ways of God. God can and will direct our paths if we are open, attentive and listening. For our part, we need to be patient, consistent in praying daily, willing to consult wise persons, and we need to regularly check our motivation. (Why am I doing what I do?)

St. Ignatius insists that a key way to know if we are doing God's will is to check on our peacefulness. We may not have many positive feelings about a decision or a direction, but if we have deep peace we can be assured that we are probably in tune with God.

We need to trust our truest self. No one else can tell us if we are on the path with God. Only our true self, that part of us that is in close union with God at the core of our being, knows this. There is this true place in all of us. Let us keep going there and trusting the Peace that resides deep within us.

Sr. Joyce Rupp, O.S.M.

True Lovers Hold Nothing Back

■ **You shall love the Lord your God with all your heart, with all your soul, with all your mind, and with all your strength.** Mark 12:30

How can we love if there is one-millionth of an ounce of self within us? Love is a person. Love is God. Where love is, God is. Our vocation is to make room for God in ourselves, to clothe God with our flesh, to again give God hands and lips and eyes and a voice.

But to do that we must die to self. God is immense. God needs much room—our whole being! Not one crevice must be left to ourselves. Otherwise, we maim Christ if we refuse him access to any part of us. And where is the lover who keeps back anything from the beloved? Such a person is not a true lover. And so that is our vocation—to burn, to die to become a flame, so as to make room for Christ to grow in us . . .

This dying to self to make room for God is painful. But dedication is seen in that pain. There is a radiance emanating from that pain which disperses the shadows in another's face. That is the essence of our vocation—to burn with love, to be a light, to be a fire. And we cannot start a fire with green wood. The fire of the love of God will not take hold in a soul that is not utterly dedicated to God.

Catherine de Hueck Doherty
Grace In Every Season

Moving Off Dead Center

■ **Behold, now is a very acceptable time; behold, now is the day of salvation.** 2 Corinthians 6:2

We live waiting for the right moment to be converted and to start to practice the virtues, to pray, or to enter some ministry. All of us are waiting for the perfect situation when at last we have the time for prayer, reflection, spiritual reading, service to others, when we can be reconciled with our disagreeable relatives, when we can forgive our enemies, our early education, the church, our mothers and fathers, and finally ourselves. This sad state of affairs must be changed, and it can be changed by allowing ourselves to see, feel, touch, taste, smell the divine presence right now. It is only our habit of not seeing God that stands in the way.

Until we live with reality in the present moment, we postpone it. Seeing the presence of Christ in the present moment is the way to transformation. . . . Just say, "Here he comes! I embrace him—hidden in this trial, in this dreadful person, in this stomach ache, in this overwhelming joy."

He is in the present moment no matter what the content of the moment is.

Fr. Thomas Keating O.C.S.O.
Reawakenings

Judging False Teaching Wisely

■ **Beware of false prophets, who come to you in sheep's clothing, but underneath are ravenous wolves. By their fruits you shall know them.** Matthew 7:15-16

The laws of human psychology would seem to indicate that few people *intend* to be false prophets conspiring to deceive. Even if their doctrine or cause clearly is false or misguided, most crusaders are well-intentioned and act because they believe they will help others. What false prophets ever saw themselves as wolves? Just as we are to be harsh on sin but compassionate with sinners, should we not be firm against false teaching but compassionate with false teachers? In any event, it would be unwise of us to judge prophets or leaders solely by their sincerity or the intensity of their devotion to their causes. We should avoid concluding that *what* one teaches *must* be right because he or she believes it so firmly.

That is why the second part of Jesus' warning is so important: "By their fruits you shall know them." We scrutinize the teaching more than the teacher. We must ask, "What is the ultimate result of their teaching? Where does it lead in the long run?" For that judgment, we should pray and study and do what we can to have an informed conscience.

Holy Spirit, help us to recognize false teaching.
James E. Adams

Our God Suffers With Us

■ **Into your hands I commend my spirit.** Psalm 31:6

When seemingly innocent people who suffer ask, "Why me?" God is strangely silent. So silent, that many deny the existence of a "good" God who would create a world where there is so much suffering. But while God may be silent in answering this question, God is not silent in giving us an example. In Jesus, God has somehow joined us in suffering. The riddle of suffering in a world God has created is not solved— it remains a true mystery—but in Jesus' humanity, God knows suffering too. This is one of the most profound mysteries we Christians celebrate this Good Friday: a God who suffers *with* us. Suffering is not ignored, dismissed, or explained away; it is not glorified or praised; it is accepted as part of God's inscrutable plan. "Into your hands I commend my spirit."

When we suffer, it is rarely consoling to complain of being singled out for misfortune, or to lament our fate. That often only makes suffering all the worse. But when we unite ourselves to the suffering Jesus, we gather strength from knowing our sufferings are shared. We are not forsaken in our suffering; we share in the sufferings of Christ as he shares in ours.

Into your hands, O Lord, I commend my spirit.

Michael R. Kent
Bringing The Word To Life

The Gospel's Awesome Power

■ **He said to them, "Go into the whole world and proclaim the gospel to every creature."** Mark 16:15

Faith is always demanding, because faith leads us beyond ourselves. It leads directly to God. The Gospel of Jesus Christ is not a private opinion, a remote spiritual ideal, or a mere program for personal growth. The Gospel is the power which can transform the world! The Gospel is no abstraction: it is the living person of Jesus Christ, the Word of God, the reflection of the Father's glory, the Incarnate Son who reveals the deepest meaning of our humanity and the noble destiny to which the whole human family is called. Christ has commanded us to let the light of the Gospel shine forth in our service to society. How can we profess faith in God's word, and then refuse to let it inspire and direct our thinking, our activity, or decisions, and our responsibilities to one another?. . .

Openness to the Lord—a willingness to let the Lord transform our lives—should produce a renewed spiritual and missionary vitality among Catholics. Jesus Christ is the answer to the question posed by every human life, and the love of Christ compels us to share that great good news with everyone.

Pope John Paul II
Make Room For The Mystery Of God

We All Have Special Gifts

■ **There is a boy here who has five barley loaves and two fish; but what good are these for so many?** John 6:9

Sometimes our "loaves and fishes"—our talents—are viewed by us or others as insignificant. We may cheerfully share money, thinking that every little bit helps. Yet when it comes time to share ourselves and the skills that perhaps only we have, we think we don't really have anything worthwhile to offer. We fail to recognize that our love, our hope, our compassion may well be unique gifts. Perhaps we have the talent of laughter. People may say, "It does me *good* to talk to you." We may have faith that can move mountains. A cheery call to someone who seems down may be just enough to give that friend hope for the future.

Any gift we have comes from God. It is given to us, but we are expected to share it. No expression of love and caring is ever lost, even though we may think our words of encouragement go unnoticed. They may well change the life of someone who needs some assurance.

Lord, whatever I am I owe to you. Grant me the grace to share myself with others in need.

Joan Zrilich

Grateful For All God's Gifts

■ **The favors of the Lord I will sing forever.** Psalm 89:2

Showing gratitude was a mainstay of good up-bringing. We were probably still toddlers when we first heard our mother's prompting as we received a gift, "Now what do you say?"

God is continually giving us gifts. And most of us find it easy to be grateful for things like finding an important paper we thought was lost or discovering that the repair cost on the air-conditioner was considerably less than we anticipated. It is easier to overlook being grateful for the routine gifts of God—our daily ability to see, to hear, to walk, to think, to speak. All these deserve a nod of thankfulness.

What is most difficult is being grateful for things that don't seem like gifts at all—living next to a neighbor who is constantly complaining, having the kids come down with measles just before summer camp, locking our keys in the car. Yet who knows? In eternity we may learn these were special gifts from God—the neighbor was saved from suicide because of our friendliness; our children missed coming under a bad influence at that camp; the locked-in car key kept us from meeting someone who meant us harm.

O God, help me to be grateful for all your gifts.
Sr. Mary Terese Donze, A.S.C.

Knowing The God We Pray To

■ May God give you a spirit of wisdom and revelation resulting in knowledge of him. Ephesians 1:17

At first this wish of St. Paul appears to be just a pious sentiment. But isn't it really a profound prayer, the full realization of which would fill the heart of a Christian to overflowing? To know *God*, to have knowledge of God—can we appreciate even in the slightest what such a grace potentially means?

Consider what it would mean to know God the Redeemer . . . to know the infinite love that gave us Christ from his birth through his Ascension. Even if we were unable to know the bounty of God the Redeemer, to know God the Creator would of itself be a blessing beyond measure! It is impossible for us to create; we can at best rearrange the something God created out of nothing. To have insight into the Almighty who made this awesome universe, to be let in on some of the divine secrets at the birth of reality, to get firsthand hints into the very essence of heaven and earth . . . wouldn't that be a profound thrill for even the most jaded among us?

When we say creeds and prayers, we address that very same Creator. If we could realize to Whom we speak, wouldn't our mouths dry up, our voices crack and our knees shake at the very thought of it?

James E. Adams

Being A Trusted Messenger

■ **The words you gave to me I gave to them.** John 17:8

I once became very embarrassed after I found in my pocket a month-old note that I was given with the request to deliver it to another person. I realized I was not a very trustworthy message bearer.

When we want to get an important message to someone, we are careful to choose the best means of communication—registered mail, trustworthy messenger, direct telephone call. God's message of love to humanity was certainly given to the most trustworthy person ever: Jesus, the Son of God in the flesh. However, when Jesus had to choose the means for God's message to be transmitted to future ages, I sometimes wonder if he really chose the best means. He chose his disciples; he has since chosen me. Does his message sometimes—often, maybe—get lost unseen in my pocket?

Jesus, you have entrusted the message of your Father to me. Help me realize what a privilege you have given me so that I will faithfully deliver your message to others.

Sr. Ruth Marlene Fox, O.S.B.

Patron Saint Of 'Good Grief'

■ **Peter was distressed that Jesus had said to him a third time, "Do you love me?" and he said to him, "Lord, you know everything; you know that I love you."** John 21:17

Peter provides much inspiration both to church leaders and to ordinary Christians because he learned so well the lesson of grieving deeply over his sins and failures—but then accepting forgiveness and moving on to respond with vigor to the next call of the Lord.

If we are caught up in denial, in remorse or in pseudo-grief, we can easily be paralyzed and unfit to meet the next challenge in our spiritual journey. How often do we wallow in self-justification, self-doubt, self-recrimination, self-hatred—maybe even despair? But when we react as Peter did in heartfelt sorrow, when we look outward to God's mercy instead of inward to our own limited resources, we can accept ourselves in joyful humility. We can look again with more objective eyes on our gifts. We can begin to see the Holy Spirit working to strengthen our meager natural abilities—and working around our disabilities. We can realize again that God wants his sons and daughters—like Peter—to be on their feet in readiness, not on their bellies in discouragement.

St. Peter, help me to grieve deeply for my sins, and to seek and accept the forgiveness of God.

James E. Adams

Taking 'Our Father' To Heart

■ **This is how you are to pray: Our Father in heaven, hallowed be your name . . .** Matthew 6:9

Walking alone in a field one day I was in great need to settle myself. I was angry and in need of space to work my way back to some much needed peace of mind. I found myself praying for a solution.

It suddenly dawned on me that I was not alone, that God was there. This sense that no one of us is alone, ever, struck me that day with such force! I did not know what else to say after that experience—so I said the Our Father, asking God simply to pray through me while I did my best to get out of the way.

The Our Father is a prayer of radical dependence upon God—radical in that it is a prayer for the deepest sources of life. It is a longing for God. Jesus asked us to pray it, and I took heart that day that he was in my heart, offering that prayer again. I have since prayed it when I found that I wanted to do things my way and tended to forget that God is within me.

Perhaps the best words are never really our own. I do not remember what, if any, solution I arrived at that day. But perhaps the best solutions are never our own, either. The Our Father helps me to remember that.

Fr. Jeff Behrens

A Demanding Faith Is Healthy

■ **Lord, teach me the way of your laws; I shall observe them with care.** Psalm 119:33

Faith makes demands on our comfort, on what we plan, what we propose for ourselves. The sickness of our time is a false idea of freedom that confuses freedom with preference and thinks that life is rich and beautiful only when we act and live in a way that gives pleasure to ourselves and conforms to our desires. Psychologists tell us that it is the absence of demands, of challenge, of opposition that runs counter to human nature, that makes us sick, and causes us to confront one another with hostility. Freedom does not consist in preference. It is foolish of us to regard the demands of faith—which make unwarranted demands on us and contradict our own will—as "legalistic" and "institutional" . . . in order to shake ourselves free of faith's demands and so to sink into the leaden emptiness of a lusterless and selfish existence that receives nothing because it gives nothing.

This thought should strike us anew: admittedly faith is uncomfortable, but only because it challenges us, compels us, to let ourselves be led where we do not wish to go. In this way it enriches us and opens for us the door of true life.

Cardinal Joseph Ratzinger
Co-Workers Of The Truth

The Refusal To Leave Home

■ **Whoever loves father or mother more than me is not worthy of me, and whoever loves son or daughter more than me is not worthy of me.** Matthew 10:37

To a Jewish audience, Jesus' words must have sounded even more terrible than they do to Christians today. Traditional Jewish life has always been family-based and to suggest the need to moderate one's love must have been shocking indeed. Why would Jesus make such a harsh statement—one which seemed like a direct attack on the family unit?

At stake here is more a matter of priorities than a mandate to turn one's back on family. To cling to one's parents can symbolically represent the refusal to leave home, to begin one's own spiritual journey. It means to clutch at the safety of the familiar so as to avoid risk and uncertainty. Clinging to one's children, on the other hand, means choosing to live vicariously through others, thus hindering their own journeys of exploration. It can mean placing one's hope in the next generation rather than working for change in the present. To follow Jesus is always a radical decision. It involves detaching ourselves from the parental home and living our own lives. Now.

Give us the gift of healthy detachment, God, that we might follow you more closely.

Elizabeth-Anne Vanek

The Key To Happiness

■ **Learn to savor how good the Lord is; happy are those who take refuge in him.** Psalm 34:9

Were we, years hence, to try and form an idea of how people lived in the 20th century, we should carry away the impression of a mortal anxiety which had seeped into every crevice of human life. This preoccupation does tell us one thing—that we are not resigned to being unhappy, that we feel it to be alien, unnatural. The struggle against anxiety is another way of bearing witness to the irrepressible need we have to be happy.

Now is the time for us to start boldly proclaiming the "glad tidings" that God is happiness, that happiness—not suffering, privation and the cross—will have the last word . . . What should be the cry with which to close our tortured millennium and prepare ourselves for the next? The note to be imprinted on the new evangelization? The human race has now become convinced that we have to choose between God and happiness. We have unwittingly made God the rival, the enemy of human joy. But this is Satan's work, the weapon he successfully used with Eve.

We can go our way with a new certainty: our climb to the Living God is also a climb towards happiness.
Fr. Raniero Cantalamessa, O.F.M. Cap.
The Ascent Of Mount Sinai

God's Will Told In A Nutshell!

■ **This is the will of my Father, that everyone who sees the Son and believes in him may have eternal life, and I shall raise him on the last day.** John 6:40

Here it is, in black and white, the answer to a question I so often puzzle over: what is God's will? What should I do? What response can I make to that person, to this pressing decision, to the many choices that come my way in raising a family, building a marriage, being part of the Church? What does God want?

According to this passage, God's will is simply that everyone have eternal life through believing in Jesus. God's will is that you and I—and everyone else—believe in Jesus, and come thereby to a life so full that even death cannot contain it.

When I make the effort to take these words to heart each day, the many other decisions I have to face seem less oppressive. Since God wants me to have eternal life, then my task today is to believe in Jesus, Son of God. If I can do that, then even the most important matters will fall into place.

Loving God, may your will be done this day.

Mark Neilsen

Living As God's Cherished

■ **No one can take them out of my hand.** John 10:28

With these words Jesus creates for us an illuminating image. Like a bird in a great protective hand, we are held, cherished and protected. If we listen to the voice that comes from a Shepherd who understands the longings of our hearts, we will learn to live with a sense of being cherished.

I invite you to let these words, "No one can take them out of my hand," become an icon for you, an image of being held in God's hands with no possibility of being snatched away. Use whatever related image is helpful, a bird held in a hand, a lamb on a shepherd's shoulder, a parent holding a child. Such simple images as these can become prayers.

As you visualize the icon of God holding you in a protective embrace, expand this very personal image to include others. Enhance your prayer by praying without words for those people in our world who need protection. Can you see them in your mind's eye? The poor? The ones with no power? The ones who are sleeping out in parks or under bridges? Your family? Someone who works for or with you? See God holding them, enfolding them.

May it come to pass!

Sr. Macrina Wiederkehr, O.S.B.

A Joy Rooted In The Spirit

■ **The disciples were filled with joy and the Holy Spirit.**
Acts 13:52

To experience joy and the Holy Spirit when all is rosy and well in our lives probably comes easy for us. This lovely text about the disciples being filled with joy and the Holy Spirit comes immediately after the disciples had experienced persecution and rejection.

There's a lesson for us here. A joy so deep that it cannot be taken away by rejection can only be a joy that has its roots in the Spirit. Jesus tells us that if we believe in him we will do the same wonders he has done. In these words he is telling us to live our lives rooted in his Spirit. This will be the cause of our joy, and our lives will not be able to hide that joy even in the midst of suffering.

This does not mean that we want to suffer or that we don't, at times, feel sorrow because of misunderstanding and rejection. It does, however, give witness to the truth that we have an immense capacity for sorrow and joy in our lives; both can be holy.

O Resurrected Jesus, fill our lives with joy and the Holy Spirit right in the midst of our sufferings.

Sr. Macrina Wiederkehr, O.S.B.

Love: A Spiritual Challenge

■ **This is my commandment: love one another as I love you.** John 15:12

Whom should we love and how much should we love them? The Old Testament gives the answers: you are to love your neighbor, normally meaning those who are in close proximity to you. The amount of love you are to give your neighbor is as much as you give to yourself. That obviously is a high degree of love. It's the love that keeps us alive through self-preservation. It may be difficult to love some neighbors and very difficult to love any as much as you love yourself.

The New Testament offers an even greater challenge. Jesus told us to love one another—everyone without exclusion. The degree of loving is also intensified. We are asked to love as the Lord loves us; a far greater love than our love for ourselves, because God's capacity to love is infinite. So how are we ever to love one another as God loves us? It's an ideal for which we can strive, even if we never fulfill it. To love in this exalted way is the deep spiritual challenge of being a follower of Jesus. Through God's grace, we can continue to strive toward perfection.

Dear Lord, help me to be mindful every day of the lofty ideal of Christian love to which I am called.

Fr. James McKarns

Don't Run From Pain Too Soon

■ **Amen, amen, I say to you, you will weep and mourn, while the world rejoices; you will grieve, but your grief will become joy.** John 16:20

There is a time for weeping. It is part of being human. And a Christian knows that time only too well. All of us have, or should have, experienced a time for weeping, the pain of being human. All of us have failed in what we believe are God's expectations of us or the expectations we place upon ourselves. We know failure; we know sin; we know what it means to be broken.

The important thing in the face of failure or sin is that we *stay with the pain* and let it teach us what God wants us to learn. To run away from pain—through drugs, sex, drinking or other diversions—results in nothing but deeper pain, guilt, and shame. We may find relief for a moment, but the long-term result is to sink deeper into the quicksand.

Jesus uses the figure of a woman about to give birth to a child and the resultant joy of this act. Joy is as inevitable in this process as the pain. So it is in the pain of life: in facing it and living and learning through it, we come at last to the joy that comes from faithfulness to God's lead.

Jesus, help me to stand firm in the face of pain, and let me learn in this what you want to teach me.

Fr. Kieran Kay, O.F.M. Conv.

The Gift Of God's Presence

■ **Did you receive the Holy Spirit when you became believers?** Acts 19:2

One day I walked out of the house to go to a meeting. I had my hand on the car door, ready to open it. Suddenly a rush of peace and well-being swept through my spirit. I immediately had this keen awareness that someone was praying for me. I felt grateful and a bit in awe. I knew in that moment that God was filling me with love. This sense of an immense Power within us is one significant way in which the Holy Spirit acts. This powerful love stirs and calls to us. This gift of God's presence unites us and supports us. We cannot force or control how or when this gift is given. We can only be open and ready to receive it.

We receive the gift of the Holy Spirit when we are baptized. We continue to receive this gracious gift each time we are open to the goodness of God in our daily moments. It is easy to miss this graced movement of God or to take these moments for granted. Today might be a good day to deepen our awareness of how the Holy Spirit guides, protects, encourages, comforts, sustains, and draws us always toward a more whole union with our Creator.

Holy Spirit, may I be aware of your presence and your action in all my moments, however ordinary.

Sr. Joyce Rupp, O.S.M.

Love Is A 'Work In Progress'

■ **What God has joined together, no human being must separate.** Mark 10:9

The human heart was made for a lasting home. Our very hearts long for so many lasting things, and above all for a lasting love. That Jesus refuses to compromise the nature of the heart comes then as no surprise. He is simply reminding us of the wondrous loving Source from whom our hearts come. The God who fashioned the human heart did so with a lasting imprint, lasting both in terms of his presence and the nature of his love.

We live in a time that has seen many commitments wither and die. We need more than ever to trust in the words with which we speak our vows. Love is a gift that needs nurturing and, above all, trust in God. To live a lasting love is to believe in it and to believe in God who provides what we need. God sustains us in good days and bad.

Love is never a finished product, but a continual rough draft, in need of wise and tender revision. Your love is a unique work in progress. Trust the Author, even though you would like to discard a few pages or an entire chapter. Keep them, live them, love from them, one day at a time.

Fr. Jeff Behrens

Carrying Others' Burdens

■ **And there people brought to him a paralytic lying on a stretcher. When Jesus saw their faith, he said to the paralytic, "Courage, child, your sins are forgiven."**

Matthew 9:2

Did you ever notice that in the Gospels people are constantly being *brought* by others to Jesus? Andrew becomes a follower of Jesus and immediately brings his brother Simon to meet him.

Even in Jesus' final days, some Greek proselytes who had come to Jerusalem for the Passover approach Philip and Andrew and are introduced to the Lord. Throughout his ministry, the sick and the needy, the blind and the ignorant are brought—at times physically carried—to Jesus for healing, instruction, forgiveness.

In our prayer, we come before God with many personal burdens, some of which weigh heavily upon us and stretch the limits of our love. But we also carry others and their needs in our arms, believing that God, through Jesus Christ, has both the power and the desire to heal in body and spirit.

Who are the people we carry to Jesus this day? What situations and needs do we hold in our hearts at this moment? Others may never know how much we care, but God does and will reward our faith with new signs and wonders.

Fr. Anthony Schueller, S.S.S.

Our Need For Reform

■ **Jesus began to reproach the towns where most of his miracles had been worked, with their failure to reform...**

Matthew 11:20

We live in days that desperately need repentance. The word renewal has been used for the last twenty-five years. It is a good word. In the Pauline context it means to return to the power of the Holy Spirit and let him make us new again. But before that renewal can occur, reform is necessary. True spiritual renewal is not simply cultural or educational. It is not simply restating truths to make them more compatible with a new age. True renewal is above all a return to God. It is a daily, ongoing repentance, an attempt to accept the Good News in all its unthinkable and incomprehensible grandeur and to pick oneself up and try to respond to that call. Renewal without reform is spiritually devastating.

Where does this reform begin? It begins with individuals. Group efforts at reform often lead to discord and even to religious war. They ignore the first step. Individual repentance and reform must happen in the life of every Christian who believes and listens to the summons to repent and hear the Good News. This is the hour of repentance and reform.

Fr. Benedict J. Groeschel, C.F.R.
The Reform Of Renewal

For Mercy's Sake

■ **If you knew what this meant, "I desire mercy, not sacrifice," you would not have condemned these innocent men.** Matthew 12:7

Jesus and his disciples were walking through a field of grain. The Pharisees became upset when the hungry disciples pulled off and ate some of the heads of grain because such activity was not permitted on the Sabbath. Jesus responded to their criticism by telling the Pharisees that he was not so concerned about the rules of the law (sacrifice) as he was about the way people relate to one another (mercy).

I know Jesus' words are true for me: I'd rather fast for a day anytime (sacrifice) than have to be kind and open to someone who has dealt me a low blow (mercy). I would rather choose my own daily sacrifices than have them come to me in the form of critical people, impatient drivers and irritable co-workers. How much easier it is to give up a piece of candy or go to church on Sunday than to stay loving toward those who mess up my day. Sacrifices I choose seem easy compared to the continual kindness Jesus requires.

Jesus, full of mercy, help me accept the difficult people of my day and respond with compassion.

Sr. Joyce Rupp, O.S.M.

A Model For Prayer

■ **She had a sister named Mary, who seated herself at the Lord's feet and listened to his words.** Luke 10:39

To keep quiet in prayer—how difficult it is! To bring the imagination, the tongue and the intelligence to silence—to keep quiet. To forbid oneself fine thoughts and bring oneself to an act of adoration like that of the host! Have you ever thought about the position of the Eucharist? It's the Incarnate Word's adoration of the Father. And how does he adore? In silence, by reducing himself to zero, by abandoning himself to sacrifice in love.

This is the true model of prayer. At the beginning of our spiritual life, we feel the need in prayer to speak a lot, to say a lot (and that's OKAY). But at a certain point, when real love wins us over, the highest prayer is silent adoration, accepting, loving, abandoning ourselves to God's action without reserve.

How difficult it is to give up our busyness, even in holiness, to give up the helm, and stay *waiting*, without making plans, without making any provision. Only in this way do we come to the certainty that it is God who must act and we must receive with love and self-sacrifice.

Carlo Carretto
Letters To Dolcidia

An Example Of Compassion

■ **When Jesus heard of [John's execution], he withdrew in a boat to a deserted place by himself. . . . When he disembarked and saw the vast crowd, his heart was moved with pity for them, and he cured their sick.**

Matthew 14:13-14

In the midst of a growing confrontation with the Roman authorities, Jesus went off by himself, perhaps wondering what would happen to him now that John had been beheaded. Filled with such thoughts, Jesus is suddenly confronted by a vast crowd. He doesn't send them away, despite how troubled his own spirit is. His compassion takes over and he responds to their needs.

Very often, we have similar opportunities to break through our own struggles and anxieties by focusing instead on the needs of those around us.

Jesus' example challenges us as it did the disciples who wanted him to send the crowd away so they could get dinner on their own. He tells the disciples to feed the crowd themselves.

Similarly, we can try to meet the needs of those around us, even though it may seem impossible. With Jesus' blessing, our efforts can be the answer to the pleas and prayers of the sick and hungry of our day.

James McGinnis

That Sinking Feeling

■ **At once Jesus spoke to them, "Take courage, it is I; do not be afraid." Peter said to him in reply, "Lord, if it is you, command me to come to you on the water."**

Matthew 14:27-28

I have long suspected that in the midst of my darkest, most stormy moments, there is someone beside me battling the stormy waters of life along with me. Someone is walking near with an outstretched hand calling to me in a voice of concern, "Take courage! You're not alone! Let go of your fear!" Seeing with eyes of faith, I reach for that outstretched hand. Yet when that faith sometimes grows dim, the stormy waters become overwhelming and I sink.

I sink when I take my eyes off that outstretched hand and try to do things on my own.

I sink when I insist on being in control of my life.

I sink when I think more about the raging waters than the presence of Jesus.

I sink when I'm reluctant to trust that all the outstretched hands around me are the hand of Jesus.

Sinking has always been, for me, a great teaching. Hitting rock bottom can be a tremendous grace.

Lord, if it is you, command me to come to you on the water.

Sr. Macrina Wiederkehr, O.S.B.

No One Is Hopelessly Lost

■ **If a man has a hundred sheep and one of them goes astray, will he not leave the ninety-nine in the hills and go in search of the stray?** Matthew 18:12

The lost sheep has a very uncomplicated role: it does not appear to be coming to its senses, calling to its master or seeking its way home. It is simply lost, perhaps going further astray by the minute. The helpful action is all on the part of the shepherd. He searches for and rescues the sheep, because he values the sheep and does not want it to come to harm. When the task is complete, the shepherd celebrates.

What a beautiful image of God's initiative! Not only is it a source of hope in our own times of being lost, it is also a profound consolation when we worry about loved ones who have wandered off. They may seem stubbornly astray, resolute in their rovings, yet they are not beyond the reach of our Good Shepherd. This we can trust: it is God's desire and God's joy to retrieve all who are lost.

Nancy F. Summers

A Whole New Self

■ **I will give you a new heart and place a new spirit within you, taking from your bodies your stony hearts and giving you natural hearts. I will put my spirit within you and make you live by my statutes.** Ezekiel 36:26-27

Jesus requires us to unmask the illusion of our competitive selfhood, to give up clinging to our imaginary distinctions as sources of identity, and to be taken up into the same intimacy with God which Jesus knows.

This is the mystery of the Christian life—to receive a new self, a new identity, which depends not on what we can achieve, but on what we are willing to receive. This new self is our participation in the divine life in and through Christ. Jesus wants us to belong to God as he belongs to God; he wants us to be children of God as he is a child of God; he wants us to let go of the old life, which is so full of fears and doubts, and to receive the new life, the life of God himself.

In and through Christ we receive a new identity that enables us to say, "I am not the esteem I can collect through competition, but the love I have freely received from God."

Fr. Henri J.M. Nouwen
Show Me The Way

Work Hard To Do God's Will

■ **"Lord, open the door for us." He will say to you in reply, "I do not know where you are from."** Luke 13:25

Just being a Catholic is no guarantee of salvation.

We cannot take our own salvation as a matter of course. It is something we must work at, and work hard. There is no room in God's kingdom for the smug or complacent person. To gain entrance into God's kingdom, more is required than mere membership in the Church. We must try to do God's will in every aspect of our lives. Today's second reading from the letter to the Hebrews emphasizes one particular aspect of God's will—his wish to discipline us as his children so that we may be worthy members of his spiritual family. Good parents know that children need discipline if they are to mature, but a child of any age can resist discipline and thwart the most conscientious efforts of his or her parents . . .

One of the worst things we can do is to revolt against the trials that God sends us. We don't have to pretend that God's discipline is fun, but we do have to see that it is necessary to make us worthy of his kingdom. . . . We must work to do God's will and to cooperate with his fatherly discipline.

Fr. Charles E. Miller, C.M.
The Word Made Flesh

Beyond Hypocrisy

■ **Woe to you, scribes and Pharisees, you hypocrites. You are like whitewashed tombs, which appear beautiful on the outside, but inside are full of dead men's bones and every kind of filth.** Matthew 23:27

Do you recognize yourself in Jesus' angry denunciation of the scribes and Pharisees? Jesus' words serve as a warning to all of us religious people, not because being religious is bad, but because it is all too easy to observe the outward forms of worship while our hearts remain stony. And Jesus reminds us that it is what's in the heart that counts.

What can we Christians do? We don't want our faith in God to be simply a self-serving means of gaining public approval or personal pride. We don't want our selfishness to destroy all our attempts to love genuinely. How can we get beyond the hypocrisy of the scribes and Pharisees without becoming smug and self-righteous ourselves?

What the scribes and Pharisees lacked was an appreciation of their need for God's mercy; they thought they were already justified through their own actions. The surest way to avoid their sin is to recognize, from time to time, how much you have in common with them, and then to throw yourself on God's mercy.

Mark Neilsen

Am I Ready To Meet God?

■ **When he reached the Ancient One and was presented before him, he received dominion, glory, and kingship.**
                                                    Daniel 7:13-14

Have you ever thought what it would be like to be presented to God? From time to time it is good to use our imagination to visualize what this might be like. We can learn a lot about our relationship with God and about how we are living our life.

Author Robert Fulghum describes going out to his cemetery plot on every birthday to sit for a while in a lawn chair and think about his presentation to God. He quickly sees what is vital and worthwhile in life and what is not.

We do not have to sit on a lawn chair on our cemetery plot to think about our "last days." Reflecting on this reality, however, can be a good thing. Rather than something morbid, it can help us anticipate union with the all-loving Being. Visualizing our moment of being presented to the One who created us with love and who receives us with love can free us from some of the clutter and clutching of our lives and be a source of renewal.

Think about it: how do you envision your presentation to God?

                                        Sr. Joyce Rupp, O.S.M.

Making Proper Comparisons

■ **When you are invited, go and take the lowest place so that when the host comes to you he may say, "My friend, move up to a higher position."** Luke 14:10

The saints sincerely felt deep humility because they compared themselves with God, and not with their fellow human beings. Their faults, their failures, their weaknesses were manifestly clear to themselves in the brilliant light of God's perfection.

If we could only learn to compare ourselves with God, how could we feel anything but humility? Pride comes from a false point of comparison. These days, it is commonplace to read in the papers or hear on television about people whose lack of morals is notorious. . . . It is easy to feel pretty proud of ourselves in comparison. The comparison makes us feel complacent, and the desire for such a comfortable feeling is behind a lot of prejudice, racial and otherwise. Looking down on others gives us a sense of personal elevation . . .

A pride that is produced by comparing ourselves with despicable people—or those we may consider despicable, is condemned by Jesus. The complacency it begets inhibits our spiritual growth. God's own perfection is the ideal toward which we must strive.

Fr. Charles E. Miller, C.M.
The Word Made Flesh

God's Underground

■ **He loves justice and right; of the kindness of the Lord the earth is full.** Psalm 33:5

Devastated by the loss of a job I loved, I approached the bureaucracy of the state unemployment office with fear and shame. The job counselor, an older man, listened to my story with patience and compassion, told me funny stories about his dog and generally cheered me up.

God has an "underground," my friend Judy says, a network of holy souls who stand ready to lift us up when the world has beaten us down. I felt I had met one that day. The stranger who stops to help with the flat tire, the nurse holding the hand of a suffering patient, the clerk who provides a kind word on a desperate day—all these are agents of grace.

If we are open to the movement of the Spirit in our daily lives, we can join this holy underground by taking the part of the kind stranger, the whisperer of hope, the courier of God's infinite, merciful love. It gives us joy to receive the healing, saving touch of God's messengers; it gives us even more joy to be able to bring a touch of divine mercy to others.

Give us, Lord, the grace to hear the call to bear your presence in our daily lives.

Denise Barker

God Works In Us

■ . . . **the Lord will bring to light what is hidden in darkness and will manifest the motives of our hearts, and then everyone will receive praise from God.**

1 Corinthians 4:5

The motives of our hearts to be made public? What a frightening thought! How often I have done a good deed with the motive of being thought well of or having people like me so that they would, in turn, do good deeds for me? What other selfish intentions are hidden in the darkness of my soul? What other manipulations, deceits, and attempts to control lie just below the surface of my smiles, my good advice, my helpfulness? How will I bear the shame of such revelations?

And yet, Paul tells us, we will all receive praise from God. In spite of our pettiness, our neediness, our mixed motives, we *have* served the kingdom. We do the work of God as well—perhaps even better—in our weakness as in our strength. Just by putting ourselves at the service of the divine will we become implements to be used in God's own way and time.

God, help me to accept myself with all my weaknesses and hidden faults and to rejoice in the way you use me in spite of them.

Denise Barker

God Is Always Near

■ **The Lord is near to all who call upon him, to all who call upon him in truth.** Psalm 145:18

What are we to understand by contemplation? Quite simply the attitude in which our whole being is totally seized by the wonder of a presence. When we understand the vast reality of the beauty of things intellectually, in one sense we have indeed been seized by it all, but that is only partial. It is the whole of our being, emotions and all, that is seized by the reality of the love of God.

Some people are in the grip of the subjective experience of the silence of God, as if the presence of God were bound to our perception and to what we feel. Can they have forgotten? God is there, too, in the times that enthusiasm evaporates and all apparent feeling vanishes. God says: Before you were born, I dreamt of you.

When we realize that God loved us first, even before we loved him, we can only tear aside the veil under which we have been hiding. The day will come when each one of us will know and perhaps even say, "No, God did not go away. I was the one who was absent. God was with me all the time."

Br. Roger of Taizé
His Love Is A Fire

The Art Of Detachment

■ **Everyone of you who does not renounce all his possessions cannot be my disciple.** Luke 14:33

St. John of the Cross, the sixteenth century Spanish mystic, uses a wonderful image to describe how our possessions can tie us down and keep us from soaring heavenward: whether a bird is tied, he explains, by a thin thread or a thick cord, it cannot fly. So it is with us: whether we give our whole-hearted attention to trifles or great riches, to relationships or careers, the results are the same: there is little room left for the Spirit.

Most of us need to learn the art of detachment from our possessions. At some point in our lives, whether we like it or not, little progress will be possible on the spiritual journey if we don't begin to let go of what ties us down. The more we are able to approach God with empty hands and empty hearts, the more the fullness of Presence will come to us.

Detachment, even from what we hold most dear, not only draws us close to God, it gives us courage for that final letting go, death itself, for we will have already tasted something of the ecstasy that awaits us.

Elizabeth-Anne Vanek

Timekeeper

■ **I tell you, brothers, the time is running out. . . . For the world in its present form is passing away.**

1 Corinthians 7:29, 31

My friend bought a new watch for herself—the old-fashioned kind with two hands, Arabic numerals and a winding stem. Each evening, she dutifully wound the watch, but noticed that the stem never grew tight as happened with her previous watches. After a year, the watch started losing time, so she returned it to the store. After inspecting it, the clerk informed her, "All it needs is a new battery."

For all those months, the wearer of the watch was convinced she was in control of the time-piece, that she kept it running with her daily ritual of winding.

In many areas of my life, I act as though I am in control of the time that is allotted to me. Even my language betrays my self-deception as I speak of "saving" time, "making" time or "wasting" time. Recognizing that I am not really in control gives me a great relief, for all the while, the unseen and unknown grace of God is directing my time from the inside.

Thank you, God, for your silent and careful creating and managing of all time.

Sr. Ruth Marlene Fox, O.S.B.

Compassionate Solidarity

■ **Be compassionate as your Father is compassionate.**
                                                    Luke 6:36

Let us not underestimate how hard it is to be compassionate. Compassion is hard because it requires the inner disposition to go with others to the place where they are weak, vulnerable, lonely and broken. But this is not our spontaneous response to suffering. What we desire most is to do away with suffering by fleeing from it or finding a quick cure for it . . . we want to make a real contribution. This means first and foremost doing something to show that our presence makes a difference. And so we ignore our greatest gift, which is our ability to enter into solidarity with those who suffer.

It is in solitude that this compassionate solidarity grows. In solitude we realize that nothing human is alien to us, that the roots of all conflict, war, injustice, cruelty, hatred, jealousy and envy are deeply anchored in our own heart. In solitude our heart of stone can be turned into a heart of flesh, a rebellious heart into a contrite heart and a closed heart into a heart that can open itself to all suffering people in a gesture of solidarity.

Fr. Henri J.M. Nouwen
The Way Of The Heart

Compassion For Others

■ **You hypocrite! Remove the wooden beam from your eye first; then you will see clearly enough to remove the splinter in your brother's eye.** Luke 6:42

Why is it always so much easier to see the faults of others than our own? It is so logical to excuse ourselves for our less than perfect behavior because we know the reasons behind it: "I am tired, my head aches, I am concerned about something else, my parents didn't love me, I was abused as a child, this is just the way I am." These may all be quite true. But should we not allow others the same benefit of the doubt when their behavior does not meet our definition of "good"?

At a recent conference, the speaker reminded us, "If you really knew and understood the pain that others bear, your compassion would lead you to tears most of your life."

What are the blinders that prevent me from seeing clearly the pain of my brother or sister? It could be jealousy, competition, anger, revenge, or even my own lack of self-respect.

Help me, O God, to take these planks from my eyes so that I may look upon others with compassion.

Sr. Ruth Marlene Fox, O.S.B.

The Forgiving Father

■ **Then let us celebrate with a feast, because this son of mine was dead, and has come to life again; he was lost, and has been found.** Luke 15:23-24

The real prodigal in this gospel story may be the father. The lost son may have spent all his inheritance on riotous living, but the father exceeds that extravagance by spending his love. While the son forfeits his reputation, the father forfeits logic. While the son loses his self-respect, the father loses the respect of his elder son.

I imagine a foolish old man, watching day and night from the hilltop, straining to see the spendthrift; a foolish old man, placing a ring on the finger of the squanderer; a foolish old man, killing the fatted calf and risking the displeasure of the older son, the penny pincher who refuses to celebrate; a foolish old man, caught between heartbreak and hope.

The father is a foolish old man, perhaps as foolish as the God who loves us in spite of everything and who lavishes care upon us, even when we stray; a foolish old man whose extravagance is cause for our own rejoicing.

Elizabeth-Anne Vanek

Jesus' Victory—And Ours

■ **Just as Moses lifted up the serpent in the desert, so must the Son of Man be lifted up, so that everyone who believes in him may have eternal life.** John 3:14-15

To his enemies the Crucifixion seems to be the hour of their triumph and Christ's defeat, but in fact it is the supreme hour of *his* triumph. When he seems to be more helpless than ever, he is, in fact, more powerful. When he seems to be more limited, more restricted, his love is boundless, his reach across the world to the hearts of all in all ages is infinite.

But for those who look on, how different what appears to be happening seems from what is really happening.

How certain it seems that Christ has been overcome. That his plan of love for the world has failed utterly, that he himself is a failure, his "kingdom" a pitiful delusion. . . . He seems to be quite alone, quite defeated, dying a useless death at the end of a useless life, the tragic life of a poor deluded dreamer . . .

"If I be lifted up, I will draw all to me," Jesus had said. Now he had done just that, he had drawn all people to him because he was dying all of their deaths for them, he was giving himself to them in death.

Caryll Houselander
The Stations Of The Cross

Custom-Made

■ **From his fixed throne he beholds all who dwell on the earth, he who fashioned the heart of each . . .**

Psalm 33:14-15

According to the Scriptural account, God made the sun, the moon, the stars, the plants, the animals, each group in a vast, sweeping creative act. Only in the creation of rational beings did God seem first to pause and deliberate. Once the reflective moment was over, the Creator came up with only one of its kind, a solitary man.

What is true of the creation of the first human is true for each of us. There is something awesome in the thought that God, the Source of might, life and goodness, takes time out, as it were, to create each individual soul in a one-on-one creative movement. It is touching to realize that we ourselves have received just such special attention.

For there is no "ho-hum" with God. Not even the most insignificant infant born to a young mother in the unknown stretches of the world is the by-product of some afterthought by the Creator. From eternity to the day we were conceived in our flesh, we were custom-made to fit the specifications of the Trinity. What love surrounded our origins! What a destiny God still has in mind for us!

Sr. Mary Terese Donze, A.S.C.

Look Within

■ **So I tell you, her many sins have been forgiven; hence, she has shown great love. But the one to whom little is forgiven, loves little.** Luke 7:47

What a wonderful message is contained in this passage, especially for our day and age! The forgiven prostitute showered Jesus with love because she, perhaps for the first time in her life, had really been loved. How had this come to be?

Jesus says very clearly that it is because she has been forgiven. But she could never have experienced this forgiveness if she had not first been able to recognize her sinfulness. This is Simon the Pharisee's problem: he cannot experience forgiveness because he does not regard himself as a sinner.

Let this not be our problem, too. Today, many voices would have us believe that prostitution is a "victimless" crime. Others would have us believe that seeing ourselves as sinful is unhealthy. But Jesus' words make it so plain that we will miss out on the joy of love and life if we cannot recognize how much we need God's mercy.

Lord, give me a greater awareness of my own sinfulness, not to "beat up on myself," but so I can ask for and receive your forgiveness and dwell in love anew.

Mark Neilsen

Hope For More

■ **If for this life only we have hoped in Christ, we are the most pitiable people of all.** 1 Corinthians 15:19

If I find in myself a desire which no experience in this world can satisfy, the most probable explanation is that I was made for another world.

If none of my earthly pleasures satisfy it, that does not prove that the universe is a fraud. Probably earthly pleasures were never meant to satisfy it, but only to arouse it, to suggest the real thing. If that is so, I must take care, on the one hand, never to despise, or be unthankful for, these earthly blessings, and on the other, never to mistake them for the something else of which they are only a kind of copy, or echo, or mirage.

I must keep alive in myself the desire for my true country, which I shall not find till after death; I must never let it get snowed under or turned aside; I must make it the main object of life to press on to that other country and to help others to do the same.

C. S. Lewis
Mere Christianity

'Mammon Sickness'

■ **No servant can serve two masters. He will either hate one and love the other, or be devoted to one and despise the other. You cannot serve God and mammon.**

Luke 16:13

We must honestly say that the Gospel has in many ways been lured into a trap by our society and culture. The Gospel is for the most part held by cultures of affluence. This is a society where we not only need more and more things, but where we keep demanding more and where we think we have a right to keep getting more. Our whole feeling of self-worth depends on our getting more, on our doing more, on our always climbing higher and higher . . .

A large part of Jesus' teaching is a critique of "mammon sickness," . . . in which those afflicted are continually driven by unrest, cares and anxiety, because the present isn't enough for them. But for those grounded in Christ, the present contains great abundance, even though we don't yet live in the full Reign of God. This is precisely the peace that the world can't give, and the peace the world can't take away from us. It's the only gift we can bring to our world.

Fr. Richard Rohr, O.F.M.
Simplicity

Beware Of Righteousness

■ **Why does your teacher eat with tax collectors and sinners?** Matthew 9:11

Gossip about individuals' faults or sins is often concluded in these scandalized tones: "And they go to church, too!" As if this were some unacceptable paradox rather than the usual way of Jesus.

I wonder about this church where such sinners have found refuge, where mercy attracts the lost like a lighthouse during a storm. It must be a place where righteousness is not necessary for acceptance, and fellowship is not the privilege of the elite. I imagine this is a church where compassion is valued more than money, where the unfathomable movement of the Spirit is superior to regulations.

If such a place actually exists, it is probably poor, perhaps shabby, of little prestige in the local community. A lot like Matthew's dining room, one might expect, where Jesus chose to be, much to the astonishment of the gossipers of his day.

Nancy F. Summers

Embracing God's Will

■ **My mother and my brothers are those who hear the word of God and act on it.** Luke 8:21

God says to each of us: "Give me your heart, that is, your will." We, in turn, cannot offer anything more precious than to say: "Lord, take possession of us; we give our whole will to you; make us understand what it is that you desire of us, and we will perform it."

If we would give full satisfaction to the heart of God, we must bring our own will in everything into conformity with his; and not only into conformity, but into uniformity also, as regards all that God ordains. Conformity signifies the joining of our own will to the will of God; but uniformity signifies, further, our making of the divine and our own will one will only, so that we desire nothing but what God desires, and his will becomes ours. This is the sum and substance of that perfection to which we ought to be ever aspiring; this is what must be the aim of all we do, and of all our desires, meditations and prayers. For this we must invoke the assistance of all our patron saints and our guardian angels, and, above all, of our divine mother Mary, who was the most perfect saint, because she embraced most perfectly the divine will.

St. Alphonsus Liguori
from *The Redeeming Love Of Christ*

Freely Praising God

■ **Accept, O Lord, the free homage of my mouth, and teach me your decrees.** Psalm 119:108

When is my homage to God truly free? Honoring God is truly free only when I expect nothing in return. On the surface, I might assert that I am not looking for any payment, but the temptation to try to manipulate God goes very deep in all of us. Does not the desire for some small favor secretly motivate my homage? Am I not, at least, hoping through my devotion to rise a notch in God's estimation? To recognize such mixed motivation can liberate and purify my worship and prayer.

Praise of God feels most free when it comes naturally and spontaneously. Like the fig tree Jesus invited to bear fruit out of season, we can produce in our hearts a harvest of homage outside of specific, designated prayer times. Communal prayer and scheduled personal prayer have great value, but free homage may come in a flash of awareness of God's greatness and graciousness.

Dear God, thank you for creating me, for giving me faith, and for granting me ever now and again those wonderful flashes of your goodness and beauty!

Nancy F. Summers

The Work Of Our Hands

■ **May the gracious care of the Lord be ours; prosper the work of our hands for us!** Psalm 90:17

Some years ago, after recuperating in the hospital from cancer surgery, I had gone to recover at our home for sick and retired Sisters.

At first, my hands—and my whole body—needed rest. As I gradually regained strength, I was attracted to the activity room where our retired Sisters, some in wheel chairs, folded towels and pillow cases fresh from the laundry. I watched wrinkled hands that had once written on blackboards, corrected papers, dried children's tears, played on the piano, and scrubbed floors now carefully fold laundry for the home. Dignity and pride were evident in their movements. Before going back to my own ministry, I was able to minister in a different way by folding towels with them.

The hands of the surgeon who operated on me, the hands of the mother who bathes her baby, the hands of the Eucharistic Minister who gives Communion, the hands of the supermarket clerk who makes change: whatever our hands do for good, may God prosper their work.

Loving God, as you hold us in the palm of your hand, help our hands to do good work.

Sr. Marguerite Zralek, O.P.

Timely Deaths

■ **There is an appointed time for everything, a time for every affair under the heavens. A time to be born, and a time to die . . .** Ecclesiastes 3:1-2

You must let go of where you've been, let go of the level of life where you are now, so as to live more fully.

Whether it's turning 21, 40 or 65, whether it's losing your health or your hair, your looks or your lustiness, your money or your memory, a person you love or a possession you prize, yesterday's rapture or today's applause—you have to move on. Essential to the human pilgrimage, to the Christian journey, is a self-emptying more or less like Christ's own emptying: time and again, from womb to tomb, you have to let go. And to let go is to die a little. It's painful, it can be bloody; and so we hang on, clutch our yesterdays like Linus' blanket, refuse to grow.

But it will not do for a Christian. You are commanded to let go. Not invited—commanded. . . . The comforting, the thrilling thing, is that you let go for a purpose. Emptying, dying, is not its own end. You let go of yesterday because only by letting go, only by reaching out into a shadowed future, can you grow into Christ, grow in loving communion with God.

Fr. Walter J. Burghardt, S.J.
Dare To Be Christ

My True Identity

■ **Vanity of vanities, says Qoheleth, all things are vanity.**
Ecclesiastes 12:8

Nothing in this world lasts. Certainly neither beauty nor youth nor the many roles by which we define our existence and security. Worker, parent, spouse, friend: these are always changing. One's true identity is not defined by gender or race, nationality or creed. Success or failure, health or infirmity, poverty or wealth: none of these will follow us to the grave.

Rather than make us depressed, the fleeting nature of our lives can prompt us to cherish each moment, for it will never be again. We can live to the fullest our various roles and circumstances, but we must hold them lightly, like a fragile glass figurine, beautiful in itself, yet still only an image of the real thing.

Who are we, then, without all our labels, images and roles, all the data that can describe us at this moment? We are creations of God's love, distinct and unrepeatable, belonging more to God than to our very own selves. This alone will last.

Nancy F. Summers

The Lazaruses In My Life

■ **If they will not listen to Moses and the prophets, neither will they be persuaded if someone should rise from the dead.** Luke 16:31

Who is Lazarus today? A street person huddling behind a "hungry and homeless" sign, dark eyes pleading between the ragged edges of a wool cap pulled down and a blanket drawn high?

Who is Lazarus today? A family evicted from their home after jobs terminate and checks bounce, leaving nothing for mortgage payments or medical insurance?

Who is Lazarus today? Teenagers robbed of hope by dead ends in the maze of drugs, violence and fear?

Who is Lazarus today? The elderly, cast off and unwanted, frail and lonely, beating time until time runs out?

Who is Lazarus today? You? Me? People we know? People we choose not to see?

The rich man failed to see beyond his own gratification. Our challenge is to be conscious of others' needs—and to help—even when we are necessarily concerned with our own requirements. For this, Jesus tell us, is obligation, not mere choice. This, Jesus tells us, will bring angels to our side when the time comes for us to cross the great abyss.

Elizabeth-Anne Vanek

Messengers Of God

■ **I solemnly assure you, you shall see the sky opened and the angels of God ascending and descending on the Son of Man.** John 1:51

Angels are most commonly associated with joyous times—as, for example, at Christmas and at Easter.

And when we hear of angels, we also think of the comfort, protection and loving support that we were taught our guardian angels provide us. So it's easy to see how we associate angels only with good times.

But there is another side to the angels, whose name means "messenger" of God. Throughout the Bible angels are also associated with severe trials, tribulations and temptations both personal and cosmic. Jacob wrestled with an angel. Michael and the archangels are locked in mortal conflict with Satan, according to the Book of Revelation. And artists have depicted an angel offering Jesus a cup to drink as a symbol of the horrors of the Agony in the Garden.

Though it may be hard for us to see angels connected with our crises and painful times, the Bible seems to teach a link between them. In faith, therefore, we know that even when we seem most alone, we may well be in the presence of friendly envoys.

Thank you, loving Father, for sending your angels to be with us in times of crises.

James E. Adams

All Is 'Borrowed Goods'

■ Yet another said to him, "I will be your follower, Lord, but first let me take leave of my people at home." Jesus said, "No one who sets a hand to the plow and looks back to what was left behind is fit for the kingdom of God." Luke 9:61-62

What folly it would be for travellers to think only of acquiring dignities and possessions in the countries through which they had to pass, and then to reduce themselves to the necessity of living miserably in their native lands, where they must remain during their whole lives!

And are not they fools who seek after happiness in this world, where they will remain only a few days, and expose themselves to the risk of being unhappy in the next, where they must live for eternity?

We do not fix our affections on borrowed goods, because we know that they must soon be returned to the owner. All earthly goods are lent to us: it is folly to set our heart on what we must soon quit. Death shall strip us of all. The acquisitions and fortunes of this world all terminate in a dying gasp, in a funeral, in a descent into the grave.

The house which you have built for yourself you must soon give up to others.

St. Alphonsus Liguori
from *The Redeeming Love of Christ*

A Faith Enriched By Doubt

■ **So the other disciples said to him, "We have seen the Lord." But he said to them, "Unless I see the mark of the nails in his hands and put my finger into the nailmarks and put my hand into his side, I will not believe."**

John 20:25

He has a firmly established reputation as "doubting Thomas." But does "doubt" fairly describe Thomas' reaction? We think of doubt as opposed to faith, but isn't doubt more the initial groping steps toward genuine faith? Isn't the "doubt" of Thomas really faith seeking to become deeply personal and real?

Thomas was under pressure just to agree with the other disciples. But a grieving and deeply disillusioned Thomas didn't go along with the crowd. He reacted from his gut. He reacted independently, honestly, courageously—and with inquisitiveness. He wasn't satisfied with secondhand knowledge; he *personally* wanted to see the risen Jesus, he wanted to know for himself, to experience for himself.

Should we imitate Thomas? Should we confront and probe our beliefs honestly and courageously? Should we long for our faith to flow from our personal experiences of Jesus rather than only from the testimony of others?

Yes, indeed, in such responses we should all be more like "doubting" Thomas.

James E. Adams

God Shares My Burdens

■ **Come to me, all you who labor and are burdened, and I will give you rest.** Matthew 11:28

To be human means to suffer. Whatever our station in life, each of us knows what it means to be anxious, exhausted and afraid, to experience pain and heartache, to be overcome by disillusionment and despair. There are times when the stresses of family life or difficulties in the workplace "get to" us, so much so that we feel like giving up. Even the thought of another day can be overwhelming.

In these moments of world-weariness, Jesus invites us to turn to him, not in a passive way, but actively. The rest he offers us is something we have to desire *before* we can receive it. If we are so preoccupied with our own problems that there is no longer room for God in our hearts, then it is almost impossible for us to surrender our burdens. If we are so diminished by hopelessness that we can no longer imagine an alternative future, then it is difficult to ask God to ease our weariness. We need to remember that God's power is greater than suffering and that God promises to *share* our burdens, not necessarily take them away.

At all times and in all places, let our hearts turn to you, O Lord.

Elizabeth-Anne Vanek

The God Of Encouragement

■ ... **God our Father, who has loved us and given us everlasting encouragement and good hope through his grace.** 2 Thessalonians 2:16

The graces of hope and encouragement have been given to all of us, but it is up to us to develop them. One way to nurture encouragement and hope is to pay attention to our images of God. If we start thinking of God as alien or unloving, the universe and our place in it begins to seem unsafe and frightening, then discouraging and even hopeless. By recalling that God is the benevolent and positive force of all creation, we reclaim for ourselves a brighter vision of life and its ultimate destiny in God.

We also become more hopeful as we develop within ourselves a healthy self-love. Rather than emphasizing our negative and sinful nature, we can practice viewing ourselves as beloved children of God, cherished in the same way God loves Jesus our brother.

Being more positive about ourselves enables us to sustain a "habit of hopefulness" regarding other people and situations. In turn, we will ourselves become more encouraged and encouraging.

Loving God, may I always remember who I am— your beloved child!

Nancy F. Summers

Help Me Endure Suffering

■ **No disciple is above his teacher, no slave above his master. It is enough for the disciple that he become like his teacher, for the slave that he become like his master.**
Matthew 10:24-25

Lord Jesus, we thank you that in our suffering you have revealed to us the depths of your boundless love. You are with us in our suffering and you give us quite undeserved comfort.

But, despite having experienced all this, I still recoil from suffering, illness and difficulties. Certainly there is no need for me to pray that you should send me further suffering. Preserve me from suffering that exceeds my strength, and give me strength to say a wholehearted "Yes" to my part of your redemptive suffering which you ask me to share; and to thank you at all times for giving creative meaning to our suffering.

Send us your Holy Spirit so that we may experience the healing and liberating power of life in union with you; and that we may play our part in lightening the suffering of others.

Fr. Bernard Haring
from *Journey To The Light*

Listening With My Heart

■ **Some seed fell on rich soil, and produced fruit, a hundred or sixty or thirtyfold.** Matthew 13:8

God's word continues to be both heard and unheard. To be the rich soil of sure returns, that soil which graciously receives the seed and nurtures it, we have to practice the art of listening—not only with our ears, not only with our minds, but, most importantly, with our hearts. Whether spoken through Scriptural texts or in the silence deep within us, God's word needs to be welcomed, reverenced and attended to, for it is, in short, seeking a home.

Listening with the heart means remembering who is speaking to us. It means cherishing what is said because of our love for God. It means trusting what we hear because we know our God is trustworthy. Listening with the heart involves laying aside our own agendas and preconceived ideas so that we can become aware of what God desires for us. It means being open to the truth, even if it is painful. It means allowing ourselves to be led, even if we would prefer to stay where we are. Listening with the heart leads us into union with the heart of God, for when we hear the word in its fullness, it forms us, shapes us and carries us home.

Elizabeth-Anne Vanek

Love Freely Given

■ **Jerusalem, Jerusalem . . . how many times I yearned to gather your children together, as a hen gathers her young under her wings, but you were unwilling!**

Matthew 23:37

Jesus came to earth to win our hearts back to God. Because Jesus is God, he could have accomplished this through a personal magnetism that would have made it impossible for us to resist his advances. Nevertheless, Jesus prefers to have us give our love freely. Though he desires it, thirsts for it with a passion, died for it, he never forces it.

Even when Christ begs for our love, he does it with divine restraint. He stands apart, as it were, waiting, hoping, gently hinting, but never surprising us into a commitment.

Anyone who has loved another deeply and has found no love in return will know something of the anguish that must crush the heart of Jesus when we reject his love. Think only of how he wept over Jerusalem. It will always be that way: a God crying for our love.

Heart of Jesus, break down my indifference, my blindness, my lack of faith. Help me to love you as you love me—beyond all bounds.

Sr. Mary Terese Donze, A.S.C.

The Awesome Love Of God

■ **Praise the Lord, who is so good; God's love endures forever.** Psalm 136:1

While it is important that we love God, it is far more important that God loves us. If God did not love us first, we would not be able to love at all. In everything God holds primacy, and without him we can do nothing. That is why he is like the parent and we are like the children dependent upon the parent's continual creative love. If God were to stop his love, we would cease to be. We live only because God continually loves us into being.

God's interest in us is unconditional and unflagging, because that is simply the way God is. That is what it means for God to be God. There is nothing we can do to eradicate God's love for us, for if we were capable of that, we would be capable of eradicating God. Of course, we may not quite understand this love, but such was the revelation of Jesus.

When we finally accept this incredible largesse, we know that we rest secure in a love that at all times permeates every part of our being and every circumstance of our lives.

O God, may I stay deeply aware of your love every day of my life.

Fr. Kenneth E. Grabner, C.S.C.
Focus Your Day

Praying As We Ought

■ **In the same way, the Spirit too comes to the aid of our weakness; for we do not know how to pray as we ought, but the Spirit itself intercedes with inexpressible groanings.** Romans 8:26

"Praying as we ought" sounds formidable. It suggests that there is a set way of praying which God requires and that our imperfect attempts to pray fall sadly short of God's expectations. There is comfort, yes, in knowing that the Spirit articulates what is already in our hearts, but we also need to look at *how* we pray and consider whether we might learn new ways of praying.

If there is any single block to effective prayer, it is our tendency to forget who it is we are addressing. Instead of making God the subject of our prayer, we focus on our own immediate needs, rattling off our intentions, forgetting God in the process. Our monologues can drown out God's voice; our lists of problems can take precedence over our relationship with God. Underneath all the pleas for help, strings of complaints and prayers of habit lie our unspoken prayers—love songs and sublime poetry which only God can hear.

Spirit of God, teach us to pray from the heart.

Elizabeth-Anne Vanek

The Mystery Of Good And Evil

■ **No, if you pull up the weeds you might uproot the wheat along with them. Let them grow until the harvest.**
Matthew 13:29-30

What are we supposed to do about the weeds? To pull them up would seem a sensible thing. Many opt for this solution. There are people who want a "clean" Church. If they had their way, sinners would be excluded. Only saints would be admitted. Such a Church would be a very small one. In any case, this would be to turn the Gospel upside down. A Church which admitted only saints would make as little sense as a hospital that admitted only healthy people.

There are also those who want a "clean" society. Naturally, they are convinced that they would survive the purge. These seem to believe that evil is done only by bad people. They blame all the evils in the world on a limited number of unredeemable evil people. They think that if we got rid of these people then we would have a perfect world. They fail to realize that evil is done not just by evil people, but by the purest and best people. If evil were done only by evil people, the world would be a far better place.

O God, help me to be patient and gentle—especially when dealing with the weeds in my life.

Fr. Flor McCarthy
Windows On The Gospel

Hope—The Forgotten Virtue

■ **Blessed are you who believed that what was spoken to you by the Lord would be fulfilled.** Luke 1:45

May we see in the Assumption our own hope of new life. May we learn to hope in God as Mary always did, especially in the great affair of our eternal salvation.

Hope has been called the forgotten virtue. A large number of Catholics do not place a high esteem on hope. They forget that hope ranks among the unique trio of virtues which are called theological because they effect the union of the soul with God. Some Catholics are not completely convinced that we cannot be saved without hoping. We must impress on our mind that these virtues are an indissoluble trinity. All three go together. You cannot have one without the other. Hope is a theological virtue and we have an obligation to practice it. If we wish to analyze our attitude toward hope we might ask ourselves how often we confess faults against hope or examine our conscience on it . . .

St. Paul startles us by saying that "we are saved by hope." The basis of our hope is the almighty power, and the infinite benevolence of God. We depend upon God and not on ourselves. With the aid of God's grace we can do all things and grace is never lacking to a person of good will.

Cardinal Terence Cooke
Meditations On Mary

Finding Buried Treasure

■ **The kingdom of heaven is like a treasure buried in a field which a person finds . . .** Matthew 13:44

One of the greatest of life's joys is finding a hidden treasure. Not only in childhood do we enjoy presents and surprises. How many of us are tempted to enter lotteries or play other games of chance in the hope of finding buried treasure? Even to see and cry out, "Bingo!" carries a certain thrill with it.

Knowing our love for surprises, God has hidden clues and traces of the kingdom within every event, in the midst of every minute. Usually, we skim along over the surface of life and forget to look for the treasure that is there. Pause right now, wherever you happen to be as you read this passage, and look around you.

What treasure do you discover that was not at first evident? A bird song, a human voice, a ray of sunlight, an aroma of coffee, a friend's face? Dig a little deeper. Do you find another buried treasure? A pleasant memory, a feeling of gratitude, a mind that can think, a heart that can respond?

God, help me to uncover the buried treasures that indicate you have passed my way today.

Sr. Ruth Marlene Fox, O.S.B.

Balancing Prayer And Work

■ **Martha, burdened with much serving, came to him and said, "Lord, do you not care that my sister has left me by myself to do the serving? Tell her to help me." The Lord said to her in reply, "Martha, Martha, you are anxious and worried about many things."** Luke 10:40-41

Martha did all the work. Instinctively, most of us side with her. She represents all those people in any parish or home who keep things going, oil the wheels, do the photocopying, keep lists, empty ashtrays, wash dishes, fix cracks in the plaster, fold chairs and sweep floors. Martha reminds us that all of those very practical tasks are also ways of showing love.

Martha and Mary really represent two dimensions of every personality. Martha represents all those things that go into the business of living. Mary brings into focus for us the times of prayer and quiet when we can pull it all together in the Lord. Both are necessary. Without Martha, Mary would starve to death. Without Mary, Martha would forget the point of it all. Martha and Mary—work and prayer. They are two dimensions of every personality, each showing love in its own way.

My Lord, may I always remember that the ultimate goal of all I do is union with you.

Fr. S. Joseph Krempa
Daily Homilies

Learning To 'Sit With God'

■ **But he did not say a word to her.** Matthew 15:23

Sitting or walking with God day after day, we come to expect that a great expansion of spiritual awareness should be our reward. So often, however, nothing seems to happen. Sometimes we wonder if the effort is worth it. Could there be a better way for us to spend our time?

Prayer is something of a paradox. Sometimes nothing seems to happen during our time of quiet prayer, but the effects of it are felt in different ways during the rest of the day. You can prove this by remembering the times when you stopped spending quiet periods with God. The more protracted the omission, the less peaceful your days became . . .

If we want the peace of God, we have to sit with him in what seems like darkness. The sitting is never a waste of time. Something happens in the sitting, and it often happens below the level of our conscious awareness. God works in the apparent darkness, and he slowly changes us . . . We have to trust him.

O Lord, may I never be discouraged when I pray and—like the Canaanite woman—at first don't get an answer from you. Help me to persevere.

Fr. Kenneth E. Grabner, C.S.C.
Focus Your Day

The Prayer Of Listening

■ **"This is my beloved Son, with whom I am well pleased; listen to him."** Matthew 17:5

"Listen to him." Is there in the Bible any more apt and succinct direction for the spiritual life of a Christian than this? Listen to Jesus, the voice from heaven says; it's clearly a command of God to all Christians, not just to the three apostles on Mount Tabor in Jesus' lifetime.

If I take this admonition as the basis for my spiritual life, I must spend time reading Holy Scripture and meditating on what it is saying to *me*. This is more than simply studying Scripture. It is opening myself to Scripture in a deeply personal way.

Then, I must pray. How can I say I am listening to Jesus unless I pray? But that must be more than "saying prayers" and it must be more than pouring out my needs and describing my troubles to God. Yes, such prayer has value. But I must be aware that it often can be little more than listening to myself.

I will begin listening to Jesus when I learn to pray silently, when I learn to sit still and wait patiently, when I learn to quiet all the noise in my heart. Listening, really listening, is not as easy as it seems. Before I can listen, I must reduce the level of background noise that drowns out the voice of Jesus.

James E. Adams

Building Up Christ's Body

■ **We give thanks to God always for all of you, remembering you in our prayers, unceasingly calling to mind your work of faith and labor of love . . .**

1 Thessalonians 1:2-3

This greeting from Paul to the Thessalonians is a great example of all we can do to build up the Body of Christ.

First of all, Paul frequently thinks of his people and thanks God explicitly for their gifts and presence in his life.

Secondly, he regularly prays for his people. Lifting up others in prayer and letting them know we are praying for them is a powerful source of strength and encouragement to people.

Thirdly, Paul affirms people for their faith and love. In a society where "put-downs" abound, noticing and taking the time to praise our sisters and brother is a great way to build up the Body of Christ. Phone calls, letters, surprise notes, an encouraging word are just a few of the simple ways we can become more effective and loving disciples of Jesus. The beloved community of God is built up daily by just such works of love.

James McGinnis

Be Holy By Trying To Love

■ **This is the will of God, your holiness . . .**

1 Thessalonians 4:3

God likes to present us with long periods of pure faith during which there's nothing we can do about it but to be silent and strive to love, to love as much as we can with this old and stinking flesh . . .

Do you want the secret of everything? Do you want a boiled-down summary of the Gospel? Do you want a tiny, tiny, easy, easy formula for running, for flying onto the road to holiness?

Here it is: Strive to love. I don't tell you to love, because it's not an easy thing. To love certain unlikable people who are living alongside us, especially in a big house, is almost impossible.

I tell you instead to "strive" to love because translating a precept into action is almost always done on the Cross. Nothing which is really good and holy is easy for us. It takes an effort. It is the Cross laid upon our poor hearts and at the touch of it life begins to flow again.

Seek every day some opportunity to love more both God and neighbor. What results you'll see! Jesus expects no more than that. The whole of the Law and the Prophets is summed up as love . . . love.

Carlo Carretto
Letters To Dolcidia

Confronting My Fears

■ ... so out of fear I went off and buried your talent in the ground. Here it is back. Matthew 25:25

Fear can be one of your greatest enemies. It can paralyze you and tie your hands behind your back with a single thought.

Often fear prevents you from finding and using your gifts. Fear keeps you imprisoned in a rut called "safe." With a firm grip on your soul, it guards you from wonderful discoveries about yourself. It whispers lies to you about your inadequacies and advises you never to take the risk of getting hurt.

Fear suggests that you bury your gifts rather than be a failure.

It is important for us to be in touch with our feelings, feelings like fear. The road to health requires that we call each fear by its name. Spend time with it. Feel it. Talk to God about it. Then perhaps God will change your fear into courage.

Courage, says Dorothy Bernard, is "fear that has said its prayers."

Is it time for your fear to say its prayers?

Sr. Macrina Wiederkehr, O.S.B.

A Promise So Consoling!

■ **Thus we shall always be with the Lord. Therefore, console one another with these words.**

1 Thessalonians 4:17-18

From time to time I become aware of a truth so beautiful that I can only feel it as a premonition. It is too great for me to grasp. But it shakes me to the core, it touches my innermost being, it gives me courage, it make me shout with joy.

I become aware of where I am bound, that heaven has been promised me if I live as I should and fulfill the task that God has given me. This promise I believe in with all my life.

Heaven!

Do we sometimes think of it? Are we aware that this earth is not the place in which to settle more and more comfortably so as to find the most carefree existence? Here, every instance of our life is a step toward another country, another kingdom, homewards where we shall forever experience the pure full happiness that we long for so ardently.

And what will it be like over there? Better not to waste words on this . . . we would only talk away the new reality with useless fantasies. But one thing we know: it will be . . . heaven!

Chiara Lubich
Journey To The Light

God's Word Is 'Scandalous'

■ **They were all amazed and said to one another, "What is there about his word? For with authority and power he commands the unclean spirits, and they come out."**

Luke 4:36

What is there about God's word that it can set our hearts on fire with love and passion for our God and, at the same time, be the source of conflict between family members, friends, different faiths, and even nations? What is there about God's word that it can be so enlightening and inspirational for some, yet frightening and divisive for others?

However comforting the word of God is to us, it can—and should—be a source of consternation as well. For the word of God is given to us as a "scandalon," a Greek word meaning stumbling block. While the word of God is certainly full of hope, joy and compassion, it is also full of wisdom that is meant to trip us up, to make us take the time to think about the path on which we walk. If we read God's word closely and prayerfully, we should be grateful for those passages that press us to reconsider our lives, however uncomfortable those words may make us feel.

Thank you, Lord, for giving us your word. May it be a constant reminder of our need to reform our lives and remain focused on you.

Steve Givens

Keeping My Faith Firm

■ ... you (must) persevere in the faith, firmly grounded, stable, and not shifting from the hope of the gospel that you heard. Colossians 1:23

We have to hang on to the fact of God's love for us. That demands courage and tenacity. There is so much in the world that seems to contradict the whole idea of a loving God; there is enough in our own lives to make us doubt it. No one has ever given a totally satisfactory explanation of why there is evil. But there are truths which point us in the right direction, and indicate where a solution is to be found.

First, we are sinners. We are free. We have to be free in order to be able to love truly. We misuse that freedom, so there is tragedy, suffering and death.

Secondly, there is the fact that God became man, accepted the human condition (except for sin) and gave it a new significance and value.

Thirdly, we have to hang on all the time to the fact that God loves us, and this is true in every crisis and however much events and facts appear to contradict that truth. We must trust God ...

God asks us, sometimes often, to go on with the pilgrimage through life in the dark, but always trusting. Trust is the proof of love.

Cardinal Basil Hume
Daily Readings In Catholic Classics

Speaking From A Calm Heart

■ ... from the fullness of the heart the mouth speaks.

Luke 6:45

There have been times when I knew that what I was speaking to another person was a blessing of love and care. I knew this because my heart felt kindness and compassion. There have also been times when I knew that what I was speaking was causing great anguish and pain to another person. At these times, my heart was also full, but it was a fullness of anger, hurt or resentment. I have learned to look carefully into my heart during an emotionally charged situation before I speak in order to search out my motivations and my desires.

It also helps to pray that my heart has a strong foundation in genuine love. Jesus is always our model for this. He spoke from the fullness of his heart, and he spoke words of wisdom, care and compassion. He also spoke words of challenge and conversion, but these words were always spoken out of love.

Each night before going to sleep, it is good to reflect on the day to recall what we have said to others and to see what kind of fullness our heart has held. We can ask: did the words I spoke match what is in my heart?

Jesus, fill my heart with the goodness of your love.
Sr. Joyce Rupp, O.S.M.

The Faithful One

■ **God is faithful, and by him you were called to fellowship with his Son, Jesus Christ our Lord.**

1 Corinthians 1:9

Monica, mother of Augustine, prayed unceasingly for the conversion of her son from his sinful ways.

Monica knew she could not control, hurry or force God to intervene and override her son's free will. Augustine himself had to accept the gift of spiritual freedom which God was offering to him. Monica could only pray, trust and wait.

Perhaps the greatest blessing of Monica's prayer was that it helped her never give up on her son. She always believed that he could grow and change. After many years of Monica's prayer, her son began to cooperate with God's grace and turned his life around.

What was it like to long so much for her son to return to God? How did she cope with her heartache and sorrow? It was her faithful prayer to the God whom she knew would always be with her. This truth sustained her and kept her hopes alive.

Many of us pray for others in the hope they will change. We cannot force them, but our faithful prayer can help us continue to believe in their ability to respond to God's grace in their lives.

Sr. Joyce Rupp, O.S.M.

Is The Soil Of My Soul Rich?

■ **But as for the seed that fell on rich soil, they are the ones who, when they have heard the word, embrace it with a generous and good heart, and bear fruit through perseverance.** Luke 8:15

When traveling once in the Outback of Australia, I met an archeologist who had recently been to the United States. He told me that he was in awe as he flew over the Midwest, seeing its rich soil and fields full of ripe grain. It was obvious that such abundance never came to the arid, sandy soil of the Outback. No wonder Jesus used the image of "rich soil" when he spoke of the seed of God's word growing within us.

God is always dropping seeds into our heart's soil. They are seeds of love, goodness, faithfulness, kindheartedness, generosity, integrity and many other Gospel virtues and values. These seeds will not take root and grow if the soil of our hearts is dry and rocky with attitudes of self-centeredness, indifference, envy, prejudice or arrogance. The seeds of God lie dormant in our hearts, ready to take root only if they are embraced. Today, let us peer into our hearts and check the soil to see if it is the kind that will allow God's love to grow.

O Divine Planter, I embrace the seed of your love in my heart today.

Sr. Joyce Rupp, O.S.M.

We All Need Patience

■ **I urge you to live ... with patience, bearing with one another through love ...** Ephesians 4:1-2

Why is it that being patient always sounds reasonable and relatively easy when I am feeling loved, rested and peaceful? It doesn't feel so when I am fatigued, discouraged, grouchy or at odds with someone. The last thing I want to do then is to extend extra forbearance and understanding to another. I especially notice my impatience when I am driving in heavy traffic. My hostile glares, beeping horn and muttered comments are enough to embarrass even myself! When I reflect on it, I see that my impatience usually happens when I am in a hurry, tired or thinking only of my own needs. That's when I can forget about "bearing with one another in love."

We always need patience. Each of us knows who or what challenges our ability to be graciously accepting, and generous in our understanding. Sometimes we most need to be patient with ourselves. It is not easy to be patient, but it is a requirement of us who call ourselves Christian. I've found that I react and respond quite differently to others when I view them as they really are—a temple of God. I remember, then, the dignity and respect they deserve.

Sr. Joyce Rupp, O.S.M.

Who Is Jesus For Me?

■ **Then he said to them, "But who do you say that I am?"**
Luke 9:20

Jesus, I've too often avoided answering that question, pretending that it wasn't addressed to me. But today I want to at least try to answer it.

You are God, the holy and the awesome, the creator who is as different from me as light from darkness. At least, that is how I want to be aware of you, even if I don't often acknowledge you as that kind of God.

You are a man, truly human, a real son of Mary, just as I am the son of my mother. That makes you, in some sense, just like me, just like every man and woman who ever lived and who ever will live. At least, that is how I want to know you, even if I often slip into the bad habit of denying your humanity.

You are messiah, my messiah, *my* savior, the one whose birth, life, death and resurrection made me eligible to be what I am—a child of God and an heir to eternal happiness. At least, that is who I want you to be for me, even if I don't act as if you are that savior.

You are friend and brother, *my* friend and *my* brother, the one who is always near me to console and to counsel, to comfort and to confront. At least, that is the friend and brother I want you to be.

James E. Adams

God Is Jealous For My Heart

■ **I am intensely jealous for Zion, stirred to jealous wrath for her.** Zechariah 8:2

Of what would God be jealous? Think for a moment of your own life and loves. Don't the people and things which threaten to come between you and the one you love arouse jealousy in you? So it is with God: the false gods of our lives make God jealous.

You may notice this as you begin to pray and grow closer to God. You begin to discover that your heart is divided: in part, you love and want to follow the ways of the living God; in part, you love and want to follow the ways of certain friends, heroes, perhaps ideas and plans of your own. If you keep praying, a jealous God will show you the faults of your friends, the weaknesses of your heroes, the emptiness of your plans.

This seems at first devastating, but you are now actually much closer to genuine well-being. False gods have less hold on your heart, while the living God is nearer to you than ever. Now you can appreciate other people for who they really are and make plans that may bear real fruit.

Jealous God, help us to turn to you in trust.

Mark Neilsen

A Source Of Blessing For Many

■ **Many peoples and strong nations shall come to seek the Lord of hosts in Jerusalem . . .** Zechariah 8:22

Zechariah looked to the day when Jerusalem would be the source of blessing for all nations. . . . As the "new Jerusalem," the Church is called to be a source of blessings to the whole world. To be a Catholic is to have a universal outlook, to go beyond the desire "to save my soul" to a concern for all of God's people . . .

We should never underestimate our importance in God's plan. He wants to make us, through our prayers and sacrifices, a channel of his grace to the whole world. As good people we pray for our loved ones in need, but we should expand our vision. The needs we see in those who are close to us are multiplied many times over. Our concern for a family which has suffered a severe tragedy should move us to pray for them and for the untold numbers of others who are suffering. When we see a friend who is confused and frustrated, one who has no faith or hope, we ought to pray for him and all those like him.

This is a deep mystery, but a great truth of our faith, that the salvation and well-being of many depends on our prayers and sacrifices.

Fr. Charles E. Miller, C.M.
Opening The Treasures

Quick Fixes Have Long Histories

■ **Jonah began his journey through the city, and had gone but a single day's walk . . . when the people of Nineveh believed God.** Jonah 3:4-5

Biblical stories of instant results often appeal to us, we who live in a world of microwave ovens, computers and cellular phones. We expect quick results, even from our prayers to God. Yet God doesn't usually work instantaneously. Just as most of us don't comprehend or know the months or years of thought and labor that have made microwaves, computers and telephones possible, so we are unaware of all the groundwork that was laid before a biblical wonder occurred. Change of heart happens slowly. It takes persistence and perseverance in prayer and action. We cannot walk a mile in one great leap. We must walk it step by step. Whether we are dealing with the abortion issue, with a family member or friend who has turned from God, or with our own faults and failings, it takes time. We need to persevere and be patient. When frustration and anger occur (and they will), we can express them to God and use them to help fuel our journey. Yes, changes of heart can happen, even if it takes a lifetime.

God, this day, I ask you to strengthen my persistence, perseverance and patience.

Charlotte A. Rancilio

Back To Basics

■ **Rely on the mighty Lord; constantly seek his face. Recall the wondrous deeds he has done, his signs and his words of judgment.** Psalm 105:4-5

When I taught kindergarten, a child once brought in a toy airliner. It was a marvelous toy, full of gadgets and gizmos. We were all very impressed. But the child wasn't. He sat dejectedly on the floor idly toying with the plane. I asked him if he were feeling sick. He said, "My parents are always giving me neat toys. But what I really want is them."

Gadgets and gizmos do not suffice when the basics are lacking. Our technological world provides all sorts of marvels. We happily use all these wonders in our lives, and we often are tempted to believe that the next program, gadget, book, tape—or whatever— will solve our ills, make us better people or enhance our relationships. These resources must be based on a solid foundation if they are to do any good for us. We need the basics first, the basics that we often tend to ignore because they seem too simple or dull.

But the "Good News" of salvation is never dull. We can have God's love. We can share God's love. God's love is more than enough for all our needs.

O Lord, be enough for me today and always.

Jean Royer

Choosing Tranquility

■ **Take care you remain tranquil and do not fear.**

Isaiah 7:4

This advice was given to King Ahaz at a moment when he was trembling with fear. We have the same choice: fear or tranquility. Do we find ourselves spending time with our fear when it would be wiser to welcome tranquility? Fear and tranquility do not mix very well. It is my guess that, when they come to visit us, most of us send tranquility away.

Recall three or four tranquil moments of the past week. This exercise may surprise you. I thought I couldn't find more than one such moment, yet when I sat in prayerful reflection, memories washed over me like raindrops.An affirming letter from a friend. The moon climbing through the tree branches outside my window. Receiving Holy Communion. Smiling at a stranger.

Receive these moments as gifts from God. Stay with each moment a little longer, allowing its blessings to follow you as you go about your daily tasks. There is something sacramental about receiving these moments as gifts, acknowledging that we didn't create them ourselves. The next time you find yourself in a moment of fear, try this: Sit down and smile! I know it sounds crazy. Do it anyway. It works!

Sr. Macrina Wiederkehr, O.S.B.

Our Need For God

■ **Salvation we have not achieved for the earth, the inhabitants of the world cannot bring it forth.**

Isaiah 26:18

What a strangely sad yet hopeful passage this is! On the one hand, all human effort, in our time as well as Isaiah's, cannot save us—from the ravages of certain illnesses, the horrors of war, the persistent problems of poverty. Modern science and technology, as wonderful as they can be in the service of human life, are themselves capable of unimaginable destruction when used for evil purposes. We "inhabitants of the world" are all too often incapable of saving ourselves from even the most preventable forms of suffering such as war and starvation.

On the other hand, Isaiah knew the truth, and so he could turn to God in prayer. Not that God will immediately save us from the aforementioned ills, but at least Isaiah could recognize that God alone is powerful enough to deal with both the powers of the universe as well as the depths of the human heart.

If we humbly face up to our need for God, our labors can be transformed from arrogant and futile attempts to build utopias to hope-filled signs of God's abundant blessing.

Mark Neilsen

Baskets Of Abundance

■ **At this, they gathered twelve baskets full of pieces.**

John 6:13

Baskets. I am reminded of the tough baskets which to this day are still lowered on ropes from balconies in southern Mediterranean countries. Filled with produce by vendors hawking vegetables from horse-drawn carts, these baskets survive years of being hoisted up and down, heavily burdened. The twelve baskets in John's Gospel are also rugged baskets for everyday use, not delicate baskets for decorative purposes. Crudely woven to withstand sun and rain, heavy loads and rough treatment, these baskets hold leftovers that can provide several hearty meals, not just dainty crumbs.

When I visualize these twelve baskets of leftovers, I am struck by God's abundance. Not only is there enough food for the vast crowd, but far more than they can eat, perhaps by implication, enough for the 12 tribes of Israel. Were we to take stock of the ways in which God nourishes us, we would no doubt find our own baskets of surplus. For God, it seems, seldom settles for the bare minimum. Spiritually and materially, there is more than enough for everyone. The challenge, however, is to share it.

Elizabeth-Anne Vanek

Doing The Work Of God

■ **"What can we do to accomplish the works of God?"
Jesus answered and said to them, "This is the work of
God, that you believe in the One he sent."** John 6:28-29

Jesus' reply, on first hearing, seems entirely inadequate, for doing the works of the Creator of heaven
and earth must surely require more than simply
believing. After all, the hungry must be fed, the
naked clothed, and the oppressed set free. Right?

Right. But those who do the most for humanity
are most often the ones whose faith is most solid.
Mother Teresa often insisted that she could not do
the work she didwithout daily prayer to nourish her
belief that in her work she was really serving Jesus
in the "disguise" of the poor. The saints and martyrs
throughout our tradition were women and men of
tremendous conviction whose deep faith was often
not understood or supported by their families and
friends.

When Jesus tells us to believe in the One sent by
God, he means total belief: with our whole heart,
mind and soul. That is the kind of belief that can
provide the source of great works of charity and
justice. That kind of belief, we soon discover, is the
work of a lifetime.

I believe. Lord, help my unbelief!

Mark Neilsen

Neglecting The Guest Within

■ **When he finds a pearl of great price, he goes and sells all that he has and buys it.** Matthew 13:46

Along the road of life, we can lose our focus. We can forget the idealistic dreams of our youth, settling instead for what is practical and expedient. We may begin to value safety over adventure, luxury over generosity, comfort over self-giving, predictability over spontaneity. Then, firmly settled in our ways, we discover we may have missed out on something— we have lost the pearl of great price.

This pearl is the divine life within each of us, the inner sanctuary where God is at home. When we neglect the wondrous mystery of God's indwelling, we neglect our guest, occupying ourselves instead with trivial pursuits which bring short-term gains. Only when we remember the pearl of great price do we let go of our empty acquisitions. One by one, our fingers release their grip on ambitions, possessions and other attachments; slowly they reach out to receive our heavenly inheritance.

Restore our vision, Lord, that we might see the treasure that lies within each one of us.

Elizabeth-Anne Vanek

Why Am I A Christian?

■ **Then Peter said to Jesus in reply, "We have given up everything and followed you. What will there be for us?"**
Matthew 19:27

I like Peter: he was honest, often blurting out thoughts that were probably on the other disciples' minds as well. Peter had just seen the rich young man walk away, keeping his wealth and his comfortable life instead of choosing to be a disciple. This must have caused all of the disciples to reflect on their decisions to follow Jesus. They had given up a lot to follow Jesus, and it wasn't easy. On especially difficult and discouraging days, they must have secretly asked themselves, "What's all this worth?"

The same thoughts are probably in our minds once in a while, too. Most of us wonder at times: What's in it for me? Is this Christianity worth it? What are the rewards for trying to be kind, generous, honest, and compassionate?

Jesus' promise of "the inheritance of eternal life" is invisible and may seem far away for us. Today is a good day to reflect on our motivation for being a Christian. Are we satisfied to live our lives simply for the joy and satisfaction of knowing we are in friendship with Jesus? Do we need more reward than this?

Sr. Joyce Rupp, O.S.M.

God's Need To Reach Out

■ **My friend, I am not cheating you. Did you not agree to the usual daily wage? Take what is yours and go.**

Matthew 20:13-14

This parable raises questions about the standard of justice in the kingdom of God. Should not those who worked more hours have been given more? Evidently, entry into the kingdom of God is not a question of merit. . . .

How do we get into the kingdom if it is not something we can earn? We enter the kingdom not by meriting but by consenting to the invitation. . . The inner nature of God is thus made manifest to us: God has to respond, so to speak, to our needs. In this parable God's response is directed to the people there in the marketplace, idle and wasting their time, gambling, drinking, gossiping, snoozing, or whatever.

The fallen human condition is where the kingdom of God is most active. We are the people for whom Jesus Christ has come in the flesh to express the infinite concern of the Father for our sins and their consequences. The spiritual journey enables us to appreciate more and more the total gratuity of the divine goodness. Acceptance of the invitation is the key to belonging to the kingdom.

Fr. Thomas Keating, O.C.S.O.
The Kingdom Of God Is Like . . .

The Joy Of A Living Faith

■ **I will give you a new heart and place a new spirit within you, taking from your bodies your stony hearts and giving you natural hearts. I will put my spirit within you and make you live by my statutes, careful to observe my decrees.** Ezekiel 36:27

People with a living faith practice what they believe. With that criterion, you can evaluate to what extent your own faith is alive. A living faith bears the fruit of love in which thought and action become one.

People who profess faith in God's loving care, but distance themselves from the needs of others, profess a faith without life. If we do nothing at all to alleviate the poverty and suffering of others, how will our faith be life-giving? Such a faith is just a facade covering up our own emptiness and lack of love.

The power to maintain a life of living faith comes from God. A humble person knows this, and that is why only a humble person can experience the joy of a living faith. It is a gift from God which enables the willing recipient to put into practice what God asks.

Lord, help me to practice what you teach me through your word and through your Spirit dwelling in me.

Fr. Kenneth E. Grabner, C.S.C.
Focus Your Day

God In The Ordinary

■ ... I saw the glory of the God of Israel coming from the east. I heard a sound like the roaring of many waters, and the earth shone with his glory. Ezekiel 43:2

Ezekiel had many wonderful visions and revelations of God. While I thoroughly enjoy these fascinating stories, I also realize that I must be careful not to expect always the same astounding and exceptional revelations in my own life. It is easy to forget that God most often makes quiet, almost imperceptible visits such as the one to Elijah when God came in "a tiny whispering sound" (1 Kings 19:12).

Most of us rarely have a "Hollywood production" visit from God like those Ezekiel experienced. Ours are usually the "tiny whispering voice" type, and we can easily miss God's presence and message to us. Expecting the unusual, we may be looking for God in the wrong place, instead of in the ordinary, ho-hum, mundane, or busy places in our lives. Yet most of God's visits to people in the Scriptures took place in ordinary, everyday places of home or work: tents, fields, tax collecting tables, fishing boats . . .

God visits in many forms and disguises. Let us look and listen closely today.

God, help me to welcome you in the way you choose to visit me today.

Sr. Joyce Rupp, O.S.M.

Keeping First Things First

■ **For great is the Lord and highly to be praised, to be feared above all gods . . . give to the Lord glory and might; give to the Lord the glory due his name!**

Psalm 96:4,7

Is God the principal aim and objective of our lives? Cardinal Newman once said, "The aim of most men . . . seems not how to please God, but how to please themselves without displeasing him."

Typically, we spend our time in three unequal parts. One part we give to God, another part goes to our neighbor, while we keep the lion's share for ourselves. We go to Mass on Sunday, to confession periodically, and to an occasional retreat, parish mission or novena. If we add to this the minutes that we spend praying, we give God just about 5 percent of an average week. We might say that we are too busy to do more—but the person who is too busy to pray *is too busy*. Much of our time is spent on our neighbor—but not *for* our neighbor or for God . . .

The purpose of life is to know, love and serve God and to be happy with him. In other words, we should have the simple intention of being saints—being friends of God. The first reason that we are here on earth is to adore and to praise God.

Help me, loving God, to become a saint.

Cardinal Terence Cooke
Meditations On Mary

Crosses Don't Feel Triumphant

■ ... he humbled himself, becoming obedient to death, even death on a cross. Because of this, God greatly exalted him ... Philippians 2:8-9

I sometimes tend to pass by the cross at Calvary and hurry on too quickly to the Resurrection. Knowing Jesus is raised from the dead and triumphs over death, I can forget that Jesus felt no triumph when he was hanging on the cross. Rather, he cried out in agony, wondered if he had been abandoned and gasped in surrendering his last breath. In my own moments of trial and tribulation, I do not feel the triumph of the cross. I do not yet know the growth or conversion that awaits me. I need a belief that God will help me resurrect in due time, but I ought not deny or ignore the pain and darkness of the moment, either.

I think of this when I am with a family gathered by the bedside of a loved one who is very ill. They pat his or her hand, reassuring him or her that "all will be well." What the person really needs is someone to say, "What you are going through must be so tough." This compassion is a great balm for the one in pain. We must all be *on* the cross before we can experience the triumph of the cross. We have the example of Jesus who gives us the courage to make our own journey toward resurrection.

Sr. Joyce Rupp, O.S.M.

In Awe Of God Most Gracious

■ **The Lord is gracious and merciful, slow to anger and abounding in love.** Psalm 145:8

A common misconception is that "fear of the Lord" means the same as being afraid of God. When one is truly afraid of God, one has no desire for a genuine relationship; rather, one seeks to appease and to avoid. The presumption that God's standards are impossible and rigid becomes the basis for self-loathing, scrupulosity and harsh judgment of others. How such an attitude must pain the heart of God!

The gift of the Holy Spirit known as "fear of the Lord" is better understood as awe. It is the feeling we get looking up into a starry sky and trying to take in the grand mystery of it all. It is allowing ourselves to be overwhelmed as we ponder God's extraordinary kindness and graciousness. Enthusiasm, trust, joy, and confidence are the proper fruits of awe; it moves us toward God rather than away.

Lord, I want to be more awed than afraid. Heal me of my fears so that I may draw ever closer to you.

Nancy F. Summers

Prayers Of Praise

■ **Rejoice, you just, in the Lord; praise from the upright is fitting. Give thanks to the Lord on the harp; on the ten-stringed lyre offer praise. Sing to God a new song; skillfully play with joyful chant. For the Lord. . . fills the earth with goodness.** Psalm 33:1-5

Contemplatives remind us that it is never a waste of time to give God glory and praise. In fact, as creatures given life by our unbelievably generous Creator God, what more appropriate activity could there be than prayers of praise and thanksgiving? While every human activity can be done in a spirit of praise, conscious and focused prayers of praise ought to be part of the rhythm and routine of all our lives.

When I am honest with myself, I realize that I need to begin my day in a contemplative mode, if that day is to be richly experienced. On my best morning walks, I lift up the dawning of the new day to God, reciting the "Gloria" slowly, phrase by phrase. Each tree becomes a spire of praise, each bird a song of praise, each breath of wind a breath of praise. I declare with the psalmist that the Lord, indeed, "fills the earth with goodness."

Glory to you, O God, in the highest . . . We worship you; we give you thanks; we praise you for your glory.
James McGinnis

The Invitation To Rejoice

■ **Well done, my good and faithful servant. . . . Come, share your master's joy.** Matthew 25:21

God rejoices in our service and invites us to share in that joy! When we have done well, do we sense God's pleasure and join in it? Or do we fear self-glorification so much that we even refuse the invitation to rejoice with God?

Sometimes we trip from one arena of servanthood to another without rest or celebration. We risk burnout, depression and exhaustion. We may end up feeling overworked and unappreciated. Perhaps we have slipped into a mode of trying to earn salvation rather than viewing our good works as free responses to grace. In that case, no wonder we anxiously dash from one task to another without pausing to rejoice!

In our efforts to avoid egotism, pride and boastfulness, we ought not neglect appreciation and respect for our God-given talents. Certainly there are occasions when we have rendered good and faithful service. At such times, we are invited and expected to rejoice along with God.

Nancy F. Summers

The 'Scandalous' Beatitudes

■ **Blessed are you who are poor, for the kingdom of God is yours. Blessed are you who are now hungry, for you will be satisfied. Blessed are you . . .** Luke 6:20-21

The beatitudes contain within them all the scandal and therefore all the power of the Gospel. The beatitudes, just as much as the parables, are a challenge to us, an invitation to faith. They call on us to step outside our preconception of reality, and to accept a whole new way of looking at things.

We begin to respond with faith when we allow these words to enter our lives to stand in judgment upon us; when we allow them to be a measure of our existence, and not the "blessings" of the world. This movement of faith is filled with the same risk and danger that faith always entails. Jesus does not offer any arguments or persuasion. He simply states on the authority of his person that this is the truth about things. The risk lies in the fact that what he says seems to go against so much of our experience and understanding . . . If we can accept this overturning of our understanding, then we have taken the first step in accepting the message of Jesus about the kingdom and about the demands of discipleship.

Luke Timothy Johnson
Some Hard Blessings

The Work Of The Passion

■ **He began to teach them that the Son of Man must suffer greatly and be rejected by the elders, the chief priests, and the scribes, and be killed, and rise after three days.** Mark 8:31

J esus is announcing here for the first time the destiny that awaits the Son of Man: great suffering, rejection, death and Resurrection. Peter refuses to listen to any of this, and Jesus sends him away as "Satan," as a seducer and gainsayer.

Jesus is revealing here the decisive work he has been sent to accomplish, a task not for him alone but for all of us, for each person who believes and follows him. The teaching found in James about faith and works acquires its full force at this point: faith without the work of the Passion is not Christian faith at all. A person whose faith involves the hope that he will be safe and avoid loss will lose everything. To want to salvage oneself is egoism, which is irreconcilable with a faith that cannot be separated from love. The core of the work without which faith is dead is the act of total self-offering, whether to God or to one's neighbor. That this act can involve suffering, even to the point of death, is beyond question. It always carries within it a kind of death—the renunciation of the "I."

Fr. Hans Urs von Balthasar
Light Of The Word

Opening Daily To God's Word

■ **This is the meaning of the parable. The seed is the word of God.** Luke 8:11

Unlike the farmer who sows the seed in season and looks forward to a later harvest, God sows the word in season and out. Constantly, God's word is available through the Scriptures, the teachings of the Church and the inspirations of the Spirit. We have many, many opportunities to receive it.

Sometimes I feel like the footpath: beaten down and hardened so that nothing can get through to me. At such times, I'm afraid, the word of God bounces off me. Other times, I hear God's word with enthusiasm, make all kinds of plans and resolutions, even undertake big projects for the sake of the Kingdom, but too often the enthusiasm gets pushed aside by the "cares of the world" and I "burn out."

My hope is in God, the faithful sower, who keeps on giving me the chance to receive the word with "a good and generous heart, and bear fruit through perseverance." My job is to make myself receptive, not once or twice, but again and again.

Generous God, help me to keep my heart open to receive your word and the strength to persevere.

Mark Neilsen

How Wholehearted Is My Faith?

■ **As Jesus passed on from there, he saw a man named Matthew sitting at the customs post. He said to him, "Follow me." And he got up and followed him.**

Matthew 9:9

J esus beckoned, and Matthew followed. Immediately, like countless others who heard the call of the teacher from Nazareth. No second-guessing Jesus' motives. No examining the implications. No weighing the demands of discipleship. Jesus called, Matthew responded.

I often contrast Matthew's readiness to follow with my own measured response to the Lord. Matthew responded *without* the benefit of a relationship with Jesus. His response was based solely on faith, on a deep-seated intuition, on the power of Jesus' person and message. I have the benefit of a lifelong relationship with the Lord. I have known his mercy and faithfulness over the years and tasted of his goodness. Yet I am so reluctant to abandon my security and place my trust in him alone.

Faith such as Matthew's is a gift. I pray each day that God gives me a deeper faith, a more lively trust and hope and the inner freedom to follow unreservedly.

Fr. Anthony Schueller, S.S.S.

Living In The Present

■ **There is an appointed time for everything and a time for every affair under the heavens.** Ecclesiastes 3:1

Time is such an elusive thing and I find myself constantly wanting to control it. It seems like I am always "running out of time" when I am working at something which holds my interest. Sometimes my mind and feelings are far into the future while I am living in the present moment. At other times, I am clinging onto the present and not wanting to go forward. If it's a difficult situation, I want to hurry and get it over with. If it's a happy moment, I want to hug it to myself and not let it go. I think that I have a continuous tug-of-war with time.

The wise voice of the author of Ecclesiastes tells us that there is a time for everything. Each event and experience of our lives has some wisdom to give us if we are open and attentive to what it is offering us. It is this present moment that counts. Nothing else. Here is where our wisdom happens. Sometimes the only way we come to believe this is when we face a serious illness or the loss of something or someone significant. The quality of the present moment suddenly takes on a new look and the present moment becomes a precious commodity.

Sr. Joyce Rupp, O.S.M.

The Astounding Faith Of Job

■ **The Lord gave and the Lord has taken away; blessed be the name of the Lord!** Job 1:21

This declaration from Job surely ranks as one of the greatest professions of faith in the Bible. It is all the more astounding because it came in a period when conventional wisdom held that the loss of material possessions was a sure sign of God's disfavor. To "bless" God in the face of personal disaster was equivalent to Job praising God even as Job felt he was being cast into hell!

To be filled with praise when "God gives" is easy for most of us. We come to expect many of the "givens" of life from God—our health, our welfare and our happiness among them. We are grateful for those, although most of us probably don't thank God often enough.

But to be filled with praise when "God takes away" is very difficult for us. When disaster strikes, our faith is very often too weak to continue seeing God as benevolent. When disaster strikes, we are tempted to say, "There is no God" or "God doesn't care" or "God must have it in for me."

When disaster strikes, pray for the gift of the faith of Job, who held fast to the belief that what God wanted for him was good even if he couldn't understand it.

James E. Adams

God Does Not Insure My Success

■ **How much less shall I give him any answer, or choose out arguments against him! Even though I were right, I could not answer him, but should rather beg for what was due me.** Job 9:14-15

After Job's lament over the disaster that befell him, his friends come by to console him. They present the standard theological explanation for his problems. The causality in the universe is strict, they say. God rewards the good and punishes evil. Therefore, Job must have done wrong and sinned somewhere, sometime in the past. Where there is smoke, there is fire.

This was the conventional wisdom against which the Book of Job protests. The problem with so facile an explanation is that it places God in a box. God becomes an insurer of success much like a cosmic vending machine into which we put our good works to get our reward. It really makes God into our image and likeness. We know that every suffering is not a punishment. That is the error of the theology of Job's friends. The Book of Job insists on God's sovereign majesty and mystery, to which we can only submit.

Lord, when we can see no earthly reason for the evil that befalls us, grant us the faith of Job.

Fr. S. Joseph Krempa
Daily Homilies

Heavenly And Earthly Hosts

■ **When he reached the Ancient One and was presented before him, he received dominion, glory, and kingship; nations and peoples of every language serve him.**

Daniel 7:13-14

Yes, I have many nations and peoples with me as I serve and worship God. Perhaps I am not as aware of them as often as I would like to be, but there they are, all the same: black, brown, yellow, white, children, men, women. Perhaps, even, inhabitants of other planets and far-distant parts of creation. And, yes, angels. I am surrounded by *all* those who serve God.

When I feel alone, it is startling, yet comforting and strengthening, to know that all those hosts of every nation are with me in spirit, serving God.

When I am suffering, I try to think of all those who are in pain and who hope in a compassionate God.

When I visit patients in the hospital, I tell them that our parishioners are praying for them at our parish Masses. They always reply, "Oh, thank you! I need that." Often they note that their own parishioners and others around the world are praying, too. The reality of the Body of Christ can seem very close and life-strengthening at such a time.

Because I am weak and need others, I am grateful for all those who serve God with me.

Sr. Marguerite Zralek, O.P.

The Gift Of Contentment

■ **But I in justice shall behold your face; when I awake, I shall be content in your presence.** Psalm 17:15

To be content in your presence, Lord—what a gift that is! It is what I seek. I have caught snatches of such contentment in places I least expected it and at times that seemed ill-suited for it. You have caught me unaware at times—and the delight I have felt is something I'd like to experience again and again.

To stay in this contented status constantly—wouldn't that literally be heaven! But I am mired here on earth, with all my cares and worries. Still, I need not be discouraged, because you, O Lord, are here also, closer to me than my skin, waiting for me to pay attention to your loving presence.

To have a quiet mind, eyes open to possibility, ears ready to hear your voice, I need to listen carefully for all the cues. I must be ready to change my way of expecting you, I must fit myself into the pattern of your comings and goings rather than trying to manipulate you. I must seek your presence in my life, and not be afraid to trust that you will take me where I need to be, keeping me close to you.

Jean Royer

All Is Gift

■ **Without cost you have received; without cost you are to give.** Matthew 10:8

"I'm not rich," we may be tempted to say when urged to give. It is easy to see wealth only in monetary terms or tangible goods. And, of course, there never seems to be enough of either to feel secure enough to share without feeling deprived. I can also try to salve my conscience by convincing myself that what I have I have earned. It wasn't *given* to me!

How true is that, when all is said and done? Everything we possess ultimately *is* a gift of a generous God. Moreover, are money and tangible goods the only gifts we receive? How about our ability to bring joy to someone, our ability to love? What about our various talents? Can't they be used to bring goodness to others? Are we afraid to give these gifts because they are too personal? Because they might be rejected or viewed as not being good enough? And then might we feel personally rejected or found wanting? Are we confident enough to take that risk?

We should strive for more confidence in our abilities and gifts and, ultimately, in the God who gives them. With that confidence we can more generously share our money, tangible and intangible goods.

O Lord, help me to be generous with all my gifts.
Jean Royer

Information Overload

■ **Come to me, all you who labor and are burdened, and I will give you rest.** Matthew 11:28

So many of us in this anxiety-ridden, compulsively work-oriented culture of ours find it difficult to enjoy silence and would rather do anything than be quiet. It's a rather non-flattering sign of our times. And it points to our insecurity and rootlessness.

Unless we are rooted in God, and rooted in the only sure way of listening to God—namely, silence—then we are doomed to spend our lives standing at the window of life and watching the world go by. The only entry into the life that God offers us and wants us to enjoy is through silence and "in-touchness" with Him who fills the world with the sounds of silence and ultimate meaning.

Information doesn't usually feed our spirit. But communion always does, and the only way to communion—with ourselves, with others, with God—is through silence.

It strikes me that most of the first part of our lives is spent filling our heads with information. The last part—the most important part—is spent emptying our heads of all that trivia so that our hearts may be free to learn wisdom—in silence.

Fr. Kieran M. Kay, O.F.M. Conv.
Common Bushes Afire With God

Spending Time With Jesus

■ **Mary of Magdala went and announced to the disciples, "I have seen the Lord," and what he told her.** John 20:18

Many stories about Mary Magdalene are not biblical, but they are told so often, people believe they are true. One woman told me she had read in the Bible that Mary Magdalene had red hair, but actually there is no account of this. These stories point to people's fascination with Mary Magdalene's character.

What we do know of her is that she was a faithful, devoted disciple of Jesus, one of the few brave ones who stood at the foot of the cross at Calvary and who cared enough to risk going to her Master's tomb early in the morning to anoint his body.

What spurred Mary Magdalene to this tremendous dedication to Jesus, so much so that she would risk her life for him? I think it came from spending so much time with Jesus, listening to him speak to the people, observing his great compassion as he healed, sensing his deep bond with his God as he went alone to pray on the mountainside. The life of Mary Magdalene calls to me in my discipleship, urging me to spend more time with Jesus as she did. My heart, too, can be ablaze with devotion and courage if I am willing to read the Scriptures and ponder the words of Jesus.

Sr. Joyce Rupp, O.S.M.

Doing The Important Chores

■ **Martha . . . said, "Lord, do you not care that my sister has left me by myself to do the serving? Tell her to help me."** Luke 10:40

In many cultures it is taken for granted that women should serve guests while men converse with guests. Even in Western societies, there are still social occasions when segregation of the sexes is normative. In Europe it is customary at formal dinner parties for women to leave the table after liquors and "retire to the powder room" while men smoke their cigars and sip port.

In households in the United States on Thanksgiving Day, men commonly watch football on TV while women do the dishes. So even by today's standards, then, Mary broke the rules. Instead of serving, she listened; instead of absenting herself, she sat firmly at Jesus' feet. Nothing was going to make her move— not even Martha's complaints.

We have much to learn from Mary. Whether male or female, we may fall into expected behavioral patterns, blocking ourselves from life-giving experiences. Often we are such creatures of habit that we miss what is most important. We prefer to busy ourselves with trivia rather than risk a change of pace. May we learn to listen. May we learn to sit still.

Lord, help us to choose the "better portion"—that is, the place closest to you.

Elizabeth-Anne Vanek

'You Have Only To Keep Still'

■ **Fear not! Stand your ground . . . The Lord himself will fight for you; you have only to keep still.** Exodus 14:13-14

Moses' advice to the Israelites came as they were fleeing Egypt with Pharaoh's army hot on their heels. Imagine how the people must have felt when Moses told them to "keep still," that God would fight for them. Surely, these were not easy words to accept as they ran for their lives and freedom. We know, of course, that God did fight for them and provided a way for them to escape their life of bondage.

"You have only to keep still." This is no easy thing when we are struggling to be in control and life keeps getting messier and more out of control. What happens if we stop grumbling and attacking our difficult circumstances? What happens when we are "still," when we surrender to the One who promises to care for us? Our situation will not change instantly, but we will have greater peace of mind and more love in our hearts. Grumbling, complaining, worry and criticism never changed anything. On the other hand, trust in God, peace of mind and love in the heart have led to profound changes.

Dear God, the next time that I am running for my life, please remind me to stop and be still, to let you handle things in your way.

Sr. Joyce Rupp, O.S.M.

Doing God's Will

■ **But the seed sown on rich soil is the one who hears the word and understands it, who indeed bears fruit . . .**

Matthew 13:23

Perhaps the most common mistake people make in assessing their progress is to judge it by the standard of feeling. If they detect a pleasing emotional experience at prayer, they conclude that all must be well. But if they are dry, distracted, "empty" in their devotion, they assume something is wrong. While Scripture surely speaks often of genuine experiences of God, nowhere does it present feelings as decisive criteria of progress or dry "emptiness" as an indication of fault or mediocrity . . .

What we do find over and over in God's word is the message that growth is shown in a concrete, down-to-earth identification of our wills with the divine will. "If anyone loves me, he will keep my word" (John 14:23). The crucial commandment, the precept of love, includes all others for the simple reason that God never decides or acts arbitrarily. The divine command always specifies what good is, what love requires in certain circumstances . . .

That specific ways of showing love have to be expressed via laws and rules is due to our sinfulness.

Fr. Thomas Dubay, S.M.
Seeking Spiritual Direction

Seeking God's Presence

■ **For everyone who asks, receives; and the one who seeks, finds; and to the one who knocks, the door will be opened.** Luke 11:10

Jesus' words seem to imply that God is a dispenser of gifts, ready to fulfill all our demands. All we have to do is to ask, seek and knock—and we will receive our hearts' desires. The reality, however, is that, while there are breakthrough moments when a new job comes unexpectedly or health is restored or disaster is averted, there are more times when nothing seems to happen despite our persistence in prayer.

Receiving, finding and being admitted are primarily spiritual experiences. The asking Jesus encourages has as its end the fullness of God's indwelling presence. The seeking he urges has to do with finding eternal life *now*. The knocking involves our being open to the immense riches of God's heavenly banquet, here on earth as well as in a future time. When people say to me, "I know that God exists, but I don't *feel* it," I respond, "First, desire God's presence, then ask for it, then wait—and when the time is right, receive." I think this type of asking is the key to understanding the promises in today's Gospel.

God of abundance, give us the wisdom to ask for those things which will increase your life in us.

Elizabeth-Anne Vanek

Cherishing Both Old And New

■ **Every scribe who has been instructed in the kingdom of heaven is like the head of a household who brings from his storeroom both the new and the old.** Matthew 13:52

The Church, like the wise head of the household, strives to bring together the new as well as the old. I didn't always appreciate that. Having grown up during the 1960s and seen the many exciting changes brought to the Church by the Second Vatican Council, I used to value religious ideas and activities according to how new—perhaps trendy—they were.

Of course, that was a bit narrow-minded: God did not suddenly become active in mid-twentieth century after being dormant since apostolic times. I didn't really come to value Church tradition until stormy times in my own spiritual life helped me appreciate the ballast of long-standing practices and beliefs.

Neither antiquity nor novelty interests Jesus. Rather, he is proclaiming the Kingdom of God, where the value of something depends not on how old it is or where it came from, but how well it reflects God and embodies the Spirit. That, thanks be to God, can happen in any age.

Mark Neilsen

A Prayer Of Contrition

■ **For I know my offense; my sin is always before me. Against you alone have I sinned; I have done such evil in your sight.** Psalm 51:5-6

I confess my sin, and deeper down, I accept the fact that I am a sinner. That is my birth, my status, my definition. I, the whole of me—my mind and heart and soul and body as they are today at this moment before you—make me a sinner in your eyes and in my own conscience. I know it well when I do the evil I don't want and when I miss the good I wish I could do.

But though I am a sinner, you are a Father. You forgive and forget and accept. To you I come with faith and confidence, knowing that you never send your children away when they come to you with sorrow and humility.

Let me feel clean again. Let me feel forgiven, accepted, and loved. If my sin was against you, my reconciliation must come from you. Give me your peace, your spirit, and your strength. Make my fall an occasion of my rising up, my drifting from you an opportunity to come closer to you. I know myself better now, as I know my weakness and my misery, and I know you better in the experience of your pardon and your love.

Fr. Carlos G. Valles, S.J.
Psalms For Contemplation

Jesus Reacts To 'Great Faith'

■ **Then Jesus said to her in reply, "O woman, great is your faith! Let it be done for you as you wish." And her daughter was healed from that hour.** Matthew 15:28

Jesus is confronted by a Canaanite woman, a person on the fringe of his culture on three counts: she is a woman, a non-Jew, and appears to be a single mother. The disciples want Jesus to get rid of her because she is a nuisance. But when Jesus takes time to listen and dialogue with this outsider, he discovers her profound faith. In fact, in all of Matthew's Gospel, she is the only person whose faith is said to be "great."

We may sometimes judge that others who are outside our Church or culture are lacking in faith or favor with God. Or we may feel that we are on the outside, the fringe, of Church, culture, family or some socially respectable group. For Jesus, this does not matter; all that matters is our faith.

God, grant me the gift of great faith to believe that you always listen and respond to me.

Sr. Ruth Marlene Fox, O.S.B.

I Have Enough Of What Counts

■ **God is able to make every grace abundant for you, so that in all things, always having all you need, you may have an abundance for every good work.**

2 Corinthians 9:8

If there is any message with which we are indoctrinated in our consumer culture it is that we never have "enough" of anything. We are always urged to acquire something more or something different, to purchase the latest commodities, the newest soap, clothing, videos, even plastic surgical procedures. So we purchase one more item and discover the following week that we still do not have enough.

This belief can even extend to our very selves: "I am not enough." Contrary to this message, God assures us that we are enough and that we do have enough of everything that counts: enough time, enough talents, enough beauty, enough goodness, enough grace. These gifts are available in such abundant quantities that we even have enough to give away in good works.

Lord, help me to appreciate the good gifts I have.
Sr. Ruth Marlene Fox, O.S.B.

No Gospel Of Easy Success

■ **For whoever wishes to save his life will lose it, but whoever loses his life for my sake will find it.**

Matthew 16:25

The Gospel is not a promise of easy success. Since my youth I have felt that the heart of the Gospel is contained in these words. The Gospel does not promise a comfortable life to anyone. It makes demands, yet it holds **a great promise**—the promise of eternal life for man, who is subject to the law of death, and the promise of victory through faith for man, who is subject to many trials and setbacks.

The Gospel contains a fundamental paradox—to find life, one must lose life; to be born, one must die; to save oneself, one must take up the cross. This is the essential truth of the Gospel, which always and everywhere is bound to meet with man's protest.

Always and everywhere the Gospel will be a challenge to human weakness. But precisely in this challenge lies all its power. Man, perhaps subconsciously, waits for such a challenge. Indeed, man feels the inner need to transcend himself. Only in transcending himself does man become fully human.

Help me to know and love the truth of the Gospel.

Pope John Paul II
Crossing The Threshold Of Hope

Loving God Above All Else

■ **And now, Israel, what does the Lord, your God, ask of you but to fear the Lord, your God, and follow his ways exactly, to love and serve the Lord, your God, with all your heart and all your soul.** Deuteronomy 10:12

God demands this of us: of all our loves his must be the dearest, the supreme love of our hearts.

It must be the deepest, filling our whole soul. It must be the most wholehearted, making use of all our faculties. And it must be the strongest, to which we give ourselves with might and main. Since it is a love by which we choose and set God upon the throne of our hearts, it is a love involving the highest choice, or a choice embracing the highest love . . .

Love resembles honor. Honors are distinguished by the varied goodness which inspires them. The highest honor belongs to the highest perfection, and supreme love to the supreme goodness.

Love in God is a love that knows no equal; for God's goodness is a goodness beyond compare. Since God alone is Lord, since his goodness is infinitely great, infinitely above all goodness, he must be loved with a love that makes us value so highly the blessing of being pleasing to him, that we prefer and care for God before all else.

St. Francis de Sales
from *Finding God Wherever You Are*

Spiritual Conflict Is Inevitable

■ **If it does not please you to serve the Lord, decide today whom you will serve ... As for me and my household, we will serve the Lord.** Joshua 24:15

Whenever we seriously acknowledge to ourselves or to others that God has called us to be something, we are bound to be thrown into conflict. It is helpful to realize that this conflict is utterly unavoidable. Any religion, which summons people to a spiritual life, must include an account of this conflict.

All serious religions attempt to deal with, reduce and solve this conflict. This pervasive conflict finds its origins in the difference between the finite and the infinite, the passing and the eternal, between what is dying and what lives in unchangeable light. Ultimately the conflict is between that which in its poverty seeks its own good and that infinite love that seeks to give itself away ...

Any relationship with the living God always leads to tension, conflict and failure and then to repentance and reform. From repentance and reform, starting over again, comes a rebirth to holiness and renewal. To this day all the spiritual descendants of Abraham struggle continually with their own reform and renewal.

Fr. Benedict J. Groeschel, C.F.R.
The Reform Of Renewal

Love Must Be Reserved

■ **You shall love your neighbor as yourself.**
Matthew 22:39

Love means an interior and spiritual identification with one's brother or sister—so that the person is not regarded as an "object" to which good is "done." Doing good in that way is of little or no spiritual value to anyone. In fact, it is a tragedy! It destroys the one who gives, and the one who receives.

Love takes on one's neighbor as one's self, and loves the neighbor with all the immense humility and discretion and reserve and reverence without which no one can presume to enter into the sanctuary of another. From such love, all authoritarianism, brutality, all exploitation, domineering, and condescension must necessarily be absent.

The full difficulty and magnitude of the task of loving others should be recognized. Love should take on one's neighbor as one's very self, and love that person with immense humility . . . I have often spoken of identification with the poor. It is an identification that only love can achieve by complete forgetfulness of self and total concern for the other person. It is an identification so deep, so complete, that it becomes part of oneself, like breathing.

Catherine de Hueck Doherty
Grace In Every Season

The Gain In Pain

■ **At the time, all discipline seems a cause not for joy but for pain, yet later it brings the peaceful fruit of righteousness to those who are trained by it.**

Hebrews 12:11

Suffering is the necessary feeling of evil. If we don't feel evil we stand antiseptically apart from it, numb. We can't understand evil by thinking about it. The sin of much of our world is that we stand apart from pain; we buy our way out of the pain of being human.

Jesus did not numb himself or withhold from pain. Suffering is the necessary pain so that we *know* evil, so that we can name evil and confront it. Otherwise we somehow dance through this world and never really feel what is happening . . .

If there is nothing in your life to cry about, if there is nothing in your life to complain about, if there is nothing in your life to yell about, you must be out of touch. We must all feel and know the pain of humanity. The free space that God leads us into is to feel the full spectrum, from great exaltation and joy, to the pain of mourning and dying and suffering. It's called the Paschal Mystery.

The totally free person is one who can feel *all* of it and not be afraid of any of it.

Fr. Richard Rohr, O.F.M.
Radical Grace

The World Is In God's Hands

■ **I, like an olive tree in the house of God, trust in God's faithful love forever.** Psalm 52:10

The thought that the affairs of the world, like those of the stars, are in God's hands—and therefore in good hands—apart from being actually true, is something that should give great satisfaction to anyone who looks to the future with hope. It should be the source of faith, joyful hope, and, above all, of deep peace. What have I to fear if everything is guided and sustained by God? Why get so worried, as if the world were in the hands of me and my fellow men?

And yet it is so difficult to have genuine faith in God's action in the affairs of the world. To refuse to believe is one of the gravest temptations to which we are subjected on this earth . . .

The will of God. That's what rules the world and moves the stars, what converts the nations, what starts all life and brings triumph out of death.

Lord, I want to believe that all reality is in your hands. Help me to believe it and to live that faith.

Carlo Carretto
Letters From The Desert

The Gospel Sparks Rejection

■ **Blessed are you when people hate you, and when they exclude and insult you, and denounce your name as evil on account of the Son of Man.** Luke 6:22

Authentic Christian witness seldom has to seek out persecution. There is something about the truth being lived boldly which draws it out. A life genuinely lived for the Gospel will inevitably involve suffering for the sake of the Gospel . . .

But the Gospel also brings out suffering because it invites rejection and misunderstanding and persecution. A world defining itself by its darkness does not want the light. A world built on a system of lies will have little patience with the word of truth. Based on what we see in Jesus, we can estimate that the more authentically and powerfully the Gospel is preached, the more it will stimulate not only faith but rejection. This should make us consider our own degree of acceptance by the world. Are we liked by our fellows simply because we are indistinguishable from them? Is our Christianity so anonymous that no one notices the difference in our values? Is there anything in our lives which might make people question the way they are living? Or do we make them feel comfortable, because the Gospel we have grown comfortable with offers them no threat?

Luke Timothy Johnson
Some Hard Blessings

Do I Know I Need Help?

■ **Those who are well do not need a physician, but the sick do.** Matthew 9:12

Part of the necessary background for acceptance of Jesus Christ as Lord and Savior is our recognition that something is always a bit off in us, in human life. There is a reluctance on our part to . . . allow God's love to work forcefully in us. We are inclined to either deny there is anything wrong, to blame it on someone or something else, or to presume that we will take care of it ourselves with a bit more education or a more determined will.

But a necessary part of life is a recognition that we do need the Physician, that we rely on and can find our ultimate freedom from all that's wrong only through the power, the love of God for us, shown in Christ. Besides our thinking it's a matter of me saving me, there is also our tendency in darker moments to think that nothing can be done about it.

The essence of our faith in the Lord is a trust that God's power and love are stronger, more penetrating, more effective than either our efforts or our failures. To recognize this is not an additional cause for despair but for great happiness. In the end, it *doesn't* all depend on my gritting my teeth.

Fr. Don Talafous, O.S.B.
A Word For The Day

The Trap Named Desire

■ **If we have food and clothing, we shall be content with that. Those who want to be rich are falling into temptation and into a trap and into many foolish and harmful desires, which plunge them into ruin and destruction.**

1 Timothy 6:8-9

This Scripture verse can be very confusing to those of us who live in a consumption-oriented economy. So much of our commercial advertising presumes that we are *not* content merely with food and clothing. And would state lotteries be as popular as they are if people renounced the desire to be rich?

From my own experience, I think St. Paul has an important point. When I was younger, I had relatively little wealth. As I began accumulating more, I found myself *wanting* more. I could sense my definition of "having enough" getting larger and larger! And my sense of security, strangely enough, did not grow with my bank account.

Contentment comes from what we can actually enjoy, things as concrete as food and clothing. On the other hand, the desire to *be rich* can never be satisfied, for we can always want something more.

Lord Jesus, help me to be grateful for and generous with the blessings of my life.

Mark Neilsen

One Who Won't Sell Us Short

■ **Why does your teacher eat with tax collectors and sinners?** Matthew 9:11

Jesus called Matthew the tax collector to be an apostle. A tax collector? Yes, even such an unpopular person as that, and, moreover, a subservient agent of the alien Roman oppressors. Our Lord doesn't seem to mind who his company is. Sinners are welcome. What kind of a person is our Lord?

He is the one who knows the intrinsic goodness of every person—because he made each of us in love. He is a friend who never gives up hope. How easily we sell ourselves short! "A poor, weak, backslider like me . . . how can *I* become a saint, be a true friend of God?" But Jesus never sells us short. He calls to us constantly, even in the midst of our daily labor. He joins us in the midst of our joys and sorrows. He came to this world, joined our human race, to call sinners and to have them as disciples and friends. He calls each one of us to banquet with him at the Eucharist and in the eternal kingdom. Let us stop focussing on our own misery and open ourselves to the call of his healing love.

Jesus, friend of sinners, be my friend.

Fr. M. Basil Pennington, O.C.S.O.

Holiness Isn't Fast Or Easy

■ **But some seed fell on rich soil, and produced fruit, a hundred or sixty or thirtyfold.** Matthew 13:8

By normal Holy Land yields, Jesus' assertion of a hundredfold yield would mean 250 bushels an acre, which is . . . impossible. So Jesus' numbers suggest a fruitfulness that is supernatural. The people who hear, understand and act on God's word are blessed with supernatural abundance . . .

This parable brings hope for all who feel down when they see painfully how little progress they seem to make. Through Baptism, there is a divine power for good deep within us, which continues to work in us despite our failures and setbacks . . .

Let's remember that the conditions of the soil for the sower aren't necessarily in four different fields; in the Holy Land at that time all conditions may have been found in one field. It's the same with us. Sometimes we can't take the word of God because our hearts are just too hard or we're enslaved by sin. But sometimes we do permit the rain of God's word to bring forth the blossoms of our love. If the results overall have been less than satisfactory, it's because we haven't matured fully enough to produce the supernatural yield of which Jesus spoke.

Fr. Harold A. Buetow
God Still Speaks: Listen!

God Doesn't Abandon Us

■ **They say, "The Lord does not see; the God of Jacob takes no notice". . . . You, Lord, will not forsake your people, nor abandon your very own.** Psalm 94:7,14

One of the worst of our fears is that God simply doesn't care about our suffering. The slow dying of a loved one, the struggle to overcome an addiction, or just a persistent feeling of unworthiness—our sufferings and trials come in so many shapes. To think that God doesn't care about them only adds hopelessness to the pain. Even believing that God is punishing us seems preferable—at least punishment is a kind of caring.

The psalmist reminds us that the truth of the matter is that whatever we might feel at any given moment, God does care and will not abandon his own. What does this mean? That suffering will soon end, that refugees will be able to return home, that new jobs will be created, that race relations will dramatically improve? Even more than that: no matter what happens, God will support us in ways we cannot even imagine.

Let us trust that, regardless of how we feel, God will walk with us today through whatever trials we are facing.

Mark Neilsen

You, Lord, Are My Hope!

■ **You are my hope, Lord; my trust, God, from my youth.**
Psalm 71:5

Yes, Lord, you alone are my hope . . . for everything fits into place in the light of your all-encompassing love. How often I have forgotten that, or been lured away from believing that what you have given me is best for me. At times, my life seems at odds with what I think I want or need. There may be pain, unsettled relationships, worries about family, employment problems.

All of this can cause me to become disillusioned about the steadfastness of your loving care.

Yet when I look back on difficult times, I see that you, indeed, carried me through. And now, because I am still loved and tremendously cared for, you will again provide me all that I need. Your love has carried me throughout my life, in the various stages of my growth. Why should I worry unduly about present difficulties? I need not fear the future nor mourn the past, for your guiding hand and supporting love will be there tomorrow as they were yesterday and are today.

I thank you with all my heart. You, O Lord, are everything I ever needed or will need; help me always to remember that.

Jean Royer

The Toil And Tears Of Life

■ **Those who sow in tears will reap with cries of joy. Those who go forth weeping, carrying sacks of seed, will return with cries of joy, carrying their bundled sheaves.**
Psalm 126:5-6

How much practical wisdom is hidden in this simple agrarian image! And how starkly different the message is from the contemporary notion of one's right to go through life with only ease and comfort!

The theme of Psalm 126 is gratitude, the unbounded joy at the Lord's "restoring the fortunes of Zion." Ultimately, what we are, have and enjoy comes from God. But by using the image of "sowing in tears, reaping in joy" the psalmist reminds us that our God-given life always follows something of a cycle—hard work before rest, struggle before success, pain before contentment, risk before reward, uncertainty before assurance, sorrow before joy. Life—all life, including the spiritual life—necessitates toil and tears, but promises a share of satisfaction. Sowing is tedious and taxing work, but the expectation of a future crop helps to make it bearable. A wise commentator has noted that the worst notion we can plant in children is that they can expect to escape pain, struggle and hardship. What we ought to help them realize instead is that toil and tears are part of a normal life.

James E. Adams

Happy For Others' Blessings

■ **After six days Jesus took Peter, James, and John his brother, and led them up a high mountain by themselves. And he was transfigured before them; his face shone like the sun . . .** Matthew 17:1-2

I never tire of hearing this story—it has such power and mystery in it. I wondered today about what might have happened "behind the scenes": how did the rest of the disciples feel about missing out on this profound moment of revelation? Surely the others would have longed to have been on the mountain, too. I suspect that they had some feelings of envy, questioning why Jesus hadn't chosen to take them along. After all, they were also his disciples.

Sometimes other people have the things we long for: money, opportunity for travel, faithful friends, good health, a marriage partner, consolation in prayer, children who are successful, and so on. What happens inside of us when we see someone else receive something we wish we had? To be genuinely happy for another's "mountaintop experience" is a sign of a truly Christian spirit.

Jesus, help me to enter joyfully into another's good fortune and success, even when I'd rather have it for myself.

Sr. Joyce Rupp, O.S.M.

Do I Accept My Crosses?

■ **Whoever wishes to come after me must deny himself, take up his cross, and follow me.** Matthew 16:24

What is our attitude when we are faced with crosses?

Our attitude is the key. We are called to accept our crosses as Jesus accepted his. Yet even before we can begin to accept our crosses, we must concede that they have a legitimate claim on us. We must acknowledge that they have a rightful place in our everyday life. How many of us these days even get past this initial psychological hurdle?

Don't we almost by instinct tend to deny our crosses or fail to grant them the status they must have in daily life? We often view crosses as obstacles to be overcome, as defects to be eradicated, rather than accepting cross-carrying itself as an essential characteristic of Christian growth. We don't get it. We think we grow *in spite of* crosses or by *dodging* crosses. The truth is we grow *with and through* our crosses. We are to take up, to carry, our crosses, not abolish them.

Jesus, help me to recognize cross-carrying as the normal duty of Christians, and, by the grace of Calvary, may I never become embittered by my crosses.

James E. Adams

Childlike Trust Has No Fear

■ **Amen, I say to you, unless you turn and become like children, you will not enter the kingdom of heaven.**

Matthew 18:3

What kind of children did Jesus have in mind? The ones who always seem like "little angels"? All parents know not even the most well behaved child always fits that category. I believe Jesus was simply thinking of the child as one who trusts. A child's trust grows naturally when it is nurtured by the love of a caring parent.

Many times Jesus emphasized that we must not fear. Nurtured by the power and the love of Jesus, there is no need to be afraid. If we believe this with the openness of a child, we can trust God, even when our lives seem to make little sense.

Trust in God's love opens our hearts to God's kingdom within us. The kingdom grows within us as our experience of God's love grows. It radiates from us and touches the lives of others.

Lord, may your love and our trust nourish the growth of your kingdom within us.

Fr. Kenneth E. Grabner, C.S.C.

A Rightful Place For Lament

■ **Pass through the city and mark an X on the foreheads of those who moan and groan over all the abominations that are practiced within it.** Ezekiel 9:4

In Ezekiel's vision, those who "moan and groan" over the infidelity of Jerusalem are spared a brutal death while those who have accepted the "abominations" perish. This passage reminds me of the important role played by people who moan and groan over such abominations as abortion, child abuse, greed and violence in our society. Sometimes I tire of hearing their lament, especially when I am near despair that anything can be done to change the situation.

But a lament serves at least two purposes: first, it calls an abomination just what it is; second, it recognizes that we cannot ignore evil just because we cannot control it. Those who turn to prayer in their lament will find a third purpose: to ask God's help in our human efforts to make a better world.

Lord God, help me to recognize the abominations of my city, to turn to you for strength and to do what I can for the sake of your people.

Mark Neilsen

Clinging To Consolations

■ **The crowds went looking for him, and when they came to him, they tried to prevent him from leaving them.**

Luke 4:42

Some crowds in the Gospel accounts reject Jesus outright. Others embraced him so enthusiastically they didn't want to let him go. Both attitudes seem extreme. In the spiritual life, it is possible to become overly attached to our consolations, making them goals rather than vehicles of growth and change. We may have a dramatic or profound experience connected to a ritual, type of prayer, spiritual teacher or religious event. These are not to be coveted, hoarded or chased after. Rather, they are to be welcomed with gratitude, experienced fully, held lightly and released without fear or regret.

A good example of this seems to be the mother-in-law of Simon (Lk 4:38-39). She received physical healing from Jesus, but did not cling to this experience at the detriment of other duties. Instead, when healed, she moved on immediately to the higher purpose of serving others. So should we. Let us courageously dedicate ourselves to moving on when we may be tempted to stop.

Lord, help me to stay on my spiritual journey without stopping and clinging to what seems comfortable.

Nancy F. Summers

Work And Prayer

■ **And he came down with them and stood on a stretch of level ground. A great crowd . . . came to hear him and to be healed of their diseases.** Luke 6:17-18

"**W**ork as if everything depended on you. Pray as if everything depended on God." I wonder if Jesus ever did that. This account in Luke seems, indeed, to be a case when Jesus did so. He had just spent the night in prayer. At dawn, he and his apostles descended the mountain to be confronted by many sick and troubled people waiting to be cured. More than likely Jesus had had no sleep, and may well have been tired. Yet the draining work of healing faced him. If he were to face this task as if everything depended on his human resources, he would have been concerned. Instead, it appears, he rose to the occasion of grace when God fills in for our emptiness.

There are times when we wonder how we are going to do what must be done, when our resources are depleted. It is then that we are invited to an occasion of grace, to rely on God to work with us and through us. Here prayer and work seem to merge. Here work seems to become prayer because, through that work, we are lifting our whole selves to God.

Lord, I place every moment before you today. May all my work and prayer be done in the Holy Spirit.

Sr. Anita M. Constance, S.C.

Do I Show Gratitude?

■ **Give thanks to the Lord, who is good, whose love endures forever.** Psalm 118:1

Speaking about gratitude to God, consider the fact that God loved you first. You've heard this, but somehow it hasn't penetrated. If it had, you would be gratefully and passionately loving him back.

How many of us truly and constantly realize the bounty of God to us, just speaking in the natural order? Do we thank God for the medical care we receive, for our clothing, our food, and our holidays? I received a letter from a woman, the mother of many children, who had broken her arm. She wrote: "Only now do I realize what it is to have two hands, both of which I need so much." We walk; we have the use of our limbs, eyes, speech, hearing. Are we grateful to God for these? Or do we take everything for granted, and grumble and mumble and complain and feel sorry for ourselves? I fear with great fear when I see a lack of gratitude. Think about it, meditate about it, pray about it, do something about it! Ours are frightening times and God is so good to us. Do we realize what we have? It is time we should. The time is now!

May Our Lady open our hearts to gratitude.

Catherine de Hueck Doherty
Grace In Every Season

A Willingness To See Truth

■ **All the ways of a man may be right in his own eyes, but it is the Lord who proves hearts.** Proverbs 21:2

This proverb is strangely consoling and disturbing at the same time.

On the one hand, it speaks to the ability we all have for self-deception and rationalization. Even when we try to be honest with ourselves, we have a tendency to find justification in what we think and do, and sometimes that leaves us blind to the truth. Ironically, this blindness may even be strongest at times when we are most convinced that we are right!

On the other hand, the Lord "proves"—establishes the truth of—our hearts. If we are deceiving ourselves, God will know it. Our beliefs and opinions are not the last word, and if we are willing to learn the truth, God will continually teach us.

In other words, we don't have to have all the answers, but only the willingness to accept the truth and follow it. God will take care of the rest.

Lord, help me to keep my heart open to the truth.

Mark Neilsen

A Humble Person's Prayer

■ **Give me neither poverty nor riches; provide me only with the food I need; lest, being full, I deny you, saying, "Who is the Lord?" Or, being in want, I steal, and profane the name of my God.** Proverbs 30:8-9

I know it's foolish to think that the quality of prayer may depend on articulating precisely the right things—as if the more cleverly worded prayers somehow had a better chance of attracting God's attention than prayers that are badly muddled.

Yet it surely can't hurt anything when our prayer is formulated with grace and precision, when our words help clarify and reveal rather than obscure what we are asking for.

This passage from Proverbs strikes me as a profoundly wise prayer—and reminiscent of that "daily bread" petition in the Our Father. It is saying something like this: "Lord, I know my weaknesses. I realize that I probably can't handle either poverty or wealth very well. So give me what I need to live day by day. If I have too much to consume, I'm afraid I'll get sated and forget all about you and my spiritual duties. If I have too little, I'm afraid I'll panic and lash out to get what I need unlawfully or unjustly."

This is a humble prayer, the plea of somebody who is content to live modestly rather than to try doing great things at the risk of falling out of God's favor.

James E. Adams

The Road Of Pure Faith

■ **"The Lord gave and the Lord has taken away; blessed be the name of the Lord!" In all this Job did not sin, nor did he say anything disrespectful of God.** Job 1:21-22

The road of pure faith enables us to find God at each moment. It is this that makes it so exalted, so heavenly, so blessed. It is an inexhaustible resource of thought, preaching and writing. It is a whole collection of—in fact, the source of—wonders. To produce such wondrous effects, only one thing is necessary: to let God act and do all that He wills according to our state in life. Nothing in the spiritual life could be easier, nothing more within the grasp of everyone. And yet, nothing could be more full of wonders, no path more full of shadows. To walk in it, we have need of great faith, all the more so because our reasoning is always so full of suspicions and always ready to make some argument against this way. The soul's ideas are confused by it, for there is nothing in it that reason has ever known or read about or been used to admiring. It is entirely new.

If we are scandalized, we show but little faith and well deserve to be deprived of those wonderful things that God is so ready to work in the hearts of the faithful.

Blessed be the name of the Lord!

Fr. Jean-Pierre de Caussade
The Joy Of Full Surrender

What Does God Want Of Me?

■ **Not everyone who says to me, "Lord, Lord," will enter the kingdom of heaven, but only the one who does the will of my Father in heaven.** Matthew 7:21

Is God satisfied with the faith that I received from my family, from my teachers, or does he want more? God wants me to be aware of the forces in me; he asks more attentiveness, more understanding, a more constant and steadfast commitment. God wants to be considered not as an agreeable and happy memory, as a theoretical power, but as a being who is present, living, acting and overflowing with tenderness.

I have received faith, I have guarded it, but God wants this faith to become truly alive in me. He wants it to be ardent and dynamic so that I may become an instrument of Christ. To have faith and to conserve it is one thing, but to live it, to be a conscious instrument of Christ, is another.

To know many truths of the faith is a richness, but to live the word of God and to believe in it enough to feel the need for conversion is the treasure that I must seek.

The Good Thief . . . believed in Jesus and did not doubt his word. He accepted it with his whole heart and in a half-hour became a saint.

Fr. Louis-Marie Parent
In Intimacy With Jesus

The God Of Tender Mercies

■ **God will wipe away the tears from all faces.** Isaiah 25:8

Today we remember our own deceased and all those who have died and crossed over to the other side of life. We come face-to-face with the mystery of what it is like to die and to enter into the realm of eternal life. Do the deceased need our prayers? Do they continue to suffer? No one has ever come back to answer these questions for us. On this day, we pray for a release of suffering for them—just in case they still have some pain on their journey Home. As we pray we have the consoling and tender words of Isaiah assuring us that God will wipe away all tears.

The Church has wisely invited us to connect with our loved ones who have died, to remember them with compassion and prayerful care. This is the day to intentionally give our loved ones into the care of a God of mercy and tenderness. On this day, I especially remember my father and my brother. I pray for them in this way: I remember what they looked like. I then picture them in the arms of God. I see God carefully and lovingly wiping away any tears that might be on their faces. I then entrust them into God's care and offer a prayer of thanks for the gift of having had these two good men in my life.

Sr. Joyce Rupp, O.S.M.

I Yearn, But God Alone Fills

■ **My soul yearns and pines for the courts of the Lord. My heart and flesh cry out for the living God.** Psalm 84:3

The truth is, I often find myself yearning for a new car and pining for a vacation cottage on the lake. My heart and flesh cry out for love, love and more love from family and friends. I know, God alone can satisfy my deepest desires, but knowing that doesn't seem to stop me from looking for another way, a way that will allow *me* to be in control.

This prayer from Psalm 84 might seem depressing at first: after all, the hunger expressed here will never be satisfied in this life. Is it a tragedy for the human heart to be burdened with a hunger it cannot satisfy? Or is the real tragedy spending a lifetime trying to acquire what cannot satisfy?

Everyone experiences moments of grace—often enough in illness and suffering, but also in deep joy—when we realize we cannot provide for ourselves what we most desire. We can only long for it, beg God for it, cherish it. Rather than being depressing, this is liberating: dependent on God, we no longer have to try to do the impossible. We can simply let ourselves do what we are most inclined to do: yearn, pine, and cry out to the One who is in charge.

Mark Neilsen

Stretching To Hear The Truth

■ **Jesus then said to the Twelve, "Do you also want to leave?" Simon Peter answered him, "Master, to whom shall we go? You have the words of eternal life."**

John 6:67-68

Most of us have had the experience of feeling rejection for something we believe in. One of the most painful experiences I had as a teacher was to have a student walk out of a theology course because she could not accept something I said. In sadness I watched her pick up her books and leave the classroom. Jesus must have felt far greater heartache when several of his followers walked out on him, for he had the greatest message of love, freedom, and salvation that they would ever hear. He must have wanted to run after them and say, "Wait! Wait! You don't understand!"

They thought they did understand, but they could not accept the challenge of his words. Picking up their fears, walking out on cold feet, they rejected grace because they were imprisoned by the limits of their own faith.

Lord, help me to be open to your action in my life as you try to stretch me beyond my own limited boundaries of faith.

Sr. Ruth Marlene Fox, O.S.B.

Asking God To Do What I Can't

■ **They were all amazed and said to one another, "What is there about his word? For with authority and power he commands the unclean spirits, and they come out."**

Luke 4:36

Have you ever experienced a helplessness in freeing yourself from a particular moral failure, no matter how hard you tried? If so, these simple yet profound words of faith are for you: "I can't. God can. I'll let him do it." If we live this way, God will fortify our weakness with the power of his healing presence. God not only creates us, he also protects us as our life unfolds. But we must open ourselves to God, we must invite God to do for us what we cannot do for ourselves. Our faith in God's healing power gives us the ability to transform our powerlessness into strength.

Our faith is a gift from God, but it seems to me that faith never works completely unless it is fortified by self-knowledge. I find it helpful to remember the failures that resulted in my life when I tried to manage by myself. And it is important for me to remember the good that God brought out of my failures in those times when I turned my life over to him.

Lord, increase my faith in your saving power.

Fr. Kenneth E. Grabner, C.S.C.

Love Of Money Brings Pain

■ **For the love of money is the root of all evils, and some people in their desire for it have strayed from the faith and have pierced themselves with many pains.**

1 Timothy 6:10

I don't normally think of money as bringing pain. I think of it as providing comfort and security. But surely Timothy is right. The love of money leads to the desire to have more and more of it, which leads to the constant temptation to do anything to get and keep it . . . which, in turn, leads to pain.

We pierce ourselves with greed and envy of others' wealth, which keeps us from being in fellowship with them. We pierce ourselves with the fear of not having money, which leads us to shun the poor and needy because they remind us of our own dark fears.

We lay awake nights worrying about having enough or losing what we have, and so we forget to pray and to trust. We drown our lives in the struggle to get and to spend, and so we drift away from the shores of grace. We contemplate our material gains, and so lose sight of God.

Instead, Timothy reminds us to "pursue righteousness, devotion, faith, love, patience, and gentleness." That surely is a relevant reminder for our times.

Denise Barker

The Truth About Troubles

■ **It is good for me that I have been afflicted, in order to learn your laws.** Psalm 119:71

When pruned, a tree, a grapevine, a rosebush appear to be all but destroyed. But afterward, there comes to the plant a surge of new life. Had the plant been spared the sharp blade of the pruning hook, it would have progressively deteriorated.

There is nothing good about illness, sorrow, pain. Christ spent much of his public life in curing people and making them whole again. But the fact remains that life is filled with such sufferings. And Christ tells us to bear these daily unavoidable crosses and let them, with his tender love to support us, prune us of the "dead wood" in our lives.

Most of all, when illness or hard times come, we need to abide by the belief that God is not punishing us for something we did. What God is doing is telling us that if we accept what life deals out to us, we can come out from under all this affliction a better person than we would have been without it. The saints, who were people just like us, would never have become great in the sight of God had they not been pruned by troubles and sorrows and pains, and then found, with God's help, indomitable courage. God grant us the grace to say with them, "All will be well."

Sr. Mary Terese Donze, A.S.C.

Ongoing Repentance

■ **If you do not repent, you will all perish as they did.**
Luke 13:3

Now Testament writers all see the Christian life as an ongoing conversion. They see it as continual repentance, a daily acknowledgment that one is unable to save oneself, and a complete turning to God.

Unfortunately, when Christianity becomes too comfortable, when it gets bedded down in a kind of pious materialism, when it forgets the powerful confrontation that one finds when Jesus preaches the Good News, it loses its sense of ongoing repentance. Devout Christians may, at such times, occupy themselves neurotically with picking out their little faults while the rest of Christianity, unmoved by the thought of repentance, blissfully accepts that everyone is saved, that we are all going to heaven in a toboggan and that there is no possibility of eternal loss . . . Christianity is based on repentance and on the awareness that we must struggle to take hold of the kingdom of God in our daily lives. When Christianity does not do this, it begins to become anemic and may even die away in some parts of Christendom. This has happened many times in the Church's history. Is it happening now?

Fr. Benedict J. Groeschel, C.F.R.
The Reform Of Renewal

The Habit Of Prayer

■ **In those days he departed to the mountain to pray, and he spent the night in prayer to God.** Luke 6:12

In prayer we express to God our feelings, our thoughts, our sentiments. We wish to love and to be loved, to be understood and to understand. Only God loves us perfectly, with an everlasting love. In prayer, we open our hearts and our minds to this God of love. And it is prayer that makes us one with the Lord. Through prayer we come to share more deeply in God's life and his love.

One of the most striking things about Jesus was *his habit of prayer*. In the midst of an active public ministry, we find him going away by himself to be alone in silence and communion with his Father in heaven. On the Sabbath, he made it a practice to go to the synagogue and pray with others in common. When he was together with his disciples or when he was by himself, he prayed to the Father, whom he dearly loved . . .

If you really wish to follow Christ, if you want your love for him to grow and last, then you must *be faithful to prayer*. It is the key to the vitality of your life in Christ. Without prayer, your faith and love will die.

Pope John Paul II
from *The Pope Speaks to the American Church*

Seeing As God Sees

■ **The law of the Lord is perfect, refreshing the soul ...
The precepts of the Lord are right, rejoicing the heart.
The command of the Lord is clear, enlightening the eye.**
                                                    Psalm 19:8, 9

Silence gives us the opportunity we need to raise our hearts and minds to something above ourselves, to be aware of a spiritual life in us that is being starved out by noise pollution, to still the raging of our limitless desires. It is a call . . . to where the vision is clear and the heart is centered on something worthy of it.

There are some things in life that deserve to be nourished simply for their own sake. Art is one, music is another, good reading is a third, but the power of the contemplative vision is the greatest of them all. Only those who come to see the world as God sees the world, only those who see through the eyes of God, ever really see the glory of the world, ever really . . . find peace in themselves.

Silence is the beginning of peace. It is in silence that we learn that there is more to life than life seems to offer. There is beauty and truth and vision wider than the present and deeper than the past that only silence can discover.

Sr. Joan Chittister, O.S.B.
There Is A Season

Grace From God's Hand

■ **The grace of God has appeared, offering salvation to all.** Titus 2:11

I am confident that the grace of God comes in many different ways.

A few years ago I received as a gift a figure of a child nestling in the shadow of the hand of God. I gave it to my sister Marie as a Christmas gift. She carried it home to California in her suitcase and later sent me a picture of it on her table. "I love your gift," she wrote. The image of herself as a child protected by a loving God appealed to her very much.

A few months ago when Marie was suffering with cancer I brought her a chain and medal with the same image imprinted on the medal. Before I left the hospital, I put the chain around her neck and asked her to keep putting her trust in our compassionate God.

When I went back for her funeral, her daughter told me that my sister had not allowed anyone to remove the medal. She was buried with it.

I feel confident saying that the grace of God *did* appear for Marie in the shape of a likeness of the hand of God with a small child being caressed in it.

Sr. Marguerite Zralek, O.P.

Opportunities To Love God

■ **Whoever seeks to preserve his life will lose it, but whoever loses it will save it.** Luke 17:33

We never know when God is going to make an appearance in our lives.

Sometimes God may show up in a heady prayer experience that envelops us in warmth and awe. More often, God appears in everyday opportunities to love one another. Too often, we're not prepared when God shows up. We might like to pursue that prayer experience, perhaps through reading or talking with a spiritual director, so that we can discern its meaning in our life. But where can we find the time? Or we may take those initial steps only to learn that what God is asking of us—to change, to grow, to strike out in new directions—involves more effort than we're willing to put forth and more risk than we're willing to take. How can we give up anything in our lives to make room for this? And when God shows up in another person, we're sometimes too preoccupied with the details in our lives to notice. So we miss opportunities to love God or to be loved by God.

Dear God, give me the strength to drop whatever keeps me from following you in an instant.

Charlotte A. Rancilio

Our Divine Source

■ **Then he told them a parable about the necessity for them to pray always without becoming weary.** Luke 18:1

Prayer is not designed to change God or the situation, but to change us.

If the external circumstances are helpful to that end, we may receive our request. If there is a possibility that our faith will grow in this mysterious dialogue between our petitions and the divine silence, we may not have our request granted. In other words, prayer is designed to increase faith, which is not a particular petition for anything, but the total surrender of ourselves to God. Faith means entrusting the whole of ourselves to the infinite Mercy of God. . . .

Faith dissolves the enormous illusion of the human condition, which is that God is absent. This great lie, the source of all human misery, prevents the free flow of the divine life and love into us and into the world. The purpose of continual prayer is to access that which is most true about us, namely, our divine Source. The divine is always manifesting itself, though mostly in secret, to those who walk in the presence of God and allow this presence to influence all their relationships.

Fr. Thomas Keating, O.C.S.O.
Reawakenings

'Follow Your Bliss'

■ **By patient endurance you will save your lives.**

Luke 21:19

I am an advocate of Joseph Campbell's motto, "Follow your bliss" (I've even got a T-shirt with those words emblazoned on it). Yet I have to admit that much of life involves putting up with what we would rather do without. I also concede that life involves doing without what we would prefer to have. Some people are blissfully ignorant and never know that life could be any different from the way they experience it. What they lack in consciousness, they make up for in contentment. Others, more awake to life and in touch with their hopes and dreams, are often thwarted from attaining them. Though they pursue their bliss with a passion, it often eludes them. All they can do is wait, in less than ideal circumstances, for things to change . . .

It is how we conduct ourselves in this waiting that determines whether we emerge successfully or in defeat. To the extent that our survival tactics include denying reality or projecting our discontent onto others, we are being defeated. When, however, we allow ourselves to be schooled by the waiting, acquiring patience and compassion in the process, our bliss will eventually find us.

Elizabeth-Anne Vanek

A High Standard Of Giving

■ **I tell you truly, this poor widow put in more than all the rest; for those others have all made offerings from their surplus wealth, but she, from her poverty, has offered her whole livelihood.** Luke 21:3-4

The poor widow's generosity puts most of us to shame. All that we have—our money, possessions, health, talents, family and friends—are really gifts from God. In our thankfulness for God's lavish bounty to us, we are asked to give back generously to God. How generously? Some of our surplus? All of our surplus? Yes, and maybe even more, especially when there seem to be so many poor people nowadays.

"But it's mine," I may protest, "and there's no long-term security these days. Then there's my needs for retirement and for my children . . ." The psalmist reminds us that "the earth is the Lord's" (Psalm 24:1). Everything belongs to God; nothing ultimately belongs to us. All that we are and have are on loan, as it were, for us to use for others as much as for ourselves. And if we are as generous as the poor widow, perhaps God will surpass that generosity—maybe even a hundredfold. Dare we take that risk?

Jesus, help us to show our gratitude by sharing out of our substance and not just from our surplus.

James McGinnis

The God Of Abundance

■ **When they had had their fill, he said to his disciples, "Gather the fragments left over, so that nothing will be wasted."** John 6:12

Our God is a mysterious God, so far, far beyond us. But he wants to be our friend; he wants us to know and love him. So he became one with us in our Lord Jesus, lived with us, interacted with us so that we can get to know him.

The event described in today's Gospel tells us much about him. He is a hospitable God: he sees a crowd coming and is immediately concerned about setting out a meal for them. He is a gracious God: he condescends to us with a gentle sensitivity. Rather than making a meal materialize out of his domain, he takes the little we have—five loaves and two fishes—and makes them do. And he is a God of abundance: the only thing that limits what he will give us is how willing we are to receive. He produced as much bread and fish as the crowd could eat. Each one could have all he or she wanted. Indeed, there were twelve baskets full of pieces left over.

Lord, expand my heart by the wonder of your goodness so that I might receive more and more of your love.

Fr. M. Basil Pennington, O.C.S.O.

Getting The Rest You Need

■ **Come to me, all you who labor and are burdened, and I will give you rest.** Matthew 11:28

What is better at the end of a rough day than a good night's sleep!

It is one of the our greatest blessings—to be able to rest and then awake replenished and ready to start a new day. If you have ever gone for more than a day without a good rest, you know how the lack of sleep can affect you. Parents know the miracle that a nap has on a grouchy kid. We all need rest.

What God offers us is a kind of eternal rest—even while we walk this earth. God offers us rest from the pressures of our labor and from the heavy burdens we all place—or have placed—on our shoulders. Ironically, God offers us rest by giving us a new burden: "Take my yoke upon you and learn from me . . . for my yoke is easy and my burden light."

Those who shrink from the call of God often do so because they do not want the extra burdens and responsibilities that being a Christian brings. They see only this new yoke that they have to place on themselves. What they don't realize, however, is that when they accept this new—and easy—yoke, their old burdens will disappear.

Steve Givens

Ready To Change My Mind

■ **"Son, go out and work in the vineyard today." He said in reply, "I will not," but afterwards he changed his mind and went.** Matthew 21:28-29

Jesus tells the chief priests and elders that tax collectors and prostitutes will enter the kingdom of God before them. Why? These outcasts had the ability to change their minds. They were open to new understandings and different ways, something the religious authorities who opposed Jesus apparently refused to do. More than being simply stubborn or narrow-minded, these church leaders believed that it was their solemn duty to their God and their faith to remain steadfast in their beliefs. They were too sure, their minds locked up—and this was their downfall.

Changing our minds is not always a sign of inconsistency or lukewarm faith. What else can we do when God comes to us in new ways, when life experiences challenge our concept of reality, when modern-day prophets offer a vision beyond and bigger than what we had believed? As we develop and grow in the Christian life, this will remain constant—from time to time, we shall be changing our minds.

Dear God, grant me the wisdom to know when to change my mind and the flexibility to do it.

Nancy F. Summers

God Is With You Always

■ **"...and they shall name him Emmanuel," which means, "God is with us."** Matthew 1:23

These words were given to Joseph while he slept. God is always with us—even when we sleep. I would venture to say that God may be even more powerfully with us while we sleep because we are not in conscious control. We finally LET GO.

When you lie down to rest at night invite Jesus into your sleep. Ask him to roam through your entire being evaluating your life and deciding what in your life has greatest need for healing. Let Jesus make the decision. Don't tell him what needs to be healed. Trust in the truth that he knows you well and will know what to choose.

When you awake let your first thought be this: I wonder what Jesus healed in me last night. Let your waking moment be one of awe and wonder. Then, in the simplicity of your heart, thank Jesus for the healing. Gratefully walk through your day knowing that something in you has been anointed with God's presence. By the end of the day, you may begin to realize, quite naturally, the healing that has taken place. Gratefully accept this healing as a gift from heaven and know that God-is-with-you always.

Sr. Marcina Wiederkehr, O.S.B.

Find A Way To Share Riches

■ **But God said to him, "You fool, this night your life will be demanded of you; and the things you have prepared, to whom will they belong?"** Luke 12:20

This parable has an important warning not only for individuals, but for societies that enjoy great wealth. We should, however, be clear about what we are being warned against. The rich man is not criticized for being rich, for he owned the land, worked it and it produced for him. Nor is he called foolish for storing a certain surplus in his barns, for he had already done this as a prudent measure against hard times. What makes him a fool in God's eyes is that, already in possession of more wealth than he could enjoy, he stored up an excessive amount, believing that his abundance had finally guaranteed him security.

But like all the rest of us, he was destined to die and face the judgment of God. Suddenly, his desire to pile up wealth upon wealth appears ridiculous—it wasn't his to enjoy after all. What, then, should he have done with his great harvest? God, we can well imagine, would have been pleased had he found a way to share it with those in need.

May we feel gratitude, not guilt, for the blessings of our lives, and simply find a way to share what we have with those who have less.

Mark Neilsen

Don't Be Quick To Find Fault

■ **. . . for they were plotting to catch him at something he might say.** Luke 11:54

I am always appalled at how verbally nasty human beings can be toward one another. That is, until I find myself doing the same thing! I always have very good reasons and excuses for why I want to catch someone else in their weaknesses. The hostility and plotting of the scribes and Pharisees isn't really all that different from my actions or from what happens in most human situations from time to time. The desire to catch others in what appears to be their weaknesses is very unkind and uncaring.

Two things help me to avoid this unloving attitude. One is to be more aware of the presence of God in the other person. I am not so quick to criticize and find fault when I really believe that God dwells within someone else. The other is to become more aware of my own motivations. Insecurity, hurt, revenge or the desire to feel better about myself can all be unloving motivations for naming someone else's weaknesses.

Jesus, I do not want to plot hostility against others. May I live with your kindness and understanding.
Sr. Joyce Rupp, O.S.M.

Our Deepest Yearnings

■ **All that is in the world, sensual lust, enticement for the eyes, and a pretentious life, is not from the Father but is from the world. Yet the world and its enticement are passing away.** 1 John 2:16-17

Without yearnings, we are like a bird that does not fly. Our yearnings define our lives. What are your deepest yearnings? In our moments of honesty, we discover a sense of incompleteness in our lives. No matter how successful we are in the material world, it never fulfills us. We yearn for something beyond. Those who see this know the meaning of wisdom.

Our deepest yearnings are for the experience of belonging, the experience of communion that goes beyond what is visible and material. Our deepest longings are the longings of the spirit—the wish to be understood, to be accepted, to be one with God at the core of our being. And in our oneness with God, we long for oneness with each other. These are the yearnings that define us at the deepest level of our existence. We respond to them through prayer and through service to each other.

O Lord, may my deepest yearnings be for you, and for communion with others in you.

Fr. Kenneth E. Grabner, C.S.C.
Focus Your Day

We Are All Neighbors

■ **"And who is my neighbor?"** Luke 10:29

Who is my neighbor?

If we stop to ponder it, who on this earth *isn't* my neighbor? Can I rule out any other human being? My neighbors live across the street and across the world. My neighbors have minds, spirits and bodies, as I do. They come in all colors and are any age, from newborn to elderly. My neighbors are made in the image and likeness of God. We often limit our neighbors to local people because our vision is limited. But God sees the world as a whole, in a way perhaps much as the earth looks from the moon.

By comparison to the millions of other suns and solar systems, planet earth is very tiny. Since we all live on this one tiny island in the cosmos, we truly and literally are neighbors. Imagine that you were taken to a foreign planet and lived alone among alien creatures. You would feel strange and isolated. But if you found another human there, regardless from where on earth he or she came, you would embrace that individual as one from your very own street.

God keeps telling us we are sisters, brothers, neighbors and members of one family. We often see only our differences and live in rejection. God sees our similarities and tells us to love one another.

Fr. James McKarns

The Secret Of Being Content

■ **In every circumstance and in all things I have learned the secret of being well fed and of going hungry, of living in abundance and of being in need. I have the strength for everything through him who empowers me.**

Philippians 4:12-13

What was St. Paul's "secret"? How did he manage, in the face of changing circumstances and resources, to keep on working, traveling, spreading the word, writing letters to Christian communities? When life throws us a curve, we may well wish we could be a little more like Paul.

Paul knows that everything that is truly important, that "empowers" him, ultimately comes from God—health, relationships, even life itself. And Paul is grateful for all the good he enjoys. When times are tough and he suffers, Paul keeps faith while struggling to go forward with his life.

This may be the "secret of the secret": having faith and patience through tough times does not mean doing nothing or simply accepting passively whatever life deals out. Instead, our ability to accomplish anything at all requires that we trust God and go forward—even when the way seems impossible. A simple secret, really, but a great blessing to all who can follow St. Paul's example.

Mark Neilsen

God's Power In The Gospel

■ **For I am not ashamed of the gospel. It is the power of God for the salvation of everyone who believes.**

Romans 1:16

What is the "power of God" in the Gospel? I think of power as an energy or an ability to move or to act. The power in the Gospel is the vision which Jesus shared. This vision has an energy or an ability to help us live our lives in union with God. It carries the power of transformation, the ability for us to change what needs to be changed so we can live as God wills.

When I think of the power of the Gospel, I see that it has had a great influence on my life. I have known consolation because of the vision of Jesus with its emphasis on the totally loving and accepting quality of divine love. I have been challenged by the words of Jesus to forgive, to go the extra mile, to let go of my harsh judgments. I have also felt called to mercy and compassion as I've heard the power in the Beatitudes and in the healing stories. I cannot be ashamed of the Gospel. Rather I am deeply grateful. I'd be a very different person today if it were not for the power of God given to me in the vision of Jesus.

Jesus, thank you for your life and your words. They bring great power into my life and help me grow.

Sr. Joyce Rupp, O.S.M.

Daily Appreciation Of God

■ **They say to me day after day, "Where is your God?"**
                                                  Psalm 42:4

Even if others don't taunt us with, "Where is your God?," do we not ask ourselves the same question when times are tough? Where is God when we are mourning, in pain or afraid? Where is God in the face of random violence, undeserved rejection and broken hearts? These are the big questions of life, thrust upon us when we are most vulnerable. In such periods, we may not be up to the task of discerning God's presence in the bad times.

But it will help if we have made a practice of noticing God's presence in the good times. What if every night we asked ourselves, "Where was I aware of God today?" Surely we would quickly accumulate a long list of God's touch upon our lives; serendipitous events, near misses, extravagant gifts of nature, quiet moments of deep communion, children's faces, good news, love, friendship and so much more. Perhaps we would come to see God pervading our lives in all times in all places. Then when the question arises, "Where is your God?," we will know: God is here!

Gracious God, forgive me for taking you for granted. Help me to know and love you more each day.
                                             Nancy F. Summers

A Roadside Lesson

■ **The wages of sin is death, but the gift of God is eternal life in Christ Jesus our Lord.** Romans 6:23

When I was a child, many old barns were covered with a Scripture quote. I remember one barn we drove past every year on our way to a little lake. On the high sloping roof in big white letters was: "The wages of sin is death." What a dismal reminder of human frailty on a sunny Saturday morning! Luckily, I was aware of the rest of the quote . . . "but the gift of God is eternal life in Christ Jesus our Lord."

We ought never to forget the second part of that oft-quoted sentence. Eternal life is our gift because Jesus has overcome sin by suffering, dying and rising from the dead for our salvation. I try to live consciously aware of this truth: my salvation is a gift. And I try to help others see that they also have the gift of eternal life. At the hospital where I visit patients, I come face-to-face with despairing people who believe that because they have sinned, there cannot be eternal life for them. They are afraid, and often bitter. For them, I try to emphasize the truth of this entire sentence from St. Paul.

Loving God, giver of eternal life, help me to realize each day that I am loved and valued by you—and help me to help others realize that they are loved also.

Sr. Marguerite Zralek, O.P.

God Hears Cries Of Agony

■ **If ever you wrong them and they cry out to me, I will surely hear their cry.** Exodus 22:22

Sometimes I am silenced by other people's pain. As I listen to stories filled with tragic events, inexplicable mishaps and devastating illness, there is little I can say. Theological reflection on the cause of suffering is inappropriate; clumsy assurances that "everything will turn out fine" are meaningless. At best, I, the listener, can only hear with compassion. There are no solutions or explanations to give. All I have to offer is the reminder that God suffers with them and that it is God alone who can be their comfort.

I often wonder what it is like to be God. If all time is present to God, then so is all suffering. The cries of all people, from all ages, pierce the heavens—and God hears. I would like to think that what makes this bearable for God is that all acts of human kindness are also held in timelessness. If so, in loving one another, we are also binding the wounds of our God.

Let our love for one another comfort you, O God.

Elizabeth-Anne Vanek

When We Haven't Got A Prayer

■ **In the same way, the Spirit too comes to the aid of our weakness; for we do not know how to pray as we ought, but the Spirit itself intercedes with inexpressible groanings.** Romans 8:26

When all is going well, when we seem to be on top of the world, when God's power seems to be flowing directly into our lives, how easy it is for us to see and feel the presence of the Spirit! How easy it is to pray! But what about when nothing seems to be going well, when we've sunk to the bottom, when God seems to be a million miles away? All we seem able to do is groan and moan, and pickle in our exasperation.

Do not despair, do not even lament that you are in this situation, but be hopeful because the Spirit is probably flying to your aid: such is the suggestion of St. Paul. It's natural to assume in such situations that the Spirit is gone, but it's not true, St. Paul is saying. The Spirit is present in our weakness. The Spirit turns weakness on its head. Our groaning, pain and exasperation do not mean that all is lost. In fact, our moans and groans may well be on their way to becoming our prayer, thanks to the Spirit.

Holy Spirit, may I never forget that you can—and want to—turn my suffering into prayer.

James E. Adams

An Advent Invitation

■ **According to his promise we await new heavens and a new earth in which righteousness dwells.** 2 Peter 3:13

Part of the tension of Advent waiting is that the reign of God is now, but still to come in its fullness. We prepare to celebrate the birth of the One who has already been born. We wait for what has already come, but look forward in hope for a new world.

For the new heavens and new earth to become a reality, we must become a new creation. Just as God's glory is revealed in the re-fashioning of the landscape—the filling in of valleys and the flattening of rugged mountains—so we, too, must undergo radical transformation. Yielding to the hands of our Maker, we need to be stripped of our false selves so that we more fully mirror the Divine likeness. This does not happen without our consent: the "yes" we utter in response to God's invitation must, like Mary's "yes," come from the depths of our being. God only leads us to where we are ready to go.

Make us a new creation, God, that your light will shine in the darkness.

Elizabeth-Anne Vanek

Divine Delight

■ **The Lord is near to all who call upon him, to all who call upon him in truth. He fulfills the desire of those who fear him, he hears their cry and saves them.**

Psalm 145:18-19

The past can haunt us: shame, regret and guilt may linger for years or even decades. We accuse ourselves in the present: "Why did I do that? How could I have been so stupid? What if I had made better choices? Wouldn't my life be wonderful if not for my past mistakes? Don't I deserve to suffer for the wrongs I have done?"

Even as we acknowledge our sins and cry out to God for relief, one last question may emerge: "How can God possibly forgive me?"

We may be tempted to think that God forgives only because it is part of God's job description! Although mercy is part of the Divine nature, we wonder if, in our case, forgiveness is dispensed only grudgingly or with many strings attached. Perhaps we need to expand or correct our understanding of who God really is. Our God forgives, not on the basis of some criteria we must satisfy, but simply and amazingly because God finds forgiving delightful. How much longer shall we deny God this joy?

Nancy F. Summers

Drawing Near

■ **Woe to the city. . . . In the Lord she has not trusted, to her God she has not drawn near.** Zephaniah 3:1-2

"The city" in the Hebrew Scriptures usually refers to the city of Jerusalem. In this passage, the prophet Zephaniah is reproaching the people for not trusting or drawing near to God. This raises questions about our own relationship with God: How does one draw near to God? Isn't God always with us?

Yes, but it is much like a human relationship. We can live with someone, be with them all the time, and yet not have much sense at all of what they are thinking or feeling. Maybe all we have are "take out the garbage" or "what time is dinner?" conversations. It is very easy to take our loved ones for granted and not spend much time in any in-depth sharing from day to day. To draw near to someone takes trust, believing they will want to respond to our efforts to share more deeply. It always takes a deliberate intention to try to connect with them.

The same is true of our life with God. We must make a real effort to pray. We must be intent upon connecting with the One who dwells within us and "draw near" every day to spend some quality time with God in order to keep the relationship alive.

Sr. Joyce Rupp, O.S.M.

Treating Others With Respect

■ **Anticipate each other in showing respect . . . be generous in offering hospitality.** Romans 12:10, 13

We often think that hospitality has to do only with the way we treat guests in our home. But hospitality means more than that. Hospitality presupposes a depth of insight into and empathy with another person. To discreetly ascertain another's needs and try to fulfill them; to accept another's faults and foibles; to create a sense of welcoming acceptance, peace and rest in one's presence no matter the place, time or people present: these are hallmarks of hospitality.

Hospitality also presupposes respect for another. Respect and hospitality belong together and are essential components of our lives lived in Christ. We need only look around our society to see the great need for these virtues in all types of relationships and environments.

Respect and hospitality seem to be relics of the past—when life was lived at a much slower pace and people weren't as rushed. But it is a mistake to blame the lack of civility on a lack of time. It is more a matter of not paying attention to the presence of God in ourselves, in others, in the work around us.

Lord, help me to be truly hospitable to others.

Jean Royer

The Key To Peace Of Mind

■ **I will say, "Peace be within you!"** Psalm 122:8

What better time to ponder "peace" than during the busy weeks of Advent as we busily shop, make plans for Christmas gatherings, attend parties, and try to write annual letters to long-forgotten relatives and friends? Ironically, it sometimes feels that peace is far away from our hearts during this frenzied time.

Peace is more than the absence of conflict. It is an attitude about life. The prophet Isaiah writes that those who trust God are the ones who have peace (Isaiah 26:3). We can't keep all the hustle and bustle out of our lives. We can't avoid some daily conflicts and difficulties but we can give ourselves in trust to God. How? Each time we feel distress, act unlovingly, succumb to anxious worrying or get caught in a whirlwind of activity, we can re-focus our inner self. We can turn our hearts toward peace by asking ourselves some questions: What will all this mean after I die? What is the value here? What do I need to let go of and entrust to God? Peace of mind and heart is simple. Isaiah knew that. It means trusting that God is with us and that this gift is all we really need for our happiness.

God of peace, do not let me forget that you are the most necessary part of my life. All I need is you.

Sr. Joyce Rupp, O.S.M.

Imitating Mary's Faith

■ **. . . for the one who is righteous by faith will live.**

Galatians 3:11

Mary's faith was the most perfect that ever existed, and most worthy of admiration and imitation.

Faith is the root and basis of our justification. It is the supernatural gift which God bestows upon the soul, to guide it toward the possession of his love on earth and of himself in heaven. Faith is a priceless gift and it is the foundation of supernatural life. It is the first thing Our Lord demands of all disciples. Faith means accepting Christ without reserve—accepting his works, his Church and his Sacraments, accepting the whole plan of Divine Providence and seeing Christ as the beginning and end of all.

As we strive to imitate Mary's faith, we must remember that faith is not only a gift but also a virtue. It is a gift of God because it is a light infused by him into our souls. **It is a virtue because the soul has to exercise itself in the practice of it.** Faith is a guide of our actions. If we really believe, we should put into practice what we believe . . . In prayer, one of the most important requests we can make is for the gift of a living faith that, through Mary, we may see Jesus everywhere and in everything.

Cardinal Terence Cooke
Meditations On Mary

Striving For Freedom

■ **Christ freed us for liberty. So stand firm, and do not take on yourselves the yoke of slavery a second time.**

Galatians 5:1

We think of ourselves as being free and independent but we are not. Much of the time we are slaves to our prejudices, habits, ethnic heritage, culture and complacency. These things blind us to the needs of others—and even our own real needs—and close our ears to God's call to change and to action. They keep us from being the loving and compassionate people God made us to be.

Jesus freed us and called us friends. We want to be free, loving followers of Jesus, yet we continually shackle our hands and feet and limp along, dragging our chains. Life is a process of letting go of the excess baggage that binds us. Prayer, reading, listening and, for some, professional therapy are all avenues we can take to freedom. Each demands an openness to change. And that can be difficult. Yet as long as we continue to strive each day to break the chains that bind us, we will make progress. And we'll all have moments when we slip out of our shackles and experience true freedom. God wants us to be free. We yearn to be free. Together, we will make it happen.

Charlotte A. Rancilio

Recalling How Near God Is

▦ Blessed are you who believed that what was spoken to you by the Lord would be fulfilled. Luke 1:45

Elizabeth was a wise woman, not only because of her age, but because of the way she perceived life. Her wisdom is evident in her greeting to Mary. Elizabeth knew there was a deeper message for her when she felt the baby kicking in her womb. She was caught up in the wonder of Mary's pregnancy. Elizabeth recognized the power of Mary's visit and how faithful God was. It was a moment of awe and joy as she exclaimed how fully God was present with them.

As Christmas draws near, it is easy to forget God's nearness as we rush around with many last-minute preparations. We need to slow down and catch Elizabeth's wisdom. She experienced a special moment and recognized it as an opportunity to know God's nearness. She knew how much strength and comfort there was in that awareness. That's what led her to trust so strongly and to love so deeply. Let us look for signs of God's nearness as we complete Christmas preparations and enter into the joy of the season.

O God, you are continually making yourself present in my life. Slow me down so that I can recognize and celebrate the many ways that you are with me.

Sr. Joyce Rupp, O.S.M.

Make Mary's Prayer Your Own

■ **And Mary said, "My soul proclaims the greatness of the Lord; my spirit rejoices in God my savior."**

Luke 1:46-47

Have you ever said Mary's great Magnificat as your own prayer? It is your prayer, too. You proclaim God's greatness by your very existence. You are a child of God, a friend of Jesus. God has looked upon you with great love in your weakness and, as a result, many people count you as a blessing in their lives.

God has done great things for you. Like you, Mary was no VIP in the eyes of the world; only her family and friends gave her any notice. She did ordinary, everyday things, just as you do. Yet she allowed God to dwell in her, and she began to see her life in a whole new light.

Great things happen in you, through you and to you. If you will make the first four verses of Mary's prayer your prayer, you will find that the following verses of praise will tumble from your lips and soar from your heart, just as they did from hers. God is a magnificent gift to you, and God has made you a magnificent gift to others.

Charlotte A. Rancilio

The Front Seat

■ Some who are last will be first and some who are first will be last. Luke 13:30

What an embarrassing situation, to be asked to get out of a seat and move to the back of the auditorium! It happened to me once. I had found an empty seat in the first row at a stage performance. While the lights were still on the usher came up to say that the seat was reserved and the ticket holder had arrived. I had to face row upon row of amused faces as I hurried to the back, to my own place.

In my dreams, I like to think of myself in the back being brought up to the front, but it doesn't seem to work that way. And the more I think about it, the more I realize that the question "how do I get the front seat?" won't really be a burning question if I am living a loving, caring and unselfish life. Mothers who are busy serving their children don't ask that question. They are usually too busy to sit down anywhere! Those absorbed in persons or in worthwhile goals outside themselves normally aren't concerned about their own status or rank.

Lord, help me to be concerned with people and realities beyond myself.

Sr. Marguerite Zralek, O.P.

Learning How To Receive

■ How many times I yearned to gather your children together as a hen gathers her brood under her wings, but you were unwilling! Luke 13:34

When I think of my unwillingness, I tend to examine what I am reluctant to give, what I don't want to do. Rarely do I consider what I might be unwilling to *receive*. Yet this seems to be a major point in Jesus' lament over Jerusalem. Jesus wanted to give all that is symbolized by a hen gathering her brood: safety, sustenance, belonging, leadership. The obstacle was Jerusalem's refusal to accept from Jesus what he offered. What is Jesus offering me today? Is it deeper faith? Forgiveness? Rest? Love? What is the root of my unwillingness to receive: fear, independence, anger, unworthiness?

God gives abundantly, eternally and extraordinarily. In our entire lifetime, we can never match God's great giving heart with a comparable capacity to accept on our part. Yet we can stretch and soften, gradually unfolding to deeper levels of receptivity. In this growing, it seems appropriate to ask regularly, "What does God yearn to do for me today, and how can I be more willing?"

Nancy F. Summers

Lord, I Want To See!

■ **"Rabboni," the blind man said, "I want to see."**

Mark 10:51

Jesus, I want to see. I want to see as you see, to see through the surface, beneath the obvious, beneath the realm of material visibility. I want to see beneath physical beauty, beyond impressive heights, below terrifying depths, to the essence, to the inner core, to the heart of your creation.

Jesus, I want to see with the heart—with *your* heart. I want to gaze with eyes of compassion, beholding the truth of each person I encounter, noting their struggles and their pain, their faults and foibles, neither judging nor excusing, but only loving.

Jesus, I want to see myself as *you* see me. I want to strip away the false selves which others see, probing the secret place where you desire to reside and where I desire to invite you. I want to see the essence of myself which is, in reality, you dwelling within, transforming remnants of ego into your presence. I want to see with eyes wide with wonder, with gratitude, with awe, but especially with love.

Jesus, I want to see your love beholding me. I want to see your face and live.

Elizabeth-Anne Vanek

Choosing Daily To Love God

■ **You shall love the Lord your God with all your heart, with all your soul, with all your mind, and with all your strength.** Mark 12:30

We must stress the importance of choosing and willing to love, for we do not just happen to fall in love with God. Indeed, we don't just happen to fall in love with anyone. We have to work at it; we must choose to love. Love is not just blind feeling. Love is an act of the intellect and an act of the will . . .

Our own love for God will never be strong enough to give us any real peace or real joy unless we choose to love him, and choose him each day and choose to love him just for himself, just because God is so lovable, worthy of all our love. One of the hymns of the liturgy says, "And let our choice be strong."

Our gift of self to Jesus must be a blank check. He writes the terms. We surrender ourselves lovingly to his will. Only then do we find true peace and joy. If we want to be real lovers, to be holy, to be saints, God and heaven must preoccupy our mind and heart. God, not things of the world, must be our chief love.

Fr. Philip Schuster, O.S.B.
Seeking God's Will

A Love Tested And Proved

■ **These are the ones who have survived the time of great distress; they have washed their robes and made them white in the blood of the Lamb.** Revelation 7:14

We tend to think of suffering, growing old and death as being tragic, our lot a cruel one, our end degrading. But no! When the farmer comes in from the field, dirty and wet with sweat; when the mechanic crawls out from under the car after work well done; when the nurse gets off duty, not looking so neat and fresh or feeling like she did that morning; when the nun comes back to the convent after a day or a lifetime of teaching, tired and worn out—are any of these a cruel sight? No! It is love that has been tested and proved true. It is harvest. It is victory.

The patient in the wheelchair or on the deathbed, wracked with pain, helpless, yet refusing to despair, clinging to Christ with total trust, hope and peace— that is a symbol of victory and beauty and love. It is like Jesus' shout of victory on the Cross. The gnarled, heavily veined hand of our mother, or the work-worn hands of the nun who has labored for years—these hands are beautiful, much more beautiful than the smooth, soft hands of a maiden. For they are hands that speak of love tried and proved true.

Fr. Philip Schuster, O.S.B.
Seeking God's Will

Giving What I'd Rather Keep

■ . . . she, from her poverty, has offered her whole livelihood. Luke 21:4

It is not easy for me to give out of my poverty. I quite naturally find myself checking to see how much I have left. The nameless widow from this Gospel has become one of my teachers. She teaches me that from time to time, it is good to evaluate my motives for giving gifts. Is my giving more of a gift to me than to the one receiving? Sometimes I am shocked at what I see in myself.

The Salvation Army becomes a way to empty my over-stuffed closet in order to make room for new clothes. My checks to charity become a write-off so as to receive something back in due time. My name listed among the contributors enhances my self-esteem. The time I render in service becomes a kind of competition with the giving of others.

Today I will make an effort to give out of my poverty. Whether giving from my possessions, my money, my time, or my presence, I will give away something I would like to keep.

O nameless widow of the Gospel, continue to be my teacher. May your lavish heart speak to my cautious heart.

Sr. Macrina Wiederkehr, O.S.B.

The Many Voices Of Praise

■ **Let everything that has breath praise the Lord.**

Psalm 150:6

What is praise except a stance of joy-filled adoring presence? Sometimes praise presents itself in the form of a joyful song, sometimes a word of affirmation. Praise can be the ecstatic music of a grateful heart or it can be the silent music of a heart in communion with the Beloved.

It is a leaning toward God in joyful abandon. It is the image of all creation standing on tiptoe giving thanks for the awesome gift of life. Let all that has breath praise the Lord. Let everyone and everything that lives because of the breath of God make visible the glory of God. Today I will focus on my breath as part of the breath of God.

In this season when things appear to be dying, I praise you, my God, for the life hidden even in death. I praise you for the Song of Life in all my breathing.

Sr. Macrina Wiederkehr, O.S.B.

When God Seems Near

■ **He will be gracious to you when you cry out, as soon as he hears he will answer you. The Lord will give you the bread you need and the water for which you thirst. No longer will your Teacher hide himself . . .** Isaiah 30:19-20

I am never sure how personally I should take such "prophecies" and try to apply them to myself. Is this passage from Isaiah a prediction of how close and intimate to God I should expect to be? If so, it should fill me with profound joy and give me much comfort.

What often happens is that such passages serve instead to remind me how far from God I normally seem to be. I don't often sense that God hears me at all—much less responds right away! I don't normally experience God giving me the bread I need or the water for which I thirst. Most of the time I very much experience a God who seems to hide—so well, in fact, that I quite easily give up looking.

Are there any times in my life when predictions of God's nearness seem on the verge of becoming true? Yes—and those times are wordless prayer. When I am faithful to regular prayer, such prophecies start to seem more believable. Indeed, there are times during prayer and after prayer that I feel God has given me the bread I need and the water for which I thirst.

James E. Adams

The Voice Of Truth

■ For this I was born and for this I came into the world, to testify to the truth. Everyone who belongs to the truth listens to my voice. John 18:37

I want to seek the truth, to know the truth, to cherish the truth, to live the truth. I want—at least I think I want—to "belong to the truth." And in a general way, I believe that I do belong to the truth.

But if I ask whether or not I have the necessary discipline to reach that goal to the extent I am called to do and to the extent that I say I want, I have reason to pause and hang my head.

I confess, Jesus, that I don't spend nearly enough time listening to your voice. May I learn to listen to your voice in nature. May I learn to listen to your word in Sacred Scripture. May I learn to listen to your messages that come to me in the celebration of Mass and reception of the sacraments. May I learn to listen more attentively to your voice in prayer.

Help me to learn the prayer of listening to your truth and to *live* the life of listening to your truth.

James E. Adams

Trusting God's Gift Of Life

◼ **Great and wonderful are your works, Lord God Almighty.** Revelation 15:3

Physicists from all over the world rejoice every time there is a discovery of what is believed to be one of the basic building blocks of matter. When this happened most recently, they gave this particle, this incredibly tiny piece of matter, a strange name—and then declared that the understanding of reality had taken a giant leap forward.

There are different ways of understanding reality. For men and women of faith, what is most longed for and most real is not fully reducible to matter, but ultimately makes sense only through a trusting response to a loving God who permeates all of life, down to the tiniest bits of matter. God asks that we trust in and respond to existence as a Gift that is being transformed through God's love and power.

There is no shared consensus—and probably never will be—regarding the ultimate nature of the real. But if we want to more nearly approach what is true and real, then we should ask God daily for the grace to love this Gift of life, down to the smallest detail.

Fr. Jeff Behrens

'One Problem After Another'

■ **My soul yearns and pines for the courts of the Lord.**
Psalm 84:3

When I was younger I didn't realize the import of these words of the psalmist. Now that I have been buffeted by the trials of life, these words have a special meaning for me. I once thought that when a problem or difficulty had been resolved, I would "live happily ever after." Now I know that when one worry has been confronted and solved, several others pop up. *Life consists of one problem after another, whether large or small.* There may be ants in the kitchen, a failing washing machine or car, a lost job, a family member on drink or drugs, terminal illnesses. That's life! True, there is much joy and pleasure to be found in life. Yet there is also pain, sorrow and sadness. We must accept the pain and sorrow—and we must thank God for the grace to make our life a time of spiritual growth and maturity.

Still, we often yearn for the battle to be over. We yearn and pine for God's courts of peace and tranquility. Those courts are our destiny as children of God, but we arrive there on God's timetable.

Meanwhile, we continue the struggle, in prayer and in trust, knowing that our final goal is, indeed, the courts of the Lord.

Joan Zrilich

The Anxieties Of Daily Life

■ **Beware that your hearts do not become drowsy from carousing and drunkenness and the anxieties of daily life, and that day catch you by surprise like a trap.**

Luke 21:34-35

Firmly now in middle-age, my days of carousing appear to be long gone. Not wanting to face another hangover, I avoid drunkenness. But, oh, those anxieties of daily life! They get me on a regular basis. First it's my family: Are they safe and healthy? Am I providing them with enough? Too much?

Then it's my relationships, especially my marriage and friendships, and my job. Any upset in these key areas can send me spinning. And if all is well close to home, I find myself switching automatically to the big list: crime, unemployment, the economy, wars and rumors of wars, AIDS.

Of course, daily life has its proper cares and it is only prudent to meet our responsibilities as best we can and make a contribution to a better world. But Jesus warns you and me against trying to control life through worry. It doesn't work, but only dulls us to the coming of the One who is really in control.

Lord, free me from worrying about what I cannot control. Help me to increase my trust in you.

Mark Neilsen

Wholehearted Discipleship

■ **Jesus said to them, "Come after me, and I will make you fishers of men." At once they left their nets and followed him.** Matthew 4:19-20

Nothing drains energy and joy faster than living a halfhearted life. The resurrected presence of Jesus touches our consciousness with friendship and power, but we never quite open ourselves fully to receive it. We are invited to a vibrant life of love and caring service, but we say to Jesus, "I'll test the waters. I'm not absolutely sure. I'll see how things turn out."

There is within us a deep-seated fear of fully committing ourselves to God. Maybe we are afraid of being cheated if we respond completely to the message and presence of Jesus. We seem to fear that trusting in Jesus will give us less fulfillment and security than trusting in ourselves. But we have experienced the results of not fully committing ourselves to the God who lovingly calls us in the depths of our hearts. Finally we have to decide for ourselves what is best for us: to endure the permanent unfulfillment of a half-committed life, or to pass through a temporary fear so that we can know the joy of a life fully committed to Christ.

Jesus, help me to follow you wholeheartedly.
                         Fr. Kenneth E. Grabner, C.S.C.
                                      Focus Your Day

How Open Am I To God?

■ **Every valley shall be filled and every mountain and hill shall be made low.** Luke 3:5

Often people complain that God is seemingly absent in their lives, or that they experience nothing in prayer because God seems remote, uncaring, indifferent. One question I ask in spiritual direction of others is, "What is blocking God's path to you?" When I ask this, people are sometimes jolted into a new set of assumptions. Whereas, they had believed that God was choosing to be distant, now they can ask themselves, "What is it *in me* that makes me less accessible to God?" In many cases, God's "absence" is the result of *our* fear, *our* resistance to change, *our* desire to be in control, *our* cynicism, *our* inability to love.

When we recognize that it is we who are blocking God's path to our hearts and that the valleys and mountains of our experience are of our own making, then we give God the opportunity to straighten, smooth and level this path. Instead of projecting blame onto God for being absent, we can face the truth that, many times, it is we who construct the obstacles which stand between us and our God.

Lord, help me to learn what obstacles I may be placing in the way of deeper union with you.

Elizabeth-Anne Vanek

Humming Your Praise And Joy

■ **And Mary said, "My soul proclaims the greatness of the Lord; my spirit rejoices in God my savior."**

Luke 1:46-47

Have you ever found yourself humming along when you are happy? Do you ever sing a little ditty as you are driving the car or working around the house or taking a shower? At times like this, the melody of a song is a spontaneous eruption of the human spirit, a way of expressing the satisfaction one feels.

Mary, mother of Jesus, and Hannah, mother of Samuel, had much to sing about—both had been surprised with the wondrous children of their wombs. Both marveled in song at how their lives had been filled with unexpected treasure. Because they were women of faith, both recognized that God was the source of their blessings. I can just hear these two women humming along as they went about their daily tasks.

As Christmas nears and so much emphasis is placed on material treasures, let us also look at our spiritual treasures and take time to proclaim the goodness of God in us. Today, choose a few lines of a favorite song or create a few lines of praise and thanksgiving to God. Hum or sing this melody as you go about your day. Praise God for all the goodness that is yours.

Sr. Joyce Rupp, O.S.M.

A Time To Wait

■ **I have waited, waited for the Lord and he stooped toward me and heard my cry.** Psalm 40:2

So much of our life seems to be spent waiting for someone or something—waiting for Christmas, for spring, for graduation, for a sick child to grow healthy, for a green light, for a lonely night to pass, for the movie to begin. Some places are even set aside just for waiting—clinic waiting rooms, train stations, checkout lines. It would be interesting to calculate how much of a typical day is spent in waiting for someone or something.

What do I do while I am waiting? Rather than pace and grow agitated, I try to realize that this waiting time may be a gift to me, a space in my day where I can pause and reflect on my life. Maybe it is an opportunity for God to enter my life and remind me that I am not in control. When I pay attention, I may hear God knocking on my waiting time and space. My whole life is in fact a waiting time and the world is a waiting place for God to fully enter my life.

God, in my waiting moments this day, may I recognize your presence.

Sr. Ruth Marlene Fox, O.S.B.

God's Awesome Generosity

■ **The virgin shall be with child, and bear a son, and shall name him Immanuel.** Isaiah 7:14

Tradition tells us that St. Francis of Assisi first began the custom of venerating the creche. In order to bring to life the memory of the Child Jesus' birth, he invited his friars and the local people in the little town of Greccio to celebrate Mass before a hay-filled crib, in the company of an ox and an ass. Written accounts inform us that the night was illumined by countless lanterns and that the nearby forest resounded with songs of praise. Most striking was Francis' proclamation of the Gospel and his joyful preaching about the birth of the Poor King.

Francis fully grasped the implications of the Child of Bethlehem's birth into poverty. By recreating the stable scene, he helped others to actually *feel* that immense Love which took on human flesh and entered the human condition in its most abject state. In the presence of humble hay and with the stench of farm animals around them, nobody was left unmoved by God's overwhelming generosity. The Birth was indeed the sign of signs, testimony to unfathomable mystery.

Fill us with wonder, O God, when we remember your love.

Elizabeth-Anne Vanek

Overcoming Holiday Blues

■ **My trust is in you, O Lord; I say, "You are my God."**
Psalm 31:15

When the celebrating winds down, fatigue, tension, and a vague sense of unfulfillment can become our companions. We may wonder why the holidays didn't quite turn out as we had wished. We may even make plans to try harder next year to achieve our holiday ideal. Do such post-holiday blues have a theological basis worth considering?

Special times call forth our underlying desires for the Ultimate, the Perfect, the "best-ever-can't-top-this" experience. But no day, no matter how special, can satisfy yearnings such as these. Only union with God can fulfill our deepest dreams and hopes. If our frenzied pursuit of holiday joy has become an unintended form of idolatry or substitute for God, perhaps the ensuing letdown reminds us that we can never be satisfied except in the Lord. Perhaps "the blues" can motivate us to redirect our attention, energy and expectation to the realm of God where peace truly reigns and abundant joy may be found.

Nancy F. Summers

Prayer Of Praise

■ **Lord, teach us to pray, just as John taught his disciples.**
Luke 11:1

When he was asked to teach his disciples how to pray, Jesus began by teaching them how to praise God. "Father, may your holy name be honored; may your Kingdom come." How natural that Jesus' prayer should begin this way! If we truly love God, wouldn't we desire that his name be honored? Isn't that what we desire for anyone we love? And if we truly love God, wouldn't we long for God's Kingdom to come? The Kingdom comes when God is present in our midst, forming a community of love. Wouldn't this also be a primary desire for one who loves?

It is only after Jesus teaches a priority for the honor of God that he tells us to pray for our daily bread. Because God is a loving presence in our lives, we can ask for the gifts we need, sure that we will receive what is necessary for our fullness and our joy.

Prayer involves an act of praise, and then we ask for our needs. Jesus' prayer invites us to examine how we pray. We always remain needy people, and so we ask the One we love for what is necessary. But how often do we forget the praise that is meant to flow from a heart that loves?

Fr. Kenneth E. Grabner, C.S.C.

The 'School' Of Affliction

■ **It is good for me that I have been afflicted, in order to learn your laws.** Psalm 119:71

A time of affliction is often a time of revelation. Truths and insights are revealed to us that we do not always see on ordinary sunny days. We find ourselves in a school of trust where all that we have said we believe is sorely tested.

The school of affliction is not something I long for, but when it comes, I want to be open to its pages of wisdom and the lessons it has to teach me.

There are places in my heart where I have not allowed myself to be vulnerable. There are feelings I've been afraid to bring to the light. The school of affliction is not always merciful. It does not ask me if I want to feel. It offers me a cup of suffering. My willingness to drink the cup often leads me to strengths and wisdoms I never knew I possessed.

Perhaps one of the greatest lessons I have learned is that it is possible to be in the furnace of affliction and yet come out with a heart that is not bitter. With the memory of my sorrow in my heart I allow the light of wisdom to surround me rather than the darkness of bitterness.

O God, in all my afflictions teach me wisdom.

Sr. Macrina Wiederkehr, O.S.B.

Our Tender, Loving God

■ **Even the hairs of your head are counted! Fear nothing, then.** Luke 12:7

There's a child's verse that concludes with these lines: *"Fancy God counting my hairs for me / How very fond of me God must be."*

We like to think that's the way it is. And it is true. At the same time there is scarcely any other saying of Jesus that is a greater challenge to faith. If God has counted the very hairs of our head, if God's concern for us is so lovingly tender, then how is it that "bad things happen to good people"?

What Christ is really telling us is that no matter what happens, no matter what tragedy comes into our lives, we will never have to face it alone. God is with us, brooding over us, ringing us round with an intimate, protective love. We anguish, and God is in our anguish. We cry, and God's ear is on our lips. We reach out, and God's strong arm supports us. Not the most minute detail of our misery escapes God's awareness. Yes, "even the hairs of your head are counted! Fear nothing, then."

O God, I thank you for the sweetness of your infinite concern for me.

Sr. Mary Terese Donze, A.S.C.

To Keep And To Ponder

■ **And his mother kept all these things in her heart.**
                                                Luke 2:51

Twice Luke says Mary "kept in her heart" the events surrounding Jesus birth and growth (2:19, 51), once with the "keeping" linked to "pondering." These two responses might well be seen as ultimately the only way for us humans to approach family life and the life of faith. How often in family life and in the life of faith are we left in the end with little else except what we keep and ponder in our hearts?

We keep and ponder because we do not understand all that happens in our families. We keep and ponder because we do not fully understand our spouses or our children—or even ourselves. Life is a mystery— and family life is an even more profound mystery! You do not ever solve—or resolve—the bittersweet realities of family life. You just "keep them in your heart" and rock them back and forth like you once tried to rock your babies to sleep.

We keep and ponder in our spiritual lives, also, because with God, the Ultimate Mystery, nothing can ever be final, nothing can be resolved or concluded. Much as we might want only answers, in this life we must keep and ponder questions in our hearts.

                                                James E. Adams

Changing Times

■ **Heaven and earth will pass away, but my words will not pass away.** Luke 21:33

Everything in life changes. When we are young we don't always realize this. But the older we get, the faster we see things change, and the more life seems to go by in a blur. Even those things that seem the most steadfast and sure can pass away—marriages, friendships, our faith, even life itself. We watch in utter disbelief as these things slowly unravel in our lives . . . parents die, old friends leave, the fire of faith seems to burn out, and marriages crumble around us. We might ask ourselves: Is *nothing* sacred?

The answer is "yes," some things *are* sacred. The Word of God and the promises God makes to us will never change. Despite the difficulties in our lives, we can rest assured that the Word of God remains solid, a place of retreat from the changing world. And even should our own faith wane, in the back of our minds and souls we should know that such changes don't change God's love for us. God is not subject to the laws of change in this world. God rides high and bright above those laws, presenting a beacon of hope for those who seek the light.

Thank you, Lord, for being our solid foundation in an ever-changing world.

Steve Givens

A Morning Prayer

O Creator of the Universe, praise be to you! I awake this day truly grateful for another day. Open my mind and my heart so that I will see the events of this day through your eyes. Open my spirit so that I can hear your voice deep within me. Open my entire being so that I can receive your love and be a bearer of your goodness to others this day. Amen.

Sr. Joyce Rupp, O.S.M.

An Evening Prayer

My God, as the sun sets, I pray that tomorrow will bring change for the better in a confused world. So much needs to be done, and I pray for the strength to dare to make a difference, no matter how small. Give peace to those who suffer, relief to those who wait, and courage to those who work for your kingdom. May I go into tomorrow with a heart full of compassion and a mind set on the Gospel. Amen.

Steve Givens

A Prayer For Courage

O God, I am afraid. I feel like a bewildered child alone and lost in the dark night. Please give me light so that I might see the path ahead of me. Let me hear your voice saying, "Do not be afraid. I am with you." Take my hand in your firm clasp. Give me the courage to walk confidently, the courage that comes from knowing you are always at my side. Amen.

Sr. Ruth Marlene Fox, O.S.B.

Scripture Citations Index

Scripture Citations Index

68, Nov 4 • 8:31-32, March 25 • 10:9, June 3 • 10:27, April 7 • 10:28, June 27 • 13:8, April 4 • 13:5, April 24 • 13:20, June 4 • 13:34, June 6 • 13:34-35, Feb 1 • 14:1-2, June 5 • 14:18, May 5 • 14:23, May 2 • 14:26, April 12 • 15:1-2, May 3, 19 • 15:12, June 29 • 15:15, April 9, May 17 • 15:16, April 11 • 16:20, May 21, June 30 • 16:23, April 14 • 16:33 April 15 • 17:8, June 20 • 18:37, Dec 17 • 20:18, Sept 29 • 20:25, Aug 6 • 21:7, April 6 • 21:17, May 7, June 21

1 John: 2:16-17, Nov 22 • 2:25, March 5 • 3:1, Jan. 4 • 4:8, Jan 16 • 4:16, Jan 17 • 4:18, Jan 31 • 4:21, Jan 18 • 5:13, March 7

Jonah: 3:1-3, Jan 13 • 3:4-5, Sept 2

Joshua: 24:15, Oct 10

1 Kings: 19:11, April 16

2 Kings: 5:11, April 1

Luke: 1:38, Jan 30 • 1:45, Aug 15, Dec 7 • 1:46-47, Dec 8, Dec 23 • 2:34-35, Jan 24 • 2:40, Feb 4 • 2:51, Dec 30 • 3:5, Dec 22 • 4:36, Aug 24, Nov 5 • 4:42, Oct 26 • 6:12, Nov 9 • 6:17-18, Oct 27 • 6:20-21, Sept 18 • 6:22, Oct 14 • 6:25, Feb 26 • 6:36, July 20 • 6:42, July 21 • 6:44, Feb 29 • 6:45, Aug 26 • 7:47, July 25 • 8:11, Sept 20 • 8:15, Aug 28 • 8:21, July 29 • 9:20, Aug 30 • 9:23, March 1 • 9:61-62, Aug 5 • 10:29, Nov 23 • 10:39, July 6 • 10:40-41, Aug 17, Sept 30 • 11:1, Dec 27 • 11:10, Oct 3 • 11:23, Jan 28 • 11:54, Nov 21 • 12:7, Dec 29 • 12:20, Nov 20 • 13:3, Nov 8 • 13:25, July 11 • 13:30, Dec 9 • 13:34, Dec 10 • 14:1, March 16 • 14:10, July 14 • 14:33, July 18 • 15:7 April 20 • 15:20, Jan 14 • 15:23-24, July 22 • 16:13, July 27 • 16:31, Aug 3 • 17:33, Nov 12 • 18:1, Nov 13 • 21:3-4, Nov 15, Dec 14 • 21:19, Nov 14 • 21:33, Dec 31 • 21:34-35, Dec 20 • 24:1, May 30 • 24:29, April 25

Mark: 1:35, Feb 6 • 1:40, Feb 9 • 2:3, Feb 21 • 3:5, March 29 • 3:34-35, Feb 22 • 4:30-31, March 8 • 4:38, Feb 24 • 5:23, Feb 3 • 6:11-12, Feb 5 • 6:31-32, Jan 8 • 6:38,

Scripture Citations Index

Jan 5 • 6:51, March 27 • 7:6, Feb 7 • 8:2, May 13 • 8:5, Feb 8 • 8:10,13, May 14 • 8:12, Feb 10 • 8:23, Feb 13 • 8:31, Jan 26, Sept 19 • 8:34, Jan 10, Feb 12 • 8:35, March 13 • 10:9, July 2 • 10:13,16, Feb 14 • 10:51, Dec 11 • 12:10, June 9 • 12:30, June 12, Dec 12 • 12:31, May 8 • 16:14, April 26 • 16:15, June 16

Matthew: 1:23, Nov 19 • 1:24, March 19 • 4:19-20, Dec 21 • 5:4, May 22 • 5:14, Jan 22 • 5:14,16, May 23 • 5:38-39, April 18 • 6:9, June 22 • 7:14, April 19 • 7:15-16, June 14 • 7:21, Nov 1 • 8:10,13, May 14 • 8:24-25, April 21, May 25 • 9:2, May 27, July 3 • 9:9, Sept 21 • 9:11, July 28, Oct 17 • 9:12, Oct 15 • 10:8, Sept 27 • 10:24-25, Aug 9 • 10:31, May 12 • 10:37, June 24 • 11:20, July 4 • 11:28, Aug 7, Sept 28, Nov 17 • 12:7, July 5 • 13:8, Aug 10, Oct 18 • 13:23, Oct 2 • 13:29-30, Aug 14 • 13:44, Aug 16 • 13:46, Sept 8 • 13:52, Oct 4 • 14:13-14, July 7 • 14:27-28, July 8 • 15:23, Aug 18 • 15:28, Oct 6 • 16:24, Oct 23 • 16:25, Oct 8 • 17:2, March 20, Oct 22 • 17:5, Aug 19 • 18:3, Oct 24 • 18:12, July 9 • 19:27, Sept 9 • 20:13-14, Sept 10 • 21:28-29, Nov 18 • 21:31-32, Feb 23 • 22:39, Oct 11 • 23:27, July 12 • 23:37, Aug 11 • 25:21, Sept 17 • 25:25, Aug 22 • 26:15-16, Feb 18 • 26:21, April 23

Micah: 7:19, Feb 28

Numbers: 6:24-26, Jan 1

2 Peter: 3:13, Nov. 30

Philippians: 2:8-9, Sept 14 • 4:12-13, Nov 24

Proverbs: 21:2, Oct 29 • 30:8-9, Oct 30

Psalms: 17:15, Sept 26 • 18:2-3, May 28 • 19:1, May 18 • 19:5, June 2 • 19:8-9, Nov 10 • 23:1-4, Feb 17 • 25:4, June 11 • 25:5, Feb 19 • 27:1, June 1 • 27:14, April 28 • 30:3-4, March 3 • 31:6, June 15 • 31:15, Dec 26 • 32:5, March 10 • 33:1-5, Sept 16 • 33:5, July 15 • 33:14-15, July 24 • 34:9, May 4, June 25 • 34:19, March 4 • 40:

Scripture Citations Index

2, Dec 24 • 40:2-3, Jan 23 • 42:2, March 22 • 42:4, Nov 26 • 46:2-3, Jan 15 • 51:5-6, Oct 5 • 51:19, March 18 • 52:10, Oct 13 • 71:5, Oct 20 • 84:3, Nov 3, Dec 19 • 89:2, May 1, June 18 • 90:17, July 31 • 94: 7,14, Oct 19 • 95:6, March 28 • 95:7-8, Feb 20 • 96:4,7, Sept 13 • 98:3, May 16 • 100:3, June 8 • 105:4-5, Sept 3 • 112:1, June 10 • 116:12, April 2 • 118:1, Oct 28 • 119:33, June 23 • 119:34, May 24 • 119:71, Nov 7, Dec 28 • 119:108, July 30 • 122:8, Dec 4 • 126:5-6, Oct 21 • 136:1, Aug 12 • 138:8, April 13 • 141:1, Jan 11 • 145:8, Sept 15 • 145:18,19, June 7, July 17, Dec 1 • 148:12-13, Jan 2 • 150:6, Dec 15

Romans: 1:16, Nov 25 • 5:5, April 17 • 6:11, May 15 • 6:23, Nov 27 • 8:26, Aug 13, Nov 29 • 12:10, 13, Dec 3

Revelation: 3:20, Feb 15 • 7:14, Dec 13 • 15:3, Dec 18

1 Samuel: 3:8-9, Jan 6 • 16:7, Jan 29

1 Thessalonians: 1:2-3, Aug 20 • 4:3, Aug 21 • 4:17-18, Aug 23

2 Thessalonians: 2:16, Aug 8

Titus: 2:11, Nov 11

1 Timothy: 6:8-9, Oct 16 • 6:10, Nov 6

Zechariah: 8:2, Aug 31 • 8:22, Sept 1

Zephaniah: 3:1-2, Dec 2 • 3:12, March 9

Author Index

James E. Adams
Jan 12, April 5, May 30, June 14, 19, 21, Aug 4, 6, 19, 30, Sept 23, Oct 21, 23, 30, Nov 29, Dec 16, 17, 30

Fr. Hans Urs von Balthasar
Sept 19

Denise Barker
Jan 23, July 15, 16, Nov 6

Fr. William J. Bausch
April 24

Fr. Jeff Behrens
June 22, July 2, Dec 18

Fr. Henri Boulad, S.J.
Jan 20

Fr. Harold A. Buetow
Oct 18

Fr. Walter J. Burghardt, S.J.
Jan 9, 15, April 8, 19, Aug 1

Fr. Raniero Cantalamessa, O.F.M. Cap.
March 28, June 25

Carlo Carretto
July 6, Aug 21, Oct 13

Fr. John Catoir
Jan 21

Fr. Jean-Pierre de Caussade, S.J.
May 19, Oct 31

Sr. Joan Chittister, O.S.B.
Jan 19, March 18, Nov 10

Sr. Anita M. Constance, S.C.
Oct 27

Cardinal Terence Cooke
Aug 15, Sept 13, Dec 5

Sr. Mary Terese Donze, A.S.C.
Jan 11, Feb 8, 14, March 7, 29, April 11, June 18, July 24, Aug 11, Nov 7, Dec 29

Author Index

Catherine de Hueck Doherty
May 10, 14, 27, June 12, Oct 11, 28
Fr. Thomas Dubay, S.M.
Oct 2
Mitch Finley
April 3
Sr. Ruth Marlene Fox, O.S.B.
March 11, April 16, 29, 30, May 16, June 20, July
19, 21, Aug 16, Oct 6, 7, Nov 4, Dec 24
Steve Givens
March 6, May 6, 20, June 7, Aug 24, Nov 17, Dec 31
Fr. Kenneth E. Grabner, C.S.C.
Jan 31, Aug 12, 18, Sept 11, Oct 24, Nov 5, 22, Dec
21, 27
Fr. Benedict J. Groeschel, C.F.R.
Jan 24, Feb 25, March 31, April 23, July 4, Oct 10,
Nov 8
Fr. Bernard Haring
Aug 9
Caryll Houselander
Jan 10, July 23
Sr. Mary Charleen Hug, S.N.D.
May 3, June 2
Cardinal Basil Hume
Aug 25
Luke Timothy Johnson
May 22, Sept 18, Oct 14
Fr. Kieran Kay, O.F.M. Conv.
March 26, June 30, Sept 28
Fr. Thomas Keating, O.C.S.O.
March 8, April 21, May 25, June 13, Sept 10, Nov 13
Michael R. Kent
March 5, June 15
Fr. S. Joseph Krempa
Aug 17, Sept 24

Author Index

C.S. Lewis
Jan 17, July 26
St. Alphonsus Liguori
July 29, Aug 5
Chiara Lubich
Aug. 23
Fr. Alfred McBride, O.Praem.
April 10
Fr. Flor McCarthy
Feb 5, Aug 14
James McGinnis
Jan 25, March 22, April 27, May 2, July 7, Aug 20, Sept 16, Nov 15
Fr. James McKarns
May 18, June 29, Nov 23
Fr. William F. Maestri
Feb 16, March 1
Joseph Martos
Jan 30
Fr. Anthony de Mello, S.J.
April 20
Fr. Charles E. Miller, C.M.
Jan 6, May 31, July 11, 14, Sept 1
Bishop Robert F. Morneau
May 24
Mother Teresa
Jan 8, Feb 17, March 14
Mark Neilsen
Feb 20, March 21, 25, 30, April 4, 15, 18, 26, May 11, June 5, 26, July 12, 25, Aug 31, Sept 5, 7, 20, Oct 4, 16, 19, 25, 29, Nov 3, 20, 24, Dec 20
John Henry Newman
June 8

Author Index

Fr. Henri J.M. Nouwen
March 4, April 22, July 10, 20
Fr. Louis-Marie Parent
Nov 1
Pope John Paul II
Jan 18, March 10, June 1, 16, Oct 8, Nov 9
Fr. M. Basil Pennington, O.C.S.O.
Oct 17, Nov 16
John Powell, S.J.
Jan 16
Fr. Karl Rahner, S.J.
March 3
Charlotte A. Rancilio
May 29, Sept 2, Nov 12, Dec 6, 8
Cardinal Joseph Ratzinger
June 23
Brother Roger of Taizé
July 17
Fr. Richard Rohr, O.F.M.
Jan 30, Feb 1, 7, 12, 23, July 27, Oct 12
Fr. David E. Rosage
Feb 19
Jean Royer
Feb 11, Apr 28, May 26, Sept 3, 26, 27, Oct 20, Dec 3
Sr. Joyce Rupp, O.S.M.
Jan 4, 26, 28, Feb 10, 13, 18, 21, 27, March 2, 12, 16, 19, 23, 27, May 4, 8, 13, 21, 23, June 9, 11, July 1, 5, 13, Aug 26, 27, 28, 29, Sept 9, 12, 14, 22, 29, Oct 1, 22, Nov 2, 21, 25, Dec. 2, 4, 7, 23
St. Francis de Sales
Feb 22, Oct 9
Fr. Michael Scanlan, T.O.R.
Jan 2

Author Index

Fr. Anthony Schueller, S.S.S.
March 15, July 3, Sept 21
Fr. Philip Schuster, O.S.B.
Dec 12, 13
Fr. Herbert F. Smith, S.J.
April 25
Nancy F. Summers
Jan 13, 14, 27, Feb 3, 4, 15, 24, April 1, 2, April 9, 13, 14, May 7, July 9, 28, 30, Aug 2, 8, Sept 15, 17, Oct 26, Nov 18, 26, Dec. 1, 10, 26
Fr. Don Talafous, O.S.B.
March 13, June 10, Oct 15
Fr. Carlos G. Valles, S.J.
Oct 5
Elizabeth-Anne Vanek (Stewart)
Jan 1, 7, 22, 29, Feb 2, 6, 9, 26, 29, March 9, 17, 20, 24, April 6, 7, 12, 17, May 5, 9, 12, 15, 17, June 6, 24, July 18, 22, Aug 3, 7, 10, 13, Sept 6, 8, 30, Oct 3, Nov 14, 28, 30, Dec 11, 22, 25
Sr. Macrina Wiederkehr, O.S.B.
Jan 3, 5, Feb 28, June 3, 4, 27, 28, July 8, Aug 22, Sept 4, Nov 19, Dec 14, 15, 28
Sr. Marguerite Zralek, O.P.
May 1, 28, July 31, Sept 25, Nov 11, 27, Dec 9
Joan Zrilich
June 17, Dec 19

■

Acknowledgments & Permissions

Bible quotations are from **The New American Bible,** © 1970, 1986 & 1991 by The Confraternity of Christian Doctrine, and **The New Revised Standard Version,** © 1989, Division of Christian Education of the National Council of Churches of Christ in the USA, both published by Oxford University Press. Creative Communications for the Parish thanks Oxford for use of these versions, as well as the following for brief excerpts from the works cited below:

Hans Urs von Balthasar, **Light Of The Word**, translated Dennis D. Martin, © 1993 Ignatius Press.

William J. Bausch, **Timely Homilies**, © 1990 William Bausch, Twenty-third Publications.

Henri Boulad, **All Is Grace**, © 1991 The Crossroad Publishing Company (English translation), Crossroad.

Harold A. Buetow, **God Still Speaks: Listen!**, © 1995 The Society of St. Paul, Alba House.

Walter J. Burghardt, **Still Proclaiming Your Wonders**, © 1984 by Walter J. Burghardt, S.J., Paulist Press; **Dare To Be Christ**, © 1991 by New York Province of the Society of Jesus, Paulist Press; **To Christ I Look**, © 1989 by New York Province of the Society of Jesus, Paulist Press.

John Catoir, **Enjoy The Lord**, © 1988 The Society of St. Paul, Alba House.

Raniero Cantalamessa, **The Ascent Of Mount Sinai,** © 1996 HarperCollins Publishers Limited.

Carlo Carretto, **Letters To Dolcidia**, © 1991 HarperCollins, English translation, Orbis Books; **Letters From The Desert**, © 1972 Orbis Books.

Cardinal Terence Cooke, **Meditations On Mary,** © 1993 The Society of St. Paul, Alba House.

Jean-Pierre de Caussade, **The Joy Of Full Surrender**, translated by Hal M. Helms, © 1986 Paraclete Press.

Joan Chittister, **Wisdom Distilled From The Daily,** © 1990 Joan D. Chittister, Harper & Row; **There Is A Season**, © 1995 Joan Chittister, Orbis Books.

Catherine de Hueck Doherty, **Grace In Every Season,**

Acknowledgments & Permissions

edited by Mary Achterhoff, © 1992 Madonna House Publications, Servant Publications. Used with permission.

Thomas Dubay, **Seeking Spiritual Direction**, © 1993 Thomas Dubay, Servant Publications.

Kenneth E. Grabner, **Focus Your Day**, © 1992 Ave Maria Press. Used with permission.

Benedict J. Groeschel, **Five Figures From The Passion**, an audiocassette tape, © 1989 Mustard Seed Productions; **Healing The Original Wound**, © 1993 Benedict J. Groeschel, Servant Publications; **The Reform Of Renewal**, © 1990 Ignatius Press.

Bernard Haring, as cited in **Journey To The Light**, editor Ann Finch, © 1993 New City Press.

Caryll Houselander, **The Stations of the Cross**, © 1955 by Caryll Houselander, Sheed & Ward.

Basil Hume, as cited in **Daily Readings In Catholic Classics**, Rawley Myers editor, © 1992 Ignatius Press.

Luke Timothy Johnson, **Some Hard Blessings**, © 1981 Argus Communications.

Kieran M. Kay, **Common Bushes Afire With God**, © 1994 Kieran M. Kay, Resurrection Press.

Thomas Keating, **The Kingdom Of God Is Like . . .**, © 1993 St. Benedict's Monastery, Crossroad; **Awakenings**, © 1990, St Benedict's Monastery, Crossroad; **Reawakenings**, © 1992 Thomas Keating, Crossroad.

Michael R. Kent, **Bringing The Word To Life**, © 1996 Michael R. Kent, Twenty-third Publications.

Joseph Krempa, **Daily Homilies**, © 1985 The Society of St. Paul, Alba House.

C.S. Lewis, **The Four Loves**, © 1960 Helen Joy Lewis, Harcourt Brace Jovanovich; **Mere Christianity**, © 1952 Macmillan Publishing Co.

St. Alphonsus Liguori, as cited in **The Redeeming Love Of Christ,** editor Joseph Oppitz, © 1992 New City Press.

Chiara Lubich, as cited in **Journey To the Light**, Ann Finch editor, © 1993 New City Press.

Acknowledgments & Permissions

William F. Maestri, **My Lenten Journal**, © 1990 The Society of St. Paul, Alba House; **My Way Of The Cross Journal**, © 1993 The Society of St. Paul, Alba House.

Flor McCarthy, **Windows On The Gospel**, © Flor McCarthy and Dominican Publications, Twenty-third Publications.

Alfred McBride, **Year Of The Lord**, © 1983 William C. Brown Publishing.

Anthony de Mello, **Contact With God**, © 1991 Loyola University Press.

Charles E. Miller, **Opening The Treasures**, © 1982 The Society of St. Paul, Alba House; **The Word Made Flesh**, © 1983 The Society of St. Paul, Alba House.

Robert F. Morneau, **Spiritual Direction**, © 1992 Robert F. Morneau, Crossroad.

Mother Teresa, **Total Surrender,** © 1985 by Missionaries of Charity & Brother Angelo Devananda Scolozzi, Servant Books; **Daily Readings With Mother Teresa**, Teresa de Bertodano, editor, © 1993 Teresa de Bertodano, HarperCollins.

John H. Newman, edited by Hal M. Helms, **Lead Kindly Light**, © 1987 Paraclete Press.

Henri J.M. Nouwen, **Life Of The Beloved**, © 1992 by Henri J.M. Nouwen, Crossroad; **Show Me The Way**, © 1992 Henri J.M. Nouwen, Crossroad; **The Way Of The Heart**, © 1981 Henri J.M. Nouwen, HarperCollins.

Louis-Marie Parent, **In Intimacy With Jesus**, © 1991 Collection Volontaires de Dieu, Editions Paulines.

Pope John Paul II, **The Pope Speaks To The American Church,** © 1992 Cambridge Center for the Study of Faith and Culture, HarperCollins; **Crossing The Threshold Of Hope**, © 1994 Alfred A. Knopf; **Make Room For The Mystery Of God**, © 1995, Daughters of St. Paul.

John Powell, **Through The Eyes Of Faith**, © 1992 John Powell, Tabor Publishing.

Acknowledgments & Permissions

Karl Rahner, as cited in **The Great Church Year**, © English translation, Crossroad Publishing Company.

Cardinal Joseph Ratzinger, **Co-Workers Of The Truth**, trans. © 1992 Ignatius Press.

Brother Roger of Taizé, **His Love Is A Fire**, © 1990 Atiliers et Presses de Taizé, The Liturgical Press.

David E. Rosage, **Beginning Spiritual Direction**, © 1994 David R. Rosage, Servant Publications.

Richard Rohr, **Radical Grace**, © 1993 Richard Rohr & John Bookser Feister, St. Anthony Messenger Press; **Simplicity**, © 1991 English translation, Crossroad Publishing Company; Richard Rohr and Joseph Martos, **The Great Themes Of Scripture: New Testament**, © 1988 Richard Rohr and Joseph Martos, St. Anthony Messenger Press.

St. Francis de Sales, as cited in **Finding God Wherever You Are**, Joseph F. Power, © 1993 New City Press.

Michael Scanlan, **Appointment With God**, © 1987 Michael Scanlan, Franciscan University Press.

Philip Schuster, **Seeking God's Will**, © 1994 Our Sunday Visitor Press.

Robert F. Smith, **Sunday Homilies**, © 1989 The Society of St. Paul, Alba House.

Don Talafous, **A Word For The Day: Reflections**, © 1992 The Order of St. Benedict, Inc., Collegeville, MN, The Liturgical Press.

Carlos Valles, **Psalms For Contemplation**, © 1990 Loyola University Press.

■